EMPIRE, MEDIA, AND THE
AUTONOMOUS WOMAN

To

*My late father, Dipankar Niyogi, whose commitment to
scholarship inspired my pursuit*

*My late mother, Pushpanjali Niyogi, whose care for my
pursuit from her sickbed got me to the end*

*My spouse, Suranjan De, without whose unflinching and
courageous support I would not have completed this book*

90 0913646 4

EMPIRE, MEDIA, AND THE AUTONOMOUS WOMAN

A FEMINIST CRITIQUE
OF POSTCOLONIAL THOUGHT

ESHA NIYOGI DE

OXFORD
UNIVERSITY PRESS

OXFORD
UNIVERSITY PRESS

Oxford University Press is a department of the University of Oxford.
It furthers the University's objective of excellence in research, scholarship,
and education by publishing worldwide. Oxford is a registered trademark of
Oxford University Press in the UK and in certain other countries

Published in India
by Oxford University Press
YMCA Library Building,1 Jai Singh Road, New Delhi 110 001, India

© Oxford University Press 2011

The moral rights of the author have been asserted

First published in 2011

ISBN-13: 978-0-19-807255-3
ISBN: 10: 0-19-807255-4

Typeset in Adobe Garamond Pro 10.5/12.5
by Sai Graphic Design, New Delhi 110 055
Printed in India at Artxel, New Delhi 110 020

CONTENTS

PREFACE

Autonomy under Empire:
An 'Untimely' Feminist Critique

This book began from a perplexity that would nag my reading of certain cultural works produced by activist thinkers in India. The works invoked the Enlightenment vocabulary of individual autonomy while elaborating the concepts in ways that *did not* fully accord with our common understanding. I noted this anomalous practice especially in works which focused on gender, women, and sexuality. Learning from the many important non-Western and Western scholars who have criticized how the liberal Enlightenment propagates empire, we have come to associate such core concepts of liberalism as autonomy and free choice with separatist and territorial notions of the human being. Focusing on that strand of Enlightenment thought, which characterizes the individual as a property-owner, we commonly view the liberal self as bounded by his/her own interests and own image. The autonomous individual is perceived to be looking upon the world as the object of self-gratification and to be measuring all others in a way vindicating his/her standard of the human.

The indigenous works I was considering departed from this model in at least two ways. On occasion they invoked individual autonomy to challenge the separation of people, bodies, societies into unequal groups and to denounce such institutions as the patriarchal nation or the capitalist empire as breeding these social and biological boundaries. Taking an even more anomalous turn, the works in question appeared to be selectively recasting the Enlightenment language such that the 'individuals' they imagined were not completely bounded and separated from others and the world. Instead, these portrayals of the self sought for ways to be human in the world and to participate in human community *unmediated* by territorial institutions and their technologies. Here and throughout this book, I use 'mediate' in both its senses: as an act of intervention which 'settles' differences between a person's agency and institutional codes, and as the technological 'medium for communicating information' so as to bring about this conciliatory 'result'.¹ To return to my point, I could not find an adequate method to account for the process I encountered here—that non-Western activist thinkers at the same time were embracing the liberal autonomous self and altering some core assumptions. This book presents one such account and it develops a critical apparatus to justify such accounts.

Let us take some representative examples from different eras of Indian modernity. I begin at the onset of literary humanism in nineteenth-century Bengal, when a modern self-reflexivity was just emerging through autobiographical writing. At this moment, we hear a prostitute by the name of Monomohini Dasi inveighing against *pakshapati* (favouritist) health laws; she calls on the colonial state to grant universal legal subjecthood irrespective of gender, social location, and chastity (1869).² Several years later, another marginalized public woman, the famed actress Binodini, shows her grasp on civil liberty by narrating how she demanded a labour *chukti* (contract) to correct her exploitative work conditions (1913).³ From another end of the colonial social spectrum, writer and philosopher Rabindranath Tagore emphasizes the 'individual person' in his English writing on nationalism and empire (1924), while in his late Bengali works he calls for recognizing the woman as a *byektibishesh* (distinct person), imbued with *manusatya* (humanity) and poised to make distinctive contributions to human history (1928).⁴ In the 1980s, dance-dramatist Manjusri Chaki-Sircar theorizes, choreographs, and performs the 'full individuality' and 'self-reliance' of women.⁵ And in our present day, filmmaker Aparna Sen maintains that her cinema is about how women could be 'private individuals'; her films show that only when individuals look upon the 'violent' racial orders of our era (such as 'pogroms' on Muslims) through ethically private eyes are they able to make human relationships 'endure'.[6]

That references to women and gender recur in indigenous engagements, such as these, with individualism, to me is far from coincidental. From their different contexts and in their different modes, all the above thinkers grapple with the problem that women themselves and allied divisions of sexuality and labour are especially vulnerable to being mediated by territorial codes and technologies. The core issue they are grappling with is the 'filiative (familial) order' of empire.[7] While this order complements imperialist individualism in Western thought, it practically *displaces* the notion of the free individual in the colonial state and in various anti-colonial nationalist contexts. Born of Victorian Social Darwinism, this evolutionary narrative of the 'Family of Man' became the colonizer's key metaphor for shaping a whole range of 'contradictory hierarchical distinctions'[8]—of race, geographic place, social status, and occupation—into one global history of human progress or regression. This temporized patriarchal view of human relations firmly re-centred the active male individual (hypermasculine, virile, or bourgeois intellectual, as the case may be). He was placed ahead of women as well as feminized states. The latter included the childlike, the natural and primitive, the aged, and the decadent. On this view, the latter categories of people and functions not only are the subordinates and properties of the central men, they are perceived to 'require and beseech' subordination within territories[9] guarded by men and determined by masculinist (male-centric) knowledge of progress. Colonial governance had entrenched this filiative logic in India by denying the people citizenship rights and market freedom and instead conceiving of colonized society as a filiative web of racial and caste-based relations. In the various eras and places of anti-colonial nationalism and diasporic cultural-nationalism studied in this book, this logic of filiation gains in orthodoxy precisely because nationalists resist Western individualism in the name of Indian family values. This orthodox logic of filiation further infiltrates native social biologies—constructing hard boundaries between sex, patriline, caste, social status, creed, ethnicity, capital and labour.

I submit in this study that for gender activists situated in contexts of postcolonial nationalism—whether in the anti-colonial, statist, or transnational era—the conception of autonomous agency presents a particular appeal. To begin with, its central liberal idea that the self is irreducible to customary filiative order constitutes for them a crucial locus from which to challenge temporized sexual subordination in all forms. Through this conceptual lens, they engage the subordination of women (whether sexually 'developed' and chastened or unchaste/ wild), of feminized workers, or/and of backward men (aged, childlike, or wild terrorist). Beyond this, the notion of individuality allows for the flourishing of feminist perspectives attentive to the filiative patriarchal view of progress born of resistant nationalism. The close readings in the following chapters will demonstrate that the struggle of feminists specific to this context of nationalism is to look for ways in which women could belong in the national community and contribute to the historical progress against the grain of sexual hierarchy. The complexity of this particular feminist struggle, in other words, is two-fold. Feminists want to invest in the indigenous nationalist's rejection of separatist individualism; at the same time, they challenge the filiative order of national history.

That said, the works I introduced above and others of their like, at first glance, could also appear to disprove the reading I am proposing. Far from relying solely on European humanistic vocabulary, they draw heavily from pre-modern non-subjective traditions of thought and from the allied familial and neighbourly practices residual on Indian modern grounds. In Tagore's woman-centred dance dramas, for example, self-actualization could come to mean fulfilling a combination of intellectual and corporeal wants in the vein of *bhava* aesthetics,[10] which eschews the control of body and nature propounded by Cartesian liberal thought. Likewise, Tagore's reflexive self-awareness and critique encompass an effacing of the property-loving self based in Vaishnava Hindu and Buddhist philosophies of self-knowledge.[11] On her part, Manjusri Chaki-Sircar choreographs psychological conflict as a collective performance wherein one woman's inwardness is shared by her companions and neighbours in struggle. Aparna Sen explores the many sides of an autonomous decision including that it could entail a woman's sacrifice of some personal wants and interests through an overflow of non-subjective compassion, the desire of *karuna* for others. And along similar lines, Binodini Dasi goes on to portray how her demands for contractual equality gave way in the face of her larger commitment to her family-like co-workers at the theatre. Without a doubt, residues of pre-modern fluid selves (as against modern reflexive selves) on the quotidian grounds of modern India account for such displacements of the interest-driven individual.

Despite these non-subjective inflections, we cannot chalk up the individualist language I quoted as misappropriating Enlightenment humanism because, at the same time, the users embrace core premises of that secular monistic language. First, they endorse the ethical idea at the basis of the Enlightenment's emancipatory vision of human rights. This idea is that the individual person is 'the substantial entity from which other categories and especially collective categories [are] derived'.[12] On this view, the fundamental substance or worth of each human individual, equally across social locations, constitutes an autonomous capacity to choose and to develop a good life in freedom from authoritative structures. And then, they want to imagine associative life as co-created by autonomous participants who act with mutual respect and support for one another's lives and labours.[13] While they may be immersing in residual non-subjective traditions of personhood, then, activist Indian modernists reflect upon ways to mobilize humanism in tandem with different historical traditions. They are seeking a future of non-hierarchal community and communication. Seen in another way, they conceive of an associative life that at the same time is replete with the nurturing practices of family and neighbourliness *and yet is devoid of filiation*, that is, of established originary and paternalistic structures.

This book will demonstrate that two presuppositions of liberal individualism attract thinkers wanting to mobilize against the complex social, economic, and moral mediations that devolve on different lives from empire and anti-colonial nationalism (in the respective eras of colonization and transnational capitalism). One is *personal autonomy*: the assumption that every individual irrespective of biological contour, social rank, and spatial location ought to be recognized as an independent agent. She must command the right to pursue a path of life and work without being exploited, discriminated, or violated. The second is *ethical* autonomy: the assumption that every seemingly ordinary individual has the potential for a responsible socio-moral vision of the world in relation to herself/himself, a principled vision unconstrained by authoritative/filiative codes.[14] The latter assumption constitutes every person as a possible emancipatory challenger of dominant social identities, be these largely subjugating or subjugated. Precisely, as they strive to realize this combination of social and ethical freedoms on non-Western postcolonial terrains, indigenous activist-intellectuals also want to refute what they see as the root of domination: the liberal-capitalist tenet of the individual as a property-owner marking boundaries and instrumentally stratifying others and the world. In their re-imaginations of the autonomous person, indigenous philosophies of the ethical self as well as quotidian non-subjective practices of association become salient concepts.

The overarching claim of this book, then, is that indigenous activist-intellectuals strive to invest in certain ethical premises of Enlightenment thought—specifically the ethics of autonomy—while refusing such other of its aspects as territorial individualism and the 'possessive' self[15] of the capitalist Enlightenment, which develops into the territorialist in the course of colonization.[16] A key phrase to be noted here, however, is that these thinkers reflexively *strive for* activist critical consciousness. None achieves perfection in this regard. To substantiate this second, related claim I take a two-pronged approach in the following chapters.

On the one hand, the chapters of this book detail the struggles of concept and of affect that transpire in the works of critical modernist thinkers. I emphasize that the struggles against visual mediation prove to be especially hard because in India as elsewhere the technologies guiding sight have been persuasive tools of empire: they reinforce biases in the guise of universal enlightenment by the way they construct images as making truth 'self-evident' to every person's eye in the most public and impartial form.[17] Chapter 1 shows that from their early days in colonial India such technologies as photography, illusionist proscenium stagecraft, and point-of-view painting reinforce the truest and best forms of womanhood and manhood in the public eye, reducing or eclipsing all other sensory ways to be and to know the world. Throughout Chapter 3 and also in Chapter 4, I lay out in what ways filiative and alienating orders of Indianness spread and change in our day through the moving image and through networks of visual imagery (television, advertising). My point is that networks of visual mediation expand hand-in-hand with a new flexible form of empire conjoined to the international sexual division of labour. Thus I examine the shaping of humanist Indian thought side-by-side in two consecutive eras of global empire. My focus is on the various locations of Indian consciousness these produce: the colony (Chapters 1 and 2); the multinationalizing nation-state (Chapters 3 and 4); transnational migration and diaspora (Chapter 3). As Edward Said reminds us, imperialism—'the practice, the theory, and the attitudes of a dominating metropolitan centre ruling a distant territory'—lingers in various cultural and financial formations long after the ending of colonial settlements.[18]

On the other hand, the contextual studies to follow delineate that critical authors and artists themselves are partially self-aware of their own filiations with masculinist and racialized boundaries and with allied media aesthetics. They strive, that is, to be self-aware about the pleasures of dominant forms of rightness, goodness, and beauty promoted by prevalent communication media. Against the grain of the dominant I read how, throughout these two eras, critical authors of Indian modernity experiment with various indigenous conceptions of autonomous agency. They seek to imagine the person who works against sexual hierarchies, at the same time embraces the indigenous activist's refusal of the bounded liberal self and looks for alternative forms of being an individual and forging association. In all the works I look at, these experiments encompass not only the content but also the form of communication. The struggle overall is to eschew the conciliatory results sought by dominant codes of mediation. In chapters to come, I explore various registers of this struggle: multi-layered autobiographical narratives by marginal and elite women of colonial Bengal (Chapter 1); the experimental woman-centred and individual-centred dance dramas and prosaic poetry that Rabindranath Tagore had produced in the last phase of his life (Chapter 2); the feminist dance-theatre, in the tradition of Tagore's works, by choreographer and performer Manjusri Chaki-Sircar and daughter Ranjabati Sircar; and the critical work with camera and narrative by feminist filmmaker Aparna Sen (Chapter 4).

That I focus this study of eclectic indigenous autonomies on aesthetic works demonstrates a larger point. To begin with, I substantiate a position taken by Wai Chee Dimock and other scholars of literary ethics—that the 'textualization of justice'[19] often allows for more creative and multifaceted explorations of democracy than the uncontextualized formulations in which legalistic discourses on rights are commonly invested. Building on this position, I explore various such textualizations in written and printed productions, visual production, and bodily performance. My point is to emphasize the importance of *reading* imagery of justice through a literary lens *as texts* consisting of multiple and conflicting layers of pleasure and persuasion. I maintain that only by approaching non-Western postcolonial contexts through this textual lens are we able to pry out conceptions of gender justice wherein *different cultures and languages* of personhood and association *overlap and clash*. Since I have found no framework to adequately account for these gendered textual politics in non-Western activist modernities, the following pages contain my attempt to develop a critical apparatus on the basis of one such account.

My study follows the trajectory of one Indian culture of aesthetic modernity and fervid debate. It commences with the inception of aesthetical humanism in colonial Bengal and winds into alterations and appropriations of humanism in contemporary liberalizing Bengal and selected North-American diasporas, Bengali and non-Bengali. Clearly, not all aspects of my study will transfer to other modern Indian contexts of aesthetic creation and theory. Arguing that 'it is historically inaccurate to maintain that the modern period in Indian literature is unrelated to its precursors', Ganesh Devy reminds us that during colonization all vernacular *bhasa* literatures of India showed various and 'constant fluctuations' in response to the varieties of social change under way in different parts of the subcontinent.[20] It stands to reason that each of these bhasa cultures has altered along a different path in subsequent postcolonial eras. The scope of my study is relatively narrow and modest in this regard. I explore in what specific ways the Enlightenment notion of the autonomous self enters, alters, or indigenizes within textualizations of gender justice in modern cultures related to Bengal. It is the apparatus I develop for reading the gendered autonomous self in non-Western postcolonial texts that ought to have wider resonance. It should be helpful for other scholars who wish to parse indigenous routes of the autonomous individual and of feminist-democratic association in postcolonial modern contexts. In its broad parameters, it should aid in understanding not only disparate Indian and South-Asian modernities, but also other non-metropolitan cultures of sexual activism.

All in all, my position is that postcolonial gender activists rethink the attitudes of masculine empire and resistance even as their own consciousness continues to be internal to empire and thus compromised. In taking this position, I broadly agree with a core assumption made by Enlightenment modernity. Liberal thought assumes that the responsible individual potentially is a transhistorical rational agent able to objectively evaluate diverse historical values and arrive at some common norms for human betterment. Yet in endorsing this assumption, I depart from at least two schools of theory prevalent today in postcolonial studies focusing on South Asia and in allied transnational feminist studies.

On the first view, scholars maintain that modern (secular) rational consciousness is constituted and codified by historical institutions; it cannot arrive at transhistorical or objective judgement. Widely influential on this school of thought has been Michel Foucault's landmark critique of the liberal Enlightenment, through his studies of how modern Western rationality is internal to and crafted by hierarchal institutions (such as the family, the state, the penal code, and the asylum).[21] For example, postcolonial theorists—Partha Chatterjee and Dipesh Chakrabarty— and transnational feminist Inderpal Grewal alike aim their scholarship at exposing how personal reasoning is constructed by histories, and how individuals who seem to be objective are complicit with empire and resistant essentialism. Scholars of this vein who wish also to theorize agency within modern contexts, by and large, do so by looking at how institutional subject positions are decentred, subverted, or hybridized by forms of knowledge alternative to the dominant and the pure. Homi Bhabha, for instance, draws on Jacques Derrida and Jacques Lacan to pursue this line of criticism, whereas Dipesh Chakrabarty conceives of indigenous quotidian knowledge also within a dichotomous framework of dominant-and-submerged. In the light of this theoretical position, my endorsement of transhistorical reasoning might appear to be a regression into the idealism of the liberal Enlightenment. It could mean that I am staking an ontological faith in a sovereign subject 'unfettered' by institutional biases and interests, and thus, capable of distilling certain truths.[22]

This postcolonial approach of engaging and decentring humanist conceptions of autonomy and reason—an approach which relies largely on critiques of the Enlightenment (such as Foucault's) internal to the Western intellectual tradition—clears the space for a second influential school of postcolonial theory. This second view affirms the potential for anti-imperialist agency in indigenous non-subjective conceptions of personhood and in fluid self-practices, which lie outside the time and space of secular modernity and its reflexive self. This view minimizes patriarchal filiations or misogynist inclinations of these non-subjective conceptions and fluid practices. Instead, the emphasis is on what in these self-practices is different from the imperialist modern self. Along the same lines, this approach does not clarify how we could distinguish all the ways that seemingly fluid non-modern practices are mediated under empire by orthodox notions of difference and resistance. Among scholars of South Asia, the most important voice for this theoretical position is Ashis Nandy, while Dipesh Chakrabarty as well pursues elements of this argument (even though the conclusions they draw are different). Among transnational feminists, Saba Mahmood has recently contended for the non-liberal feminine agency of Islamist Egyptian women against the grain of rights-based secular-left politics. In my Introduction and my Conclusion, I will return to the specifics of these important arguments. For the moment, I acknowledge that the foundational anti-Enlightenment position upon which these various thoughtful scholars base their critiques of Western modernity makes my claims about indigenous autonomy appear not merely irregular but politically suspect.

In response to this foundational position, I must raise some practical questions: if we assume that the reflexive activist's reasoning is invariably institutional, how do we explain that many histories of intellectual and social movements have improved *some* material and conceptual conditions for women and the marginalized, in modern India and elsewhere in the world? In view of these activist histories, I cannot but agree with postcolonial feminists, such as Rajeswari Sunder Rajan and Chandra Talpade Mohanty, who insist on the importance of pursuing the Enlightenment ideas of democracy and autonomy against the grain of their institutional articulations. Gayatri Spivak's recent work also reminds activist scholars to keep before them an 'axio-teleology (a value system with an end in view)'.[23] To these critical feminist positions also I shall return in my contextual chapters and my Conclusion. For the moment, I must follow up with another basic question: might it not be more intuitive to assume instead that a responsible agent is *partially objective* in evaluating injustices and coercions, in reference to a common human end, and in another part *not?* Following this intuition, I present in my introductory chapter what I consider to be a more realistic critical apparatus for situating responsible voices in the world. As noted earlier, I read as texts the multiple and messy strands in these voices. Subsequent contextual chapters demonstrate the partial yet cumulative character of humanist normativity, as this is textualized through the modern Bengali and Anglophone aesthetic works I study. I delineate that in these various works, activist reasoning *intermingles affect with causality.* The multiple strands of written and expressive thought I examine (printed matter, camera work, bodily performance) refer to the different affective relations and conceptual presuppositions on non-Western modern grounds.

By now it should be evident that the study to follow constitutes what Wendy Brown has called in another context 'untimely' critical work, insofar as timely thought comprises a sense of appropriateness 'about when, how, and where one raises certain issues or mentions certain problems'.[24] Certainly, in our dark times of neoliberal empires the discourse of choices and rights is being deployed widely to promote coercive consumerism, to justify violations, and to mask abjection. Now more than ever, it seems appropriate for critical scholars to demystify the rationalities governing individual choice and human agency, whether these stem from Indian communalist contexts or from jingoistic Euro-America. It is equally urgent that we explore where and when personhoods and epistemologies differ from dominant individualism. Indeed, the feminist and race-conscious students who come to my classroom hoping that academic learning and social activism will go hand-in-hand, do engage with whole-hearted zest in subversions of the imperialist self. Yet ever so often the animated discussions in feminist classrooms tend to run aground on the all too familiar modernist question of personal agency. Activist young scholars also ask for ways to conceptualize feminist agents of history. They seek for critical frameworks through which we are able to correct the rampant biological prejudices and gendered violations of our times and bring about more sexually equitable forms of belonging.

It is my hope that activist students and scholars who are raising such concerns as these will find the following study to be of some use. As Wendy Brown further observes, untimely critical work is a restorative endeavour—it is a 'bid to reset time' by opening up prevalent trends of thought to further deliberation and possible re-orientation. In this restorative critical spirit, my book re-opens the liberal concept of autonomy. I deliberate upon differing cultural approaches and political economic contexts of this self-conception. And, I maintain that interpretations of individualist ethics can very well depart from the dominant.

ACKNOWLEDGEMENTS

I would like to thank the many whose encouragement or active help got me to the end of this challenging project. The late Miriam Silverberg of the University of California, Los Angeles (UCLA) had been the one to say that I must write a book about 'decolonizing the individual'—and to instil in me the courage that I could. To Miriam my intellectual and personal debts are immeasurable. Ketu Katrak of University of California, Irvine held my hand through every up and down of my pursuit, ensuring that I kept at it even though my ideas were controversial. For her untiring companionship and her feminist enthusiasm, I remain deeply grateful to Ketu. The manuscript would not be in its present shape without Thu-Huong Nguyen Vo's rigorous readings of earlier drafts and her theoretically perspicacious feedback. And Vinay Lal's respectful support for my endeavours went hand-in-hand with his many resourceful suggestions in turning me into a scholar of Indian culture.

Also at UCLA, I have gained enormously from interacting with several other colleagues and with students. Shu-mei Shih's faith in this project and in me as a scholar has constituted a valuable anchor; the late Teshome Gabriel made me believe in myself as a film scholar; my inspiring conversations with Marta Savigliano inclined me towards dance studies; the respect I received from Women's Studies colleagues, notably

Sondra Hale, gave me the confidence to pursue feminist research; and the support for scholarship I received from Bruce Beiderwell's protective attitude towards my time gave me the opportunity to sustain the research. And last, but certainly not the least, students from my Ph.D. course on 'Feminist Knowledge Production' raised questions about 'theory' and 'feminist agency' radical enough to convince me of the necessity for rethinking available theoretical models. I owe a debt of inspiration to my students.

A number of other interactions outside UCLA have made my book what it is. Gayatri Chakravorty Spivak was the first to urge that I must incorporate indigenous Bengali scholarship. Her constructive criticism as well as helpful pointers made me think more self-critically about my own work. Amiya Deb's helpful guidance set me on the right track, and the anonymous reviews I subsequently received from the Readers of Oxford University Press pushed me to extend my scholarship in several directions. My thanks go to the editors at Oxford University Press for steering me through the revisions in a way that has yielded a better book. My gratitude extends also to Satya Mohanty who was the first to point out that I must think more rigorously both about humanism and about knowledge. Throughout the years of researching and writing this book, I have been greatly energized by the faith shown in my work by Asif Agha and Karen Leonard and the deep friendships of Beheroze Shroff, Anju Relan, and Ghazala Mansuri.

Versions of this book have been presented at UCLA, Stanford University; the Modern Language Association of America (MLA) Conference; University of Delhi; Indira Gandhi National Open University; the India International Centre, New Delhi; Hyderabad University; and East-West University, Dhaka. I have gained substantially from the vibrant responses I received from audiences at these venues, and notably from the astute remarks I received from my commentator Savita Singh at the India International Centre.

Research for this project was partially funded by UCLA Faculty Development and Diversity Grants and by a UCLA Women's Studies research grant. I thank UCLA and especially Christine Littleton, former Chair of Women's Studies, for the support. Research for this book was conducted at the National Library and the Bangiya Sahitya Parishad at Kolkata, and the libraries of UCLA and the University of California at Berkeley. I thank all the library staff for their assistance, and I especially thank the Director of the National Library, Kolkata, for granting me permission to avail of the archival facilities. Without the timely help of two astute and committed graduate assistants at two different locations—Khanum Shaikh in Los Angeles and Angshumaan Bhowmick in Kolkata—I would surely have missed some of the key resources that have gone into this study.

An earlier version of the Introduction appeared in *diacritics* and a portion of Chapter 3 was published by *Feminist Media Studies*. I thank Johns Hopkins University Press and Routledge for permitting me to use my previously published articles in this book. For giving me the permission to use photographs or stills, I express my thanks to Kumkum Bhattacharya of Visva-Bharati Press; Rajesh Agarwal of Suravi Films; Bipin Vohra of SPS Arts and Entertainment; Vikramjit Roy of the National Film Development Corporation of India; Devajit Bandyopadhyay, archivist of Binodini Dasi's photographs; Sasikala Penumarthi of the Academy of Kuchipudi Dance, Atlanta, USA; and Avinash Pasricha, photographer of Indian dance. I am thankful also to Jonaki Sarcar—Director of the Dancers Guild, Kolkata—for generously sharing her time, resources, and insights with me. And my gratitude to Aparna Sen is lasting—for the profoundly illuminating conversation I had with her a few months ago, and for the deep inspiration her films have provided for this study.

Without the active help and the nurturance I received from my family, this book would not have been written. My father, Dipankar Niyogi, initiated the contacts I needed to conduct research in Kolkata and even after her cerebral attack, my mother, Pushpanjali Niyogi, helped with the translations while also ensuring that I had the time and the space to write. And to my partner Suranjan my debt is boundless—for his unflagging enthusiasm for this project and my intellectual growth, his energetic assistance with the translations as well as the research, his astute comments on my writing, and above all, for being there for me at all costs.

INTRODUCTION

Individuation across Cultures:
The Blind Spot of Postcolonial Theory

Is it possible to appropriate the liberal conception of autonomy as a modality of decolonization in non-Western indigenous terms? And how? This chapter initiates my conversation, running through the rest of this book, with postcolonial and subaltern theoretical models of agency founded on a position against Enlightenment individualism.[1] I also examine some Western intellectual premises of this position, notably Michel Foucault's formulations. While I demonstrate all the ways I have learnt from the schools of thought subscribing to this position regarding how to read modern Bengali and Anglophone texts, I also point out where I find the basic position inadequate for such accounts. As shown below, some models of agency offered by the anti-Enlightenment schools prove inadequate, particularly in accounting for the pressure points and the challenges levelled at sexual hierarchies by indigenous cultural producers. Likewise, they fail to provide a framework adequate for alternative indigenous imaginations of the feminist autonomous self.

The bulk of this Introduction delineates a critical apparatus for reading how individual autonomy and transhistorical agency elaborate on material grounds at the same time, making the author's objectivity limited and fragmented by self-oriented idealism. I have been inspired in this line of thought by critical scholarship on some enabling aspects of the Enlightenment and on how these aspects have travelled to the Indian subcontinent and interacted with indigenous thought. In the light of these critiques, I underscore that we must be attentive to two things: first, authors' evaluations work and change within the content of the text and also in and through the communicative mode; second, these changes inflect to alterations in the political economic conditions of the productions. To clarify how to read the inflections, I juxtapose two works, which are born in the respective eras of Indian modernity I study and are produced in different media: written word and cinema. My point is that we must be attentive to the differing ways in which aesthetical imaginations refer to material arrangements and how they intersect with communicative media in the consecutive eras of empire. Thereby, we account for differences between the modalities of ethical autonomy and of intellectual decolonization in the respective contexts. Overall, this chapter uses brief close readings of selected text and imagery to introduce a number of features of my formulation of 'transcultural individuation'. These features will be used throughout the book to map various responses to humanist modernity by Indian aesthetic thinkers under different political economic conditions.

Reprising the Individual? Postcolonial Theories and Anti-enlightenment Critique

In 1924, Rabindranath Tagore wrote an article in *The Manchester Guardian* rebutting attacks by British journalists on his play *Red Oleanders* (*Raktakarabi*). A typical attack, published in the *Sheffield Telegraph*, argues that since the play appears to Western readers to be 'absolute nonsense', it would be 'very interesting to hear what it is all about' if the author could possibly 'follow the workings of his own brain'[2] and explain. Tagore's response is complex enough and merits a lengthy quotation:

There was a time when, in the human world, most of our important dealings with our fellow-beings were personal dealings, and the professional element in society was never hugely disproportionate to the normal constitution of its life ....

Today, another factor has made itself immensely evident in shaping and guiding human destiny. It is the spirit of organization, which is not social in character, but utilitarian. Christian Europe no longer depends upon Christ for her peace, but upon the League of Nations, because her peace is not disturbed by forceful individuals so much as by organized Powers. Naturally, in all organizations, variation of personality is eliminated, and the individual members insofar as they represent the combination to which they belong give expression to a common type ....

I am not competent to say how Europe herself feels about this phenomenon produced by her science. Very likely, her stout-hearted Jack is already busy making breaches in the walls of this fortress. But I can say on behalf of inarticulate Asia, what a terrible reality for us is the West, whose relation to ourselves is so little human. The view that we can get of her, in our mutual dealings, is that of a titanic power with an endless curiosity to analyse and know, but without the sympathy to understand; with numberless arms to coerce and acquire, but no serenity of soul to realize and enjoy.

It is an organized passion of greed that is stalking abroad in the name of European civilization.... Such an objectified passion lacks the true majesty of human nature.... It barricades itself against all direct human touch with barriers of race pride and prestige of power ....

Once our people had either an Akbar or an Aurangzeb to deal with; now we have an organized avarice—frightfully simple in its purpose, mechanically complicated in its process. Its messengers who come to us—be they Lord Birkenhead or Lord Curzon—are never for us our fellow-beings in flesh and blood, as were Julius Caesar and Antony who could easily find their immortal places in Shakespeare's drama ....

... I am told that science has become a principal subject for some notable poets in Europe. That is natural, for science has permeated Western life; it no longer has its own cradle in the secluded cells of the learned. In a similar manner, the hungry purpose, having science for its steed, running about unchecked, trampling our life's harvest, is not an intellectual generalization unfit for imaginative literature.... It is the principal hero today in the drama of human history; and I trust I have the right to invoke it in my own play, not in the spirit of a politician, but of a poet ....

I am glad to find that my critics readily acknowledge that Nandini, the heroine of the play, has definite features of an individual person. She is not an abstraction, but is pursued by an abstraction, like one tormented by a ghost. Nandini is a real woman who knows that wealth and power are *maya*, and the highest expression of life is love ....

I can assure my readers that I never meant to use this book as propaganda. It is a vision that has come to me in the darkest hour of dismay.... This personality—the divine essence of the infinite in the vessel of the finite—has its last treasure-house in woman's heart. Her pervading influence will some day restore the human to the desolated world of man ....[3]

How do we read the epistemic implications of writing such as this, born at the heart of empire and using humanistic tropes that at the same time are awkwardly indigenized? Let me begin to answer this question by reading the passage through approaches presented by the anti-Enlightenment schools of postcolonial thought.

One way to read the passage would be to focus on textual elements which suggest upfront that Tagore lacks in the agency for transhistorical evaluation. While he criticizes and resists Western masculine imperialism, his resistance is not objective towards empire but rather compromised by the paradigmatic concepts even as he reiterates the paradigm in altered form (see my discussion of the imperialist paradigm in the Preface). While Tagore criticizes the Western imperialist's possessive 'greed', at the same time he seems to be charting a separate territory for Asia's own civilization. Arguably, he also asserts a filiative or biological order of civilizations by pitting the spiritual-sexual humanism of Asia—embodied in the 'individual' knowledge of the essentially un-Westernized woman—on an evolutionary plain higher than the aggressive masculine individualism of the West. Focusing on the Orientalist bent of Tagore's imagery, we could also read how he is reducing the Asian woman into a timeless symbol of the quintessential human spirit of self-surrender, foreclosing the possibility that various women on the grounds of India and Asia can claim agency in time, that is, in particularized historical contexts. In this regard, Tagore's sexual symbolism in this passage could also be seen as paralleling the binary aesthetic attitude of the European Romantics with whom he is often aligned. Not unlike Tagore, a William Hazlitt or a Percy Shelley was resisting the ills born of capitalist societies and utilitarian norms. Even though they wrote at length about 'fellow-feeling'[4] and 'social good',[5] however, these principles got compromised in their texts. Their aesthetic drive was to possess people and nature with reference to their own gender, class, and race interests. Likewise, Tagore's symbolism of the 'individual person' appears to utilize the loving woman as an instrument referring to his own masculine national rivalry with the Western territorial man. In all these respects, Tagore's resistant reason could be analysed as entirely crafted by the institutional paradigms of empire and rivalrous masculine nationalism.

In reading along these lines, we would be amplifying the subaltern critique of historicist reason as presented by Partha Chatterjee. In his perceptive historical account of instrumental reason, Chatterjee emphasizes that essentialist humanism—born of the 'bourgeois-rationalist conception of knowledge'[6] in Enlightenment Europe—was propagated worldwide through empire and capitalism. He maintains that even though anti-colonial activists (such as Tagore) challenged Western 'political domination',[7] they simultaneously imbibed an instrumental and self-referential way of thought. Thus they voluntarily 'aligned' indigenous knowledge—the Hindu Vaishnava ethic of self-yielding love, in this instance—with Western models of discipline so that they erected 'parallel' yet different national identities to rival the imperialist.[8] The thrust of this position has been reaffirmed by Partha Chatterjee's recent commentary on the 'governmentalized' nature of democracy in contemporary India.[9] He argues that even though the Indian nation-state grants agency to population groups which transgress the legal structure of rights and claim legitimacy on the basis of alternative beliefs and practices, the state's normative modernizing project eventually normalizes the transgressions; the subaltern groups themselves 'also embark on a path of internal transformation'.[10] The point of this critique is that even though modern individuals (elite or subaltern) transgress institutional codes, their transgressions and resistances as well come to be codified anew by prevailing institutions.

Underlying this critical path of demystification—that is, of uncovering the historical complicities of modern self-consciousness, despite its mystique of transhistorical reason—are two interrelated assumptions regarding the Enlightenment self-proposed by Michel Foucault. The first is that modern self-reflexivity is unstable and double-edged—on the one side it wants to fold back on, question, and 'transgress' the institutional discourses which shape its reasoning, on the other it accepts the discursive limits.[11] The second assumption, following from the first, is that normative judgements—including ethical choices between right and wrong staked in social movements—fail to overcome institutional interests. Instead, they are consequential to and instrumental in particular historical struggles for power.[12] The implication, as I demonstrate through my reading earlier, is that such activist-thinkers as Tagore who self-consciously want to think freely of imperialist conceptions of self and community are merely transforming and readjusting the paradigmatic imperialist concepts of separatism, territorialism, and filiation. They are not able to conceive any philosophical and social change unmediated by pre-existing cognitive structures.

As against this emphasis on the complicity of transgressive thought, we could read the passage quoted earlier on the presupposition that despite complicity not all knowledge forms on the heterogeneous grounds of postcolonies are or can be normalized. We could focus on how Tagore's translations of heterogeneous reality into possessive self-oriented terms are being ruptured and hybridized through his text's affective linkage with the popular practices embedded in the everyday lives of bourgeois Bengalis of his time. Drawing on Derrida and Lacan, Homi Bhabha propounds that postcolonial (ethical) agency ruptures and hybridizes modernity's pedagogical narratives. On this view, we could examine how Tagore's binary voice is being split up through a 'performance ... of cultural time' that re-inscribes 'lessons from the past' into the fabric of the dominant present.[13] On Bhabha's terms, Tagore's hybrid lessons could be seen to comprise 'ancestral memory',[14] the Vaishnava ethic of self-yielding love permeating myriad women-centred religious and social traditions in his life-world and also various 'contra-modern' Asian legacies of liberation struggle against European colonizers.

Along a line not entirely dissimilar from Bhabha's, we could also look for the ruptures in Tagore's rational voice in the light of Dipesh Chakrabarty's model of agency. Through this lens, we would focus upon Tagore's emphasis on the woman's rejection of *maya* or desire for worldly materials, and on a love, such as hers, unconditioned by interests. We would consider in what ways village Bengali traditions of Vaishnava *bhakti* inflect these words. Chakrabarty argues that since reason is exclusive and self-referential so long as it 'colludes with the logic of historicist thought', a different agency should be sought not in rational choices but in the 'preanalytical' cultural 'training' maintained by non-Western people in the processes of living.[15] In contrast to Homi Bhabha, whose lessons from the past encompass both non-modern temporality and counter-modern liberation struggle, Chakrabarty clearly bifurcates the framework of historical reason from non-Western quotidian reasoning by eliminating mediation—in his words a 'universal middle term'.[16] Clarifying that this view does not subscribe to cultural relativism because cultures were permeable in pre-modern times (which are residual on the grounds of non-Western modernities), Chakrabarty stresses that the need to guard cultural homogenization arises only with the 'privileging of the analytical over the lived'[17] under Enlightenment humanism. From this perspective, Chakrabarty identifies a subversive agency in the 'uncanny' poetic eruption of the *chirantan* sensibilities of Bengali Hindu village life in Tagore's imagination, while he bifurcates this poetic agency from Tagore's prosaic investment in a utilitarian's struggle to 'align the world with the real and rational'.[18] Through the same frame, we could read Tagore's feminine bhakti-inflected imagery above as erupting to disturb the coherence of his anti-colonial male rivalry with the utilitarian Westerner.

The approaches to trangressive agency taken by such critics as Bhabha and Chakrabarty position individual reason and institutional language somewhat differently from Partha Chatterjee's approach. Rather than viewing text production by an individual subject as an entirely inner idealistic process—which reduces the surrounding world to only a 'philosophy inherent in the mind'[19] of the rational thinker—each critic in his different way reads texts as psychosocial processes wherein multiple voices and material realities interact. At the same time, their models of transgressive thought converge with Chatterjee's in one crucial respect— all three critics assume that modern self-conscious reason is shaped by historical institutions and biases, whereas the non-modern or critical elements of social consciousness are peripheral to mainstream thought or even repressed under it. This *counter-normative approach* to historical reason resonates with the internal limitation placed by Michel Foucault on what he considers to be the Enlightenment idea of critique.

Foucault maintains that European modernity's 'Enlightenment' lies in making every 'individual … responsible' for using reason in a way not subjected to authority so that they level a 'permanent critique' at themselves and their 'historical era'.[20] He distinguishes this counter-normative spirit of responsible critique from the normative humanism born also of the Enlightenment. His argument is that humanism's efforts to objectively 'articulate … universal' structures of good and bad knowledge and 'programmes' of social change[21] are mired in the metaphysics of self-presence and self-serving-reference. This poststructuralist view of responsible 'critique' forecloses the more holistic form of critique Tagore appears to be exploring in the passage above. His critique seeks to correct injustices and restore the times, that is, to enable a better future for the human whole (see my discussion of the concept of 'critique' in the Preface). Foucault's wholesale challenge to modern secular normative reason, when transposed to the study of non-Western contexts, also makes room for such conservationist approaches to historical difference as Chakrabarty's. Chakrabarty's model constitutes cultural reasoning as repressed within the lived *habitus*—as functioning in the realm of the 'uncanny'. Chakrabarty ascribes this encrypted status to alternative reason which precludes that non-Western people either can mobilize through local cultural legacies against imperial teleology (that is, through such intellectual and embodied legacies as the bhakti tradition Tagore invokes) or that they are able to evaluate possibilities for a better future from a site *provisionally outside* or beyond empire.

These poststructuralist and post-modern positions view non-subjective or pre-modern selves as critical perspectives from which to demystify dominant subjecthood. We could also read Tagore's words to reclaim his non-Western outlook, taking a normative approach towards alternative rationality. We could maintain that Tagore transplants the English words 'individual' and 'human' into an irreducibly indigenous frame of reference. In order to correct the hypermasculine self-orientation of humanist norms, as informed by European science and capitalism, Tagore objectively embraces the feminine principle of self-surrender indigenous to the ethics of Indian culture and embodied in Hindu women's everyday practices. With principled self-consciousness, he posits this fluid and surrendering pre-modern self as the alternative to the possessive and territorial male individual of the West. In reading thus, we would be in line with Ashis Nandy's traditionalist model which takes cultural bifurcation to its logical conclusion. He positions non-modern ethics clearly above post-Enlightenment secular modernity. Ashis Nandy presents a radically evaluative, communitarian approach: 'Under oppression,' he states, emphasis on a 'parochial' cultural existence rather than on a relational one that dominates and 'distorts ... could protect some forms of universalism more successfully than does conventional universalism'.[22] Invoking the 'authenticity and authority of the [surrendering] feminine self ... as an organizing principle of the Indic civilization',[23] Nandy states that we ought to see this principle as enshrined in such Hindu mythic notions as self-immolation of the sati (the goddess/widow). At the same time, we ought to and are able to distinguish this norm of the feminine sacred from its 'inauthentic' secular offspring, the homicidal widow-burnings which proliferated through market economy.[24] Tagore's description of the woman's individuality as a 'divine essence in the vessel of the finite' could indeed be read as an invocation of the feminine principle indigenous to India. In so reading, we would assume that Tagore is completely successful in differentiating between authentic indigenous ideas and principles and secular politics of sexual oppression around him. This would mean that we are placing an ontological faith in the exceptional capability that such thinkers as Tagore or M.K. Gandhi had of overcoming complicity in contemporary global identity politics (imperialism versus resistant male nationalism) and arriving at an ideally objective view of cultural difference.

There is little doubt that the postcolonial approaches I sketched earlier, resting on a foundational anti-Enlightenment position, account for several key aspects of Tagore's text. Indeed, my own readings in this chapter and throughout the book remain indebted to the critics I quote. I find the poststructuralist approach to be indispensable for thinking carefully about how ways of reasoning change with empire, capital, and allied structures of mediation. From Nandy's traditionalist approach I have learned to be attentive to the radical potential of alternative cultures, and to look for conflicting self-practices on quotidian non-Western grounds. That said, next I would like to point to aspects of the Tagore text which cannot be captured by either of the postcolonial schools presented earlier. Quite simply, their respective assumptions about human agency and normative evaluation, and more broadly, about the evaluating mind's relation to historical reality, stand in the way.

My immediate purpose in the next section is to consider what hermeneutic selections are prompted by assumptions underlying these anti-Enlightenment models, and how else we could approach the complexities of indigenous activist texts, such as Tagore's, and their epistemological moves. My larger goal through the following sections is to arrive at a more well-rounded apparatus for the 'critique' of gendered empire from a postcolonial perspective—an apparatus of critique that not only undermines and dismantles orthodox Western or Westernized frameworks, but also moves towards a more equitable gendered world. The discussion below addresses some other critical perspectives on Tagore and colonial Bengal that are less dismissive of Enlightenment modernity. Since I deal further with *Red Oleanders* in Chapter 2, here I will make only a few brief points.

Critiquing Modern Time: The Enlightenment and a Gendered Indigenous Engagement

If we read the above-mentioned passage with the intent only of identifying in what ways Tagore's consciousness is homogenized by imperialist history and/or how it uncannily transgresses historicist analysis through poetic perceptions (a phenomenon Tagore himself seems only fleetingly to comprehend when he names himself a 'poet'), we fail to explain the *canny* objectivity he also reveals. We have no vocabulary to explain (a) how Tagore draws normative connections between cultures and (b) how he also makes critical choices between cultural values.

Note that, on the one hand, Tagore is analytically linking the conceptual framework of orthodox European science with Euro-American socioeconomic and aesthetical practices. He interconnects such key principles of European science and philosophy as the 'curiosity to analyse and know' and the 'objectification' of (corporeal) passion with the production of 'abstractions' or idealistic templates for knowing and for quantifying everyday realities (for casting the quotidian into 'common types'). Moreover, he discerns in these principles a causal structure for the West's dehumanizing proclivities. Tagore is analysing in these causes several imperialist Western proclivities: first, the intention to organize societies into 'mechanically complicated' national powers, that is, to subject the myriad aspects of social interaction to the homogenizing technologies of capitalist nation-states; second, the drive to 'coerce and acquire' fuelled by a 'hungry purpose'—that is, to possess and to consume nature and the world as instruments of self-gratification; third, the tendency to erect 'barriers of race pride'; and fourth, the inclination to create poetry in the same scientific way, that is, to similarly objectify and mediate lived realities in aesthetic imagination. On the other hand, an attentive reading of the passage also reveals that Tagore's analytical imagination is moving by way of an internal critique of historical domination to transhistorical evaluations of alternative norms of knowledge that could redress domination and division. Among these normative alternatives of the self and knowledge we find pre-secular elements.

Poststructuralist and post-modern vocabularies cannot convincingly account for this objective analysis by Tagore of dominant institutional knowledge. They are even less equipped to explain the way his knowledge travels transhistorically to non-modern alternatives, in the quest for some criteria for bettering the overall human condition. Do we agree then that Tagore is taking a discrete rather than a monistic approach to civilization and history in the vein that Ashis Nandy suggests? That is, do we read into this passage that Tagore is objectively selecting traditions of the self from non-modern India and pre-secular Europe as salutary alternatives to contemporary Western individualisms? And do we take it that in the process Tagore is able to transcend the pervasive inclination of his time to mediate and homogenize indigenous heterogeneity and produce divisive national identity politics? Two aspects of the passage also deter me from settling for this reading of a parochial and idealized frame of reference. First, Tagore desists from endorsing absolute civilizational difference at the same time that he partially indigenizes his vocabulary of human agency. Second, far from being perfectly objective, his transcultural evaluations of the emancipatory individual to an extent continue to be complicit with masculine mystiques of authenticity and superiority.

The passage above embraces a monistic or indivisible view of humanity, characteristic of Enlightenment humanism, rather than differentiates between human contexts. To begin with, Tagore draws links across selective cultural spaces and times. He is pursuing what I call in this book a critical *transcultural* endeavour for emancipatory knowledge. Thereby, he pointedly eschews a moral demarcation of civilizations and personhoods (a practice current in both the imperial Euro-America and the nationalist India of his time). Through his cultural choices, Tagore assembles several *disparate yet interlinked* alternatives to the dehumanization he diagnoses in imperialist Euro-American societies. These include such non-modern references as the Vaishnava *bhakta* (devotee) who surrenders self-centred maya (desire) for worldly advantages and transcends into *prem* (divine love);[25] the Mughal monarchs of the pre-capitalist Indian subcontinent who did not 'covet assimilation'[26] and statist homogenization in the same way that modern colonial bureaucrats do; and the pre-bourgeois European Christian self. No doubt the focal point of these assembled references, as revealed at the close of the passage, is the self-surrendering prem (love) of the woman. This draws on a monism that is spiritual rather than of this world, since the monism of the bhakti tradition assumes that the human *atman* (inner soul) reclaims its oneness with the universal divine or *paramatman* through reneging the *maya-shakti* of material desires. Bhakti monism enabled relatively egalitarian human relations only on the fringes of hierarchal Hindu societies in Tagore's Bengal and elsewhere in the subcontinent. The concept is constitutively at odds with the humanistic monism of the Enlightenment which presents a temporal framework for human oneness, that is, it allows persons to mobilize within secular time and mainstream history and also against its unjust divisions. What is peculiar to Tagore's transcultural linkage, however, is that conversely it juxtaposes with the pre-secular bhakti imagery of early-modern Shakespearean portrayals of 'flesh-and-blood' human beings who palpably live and act in the world. Even more significant is that his vision encompasses the modern European 'stout-hearted Jack' who critically mobilizes for change in contemporary secular time, 'making breaches in the walls' of the European norms that produce divisive and possessive individualisms in the first place.

This interlinkage suggests to me that Tagore is attempting to decolonize the monistic notion of the human being and to reclaim its emancipatory potential through a transcultural interweave of ethical selves. On the one hand, he embraces forms of the 'human being' antithetical to contemporary scientific genres of agency as much in pre-Enlightenment Europe (early Christianity or Shakespearean humanism) as in the self-critical interstices of post-Enlightenment secular Europe. On the other hand, he invests the pre-secular personhood of bhakti tradition with agency in this world. He suggests here, and demonstrates in the allegorical play itself, that the woman's 'love' is active within history, in the vein of the empire's other 'stout-hearted' internal critics. For she is brought into a land/state mired in the rationality of accumulating and governing wealth at the same time that she mobilizes the people of the land to rise up against imperialist capital and governance. This woman, Nandini, is described to be embodying a *nabeen* (youthful) time—a re-conception of modern temporality which embraces certain attitudes of bhakti-centred egalitarian fringe communities as well as of indigenous agrarian societies within a transcultural revolutionary vision of progress. Tagore's point of melding the non-modern person with a historical ethical individual, then, is to correct possessive and territorial identities from within the imperial-capitalist history rather than idealistically to turn to pre-modern and agrarian civilizations at odds with modern history.

All told, Tagore's conception of the woman's 'individual' love constitutes what I see as the *first step of activist 'transcultural individuation'*: he is extending and enriching the parameters of the autonomous self of secular progress through selectively incorporating difference. There is a second step to individuation that is crucial from the gender perspective. To that I turn below. Let me note for the moment some ways in which my reading of Tagore's transcultural humanism resonates with another line of postcolonial scholarship, one which focuses on the inflections in temporal and spatial self-consciousness of such anti-imperialist thinkers as Tagore. This scholarship connects Tagore's reflexivity to his critical engagement with the norms of Enlightenment modernity rather than to divergence from its normative assumptions.

In his prescient study of the drama, Sankha Ghosh suggests that Tagore's conception of the *adhunik* (modern) rests on a critical inclination to consider *samprotik* (contemporary) life conditions from an evaluative distance and to engage with the disruptions brought on by imperialist modernization in the various life-worlds he traversed.[27] Ghosh's commentary on the play in question (*Red Oleanders*) leads me to think that we could include in Tagore's disruptive experiences with modernity his travels in the West and encounter with the instrumental

attitudes of American capitalism.[28] We learn from Sankha Ghosh
that Tagore's metaphorical portrayals of time and space—such as the
juxtaposition above of the infinitude of feminine individuality with
the ruinous finitude of urban masculine empire—ought to be seen
as his aesthetic of critiquing the discontinuities imposed by empire
on quotidian life and restoring a more processive attitude towards
progress. These metaphors emphatically ought not to be interpreted as
a *saral* (naïve) and idealistic call to return to the village and its pristine
indigenous values.[29] Ghosh is one among a number of Tagore scholars
who are in broad agreement about the bent of Tagore's engagements
with modernity and indigenous tradition. As Abu Sayeed Ayyub states
with clarity, notably in the post-First-War phase from which the passage
above is drawn, Tagore's texts manifest an explicit 'sense of time and
consciousness of [needful social] activity' for change.[30] Whereas Ayyub
himself focuses on a philosophical tension internal to Tagore's late
poetry—between a Kantian ethic of non-interested responsibility and an
aesthetical ethic of human universality[31]—the additional point he makes
regarding the role of the indigenous in Tagore's temporal consciousness
has wide relevance. It is germane to the more politicized analyses of such
recent critics as Sankha Ghosh. Ayyub avers that while 'uniqueness is
more striking than the continuity of the Indian tradition of thought'
in Tagore's aesthetic consciousness, we fail to understand this unique
(autonomous) modern aesthetic unless we account also for its 'strong
and extensive ... roots'[32] in indigenous conceptual ground. Also in line
with this critical modernist postcolonial scholarship, subaltern theorists
Ranajit Guha and Sudipta Kaviraj situate Tagore's eclectic cultural
vocabulary vis-à-vis historicist thought.

A careful reading of how the above passage weaves in polemic with
imagery and intonation reveals that Tagore is approaching the bhakti
vocabulary of non-possessive love in what Ranajit Guha has characterized
as his habitually 'secular' way.[33] He is opening up indigenous religious
thought as an 'inexhaustible source'[34] for critiquing the 'object-historical
conventions' of the dominant historiographical trends of his time.[35]
Guha has argued that Tagore sought for a restorative notion of non-
possessive individuality in the 'second degree',[36] an approach resonating
with a neo-Kantian tradition that goes back to Fichte.[37] Along these
lines, he was conceptualizing a way to know and to see 'unmediated'[38]
(made 'finite', in Tagore's word) by epistemic conventions ('barricades',
in Tagore's metaphor) which compel the individual to encounter others,
the world, time, and space as objects to be quantified and possessed. In a

similar vein, Sudipta Kaviraj maintains that Tagore took a 'disenchanted' approach to religious vocabulary, mobilizing it 'against atomic individualism' and as an 'essential principle' of the modern reflexive historical self.[39]

While my reading of Tagore's transcultural notion of the 'individual person' so far resonates with this critical modernist scholarship, on his self-consciousness regarding historical individualism and alternative tradition, I now must further complicate the picture by attending to the gender rhetoric in Tagore's above-mentioned passage. For there is a second way in which Tagore is endorsing the core Enlightenment view of a human monad responsibly enacting a common (rather than differentiated) world history. He is casting himself as an *actor inside* the contentious *masculine* 'drama of human history'. The implication of this imagery is that at present no man nor male-dominant place can be made entirely parochial, conserved from the imperial reach of scientific capitalism. For Tagore's imagery poses not merely an opposition between the infinite and the finite, it also makes this opposition openly self-critical through a gendering of the image. Note also that Tagore indirectly reasserts his monistic approach to the problem of dehumanization by discarding the proposition that the play *Red Oleanders* is a 'propaganda' against the West. In this vein, we must also read that he depicts the play's theme through a tension-filled image which is doing two things—it is privileging the woman as the 'individual' with an 'infinite' potential for autonomous agency and antithetically it is implicating the male author (all male authors) in 'finite' biopolitics. This politics of possessive identities pervades, in his words, the 'desolated *world of man*'(my emphasis). As further discussed in Chapter 2, self-critical responsibility for a gendered betterment of humanity is quite evident in Tagore's depiction of the compromised yet conflicted persona of the male protagonist of *Red Oleanders*, the king of the land of accumulation. Tellingly, Tagore himself had wanted to perform the part of the male protagonist in his initial plan to stage the work.[40] In the light of this self-critical tension in the gender imagery, we could extend Abu Sayeed Ayyub's observation that Tagore's late philosophical poems evince an 'unfinished' identity struggle;[41] this aesthetic identity struggle could also be seen as encompassing Tagore's striving against the material sexual politics of nationalism in his later life. Feminist critic Tanika Sarkar has powerfully argued that in the woman-centred works Tagore produced in the early twentieth century, humanism was being mobilized against the misogyny of Hindu filiative nationalism.[42] We could place

Red Oleanders as well in this critical framework by reading its gender metaphors as pressure points upon masculine capital (imperialist and nationalist). Chapters 1 and 2 contain more extended discussion of transcultural gendered struggles against sexual nationalism in nineteenth and twentieth century Bengal.

For the present, I emphasize that what the tension-filled gender imagery in Tagore's passage encapsulates for me is the *second step of activist transcultural individuation* in any postcolonial context, a step I consider to be crucial for enabling the voices of women and the marginalized in global history. This step of self-activism constitutes an unconcluded dialectic. It inscribes the awareness that in a world of personalities 'barricaded', as Tagore so nicely puts it, by separatist and possessive norms of social behaviour (and filiation), cognitive individuality cannot be a given. Rather, it is a matter of struggle and of only partial achievement. In my view, the gender metaphorics of the passage above stages this dialectical endeavour to fulfil the *potential* objectivity of an agent whose knowledge indeed tends to be mediated (made 'finite') by dominant terms of possessive and objectified knowing. Reading through this lens of struggle and dialectic, we are also able to account for Tagore's conflicted voice in the passage (and indeed, throughout much of his woman-centred gendered imaginations, as we will see in Chapter 2).

I am in agreement, in other words, with the brief poststructuralist reading I presented earlier, to the extent that it reveals that Tagore's objectivity remains imperfect in this passage. His analytical imagination continues to be invested in an idealistic nationalism resting upon a gender binary regarding the authentic/eternal 'individuality' of the self-surrendering woman. As my subsequent discussion should also have demonstrated, Tagore's evaluations of individual agency at the same time critique his own inclination for idealistic humanism. This critical reflexivity exemplifies Edward Said's emphasis that, at its best, humanism is non-conformity; it constitutes a continual 'effort ... [or a] dialectic of opposites' between predetermined historical circumstances and the individual.[43] I must add to Said's critical humanism the point that on the grounds of non-European cultures and languages, humanistic evaluations also travel across epistemic borders to draw on alternative social selves, seeking at once to correct and to extend the monistic European understandings of individuality and collectivity.

The conflicting rational accents I discern in Tagore's passage are inexplicable through any of the postcolonial approaches I reviewed in the previous section. As already suggested, they all settle, albeit in their different ways, precisely for the premise of Enlightenment thought which they also debate. They all reconcile with the idealistic assumption prevalent in certain strands of Enlightenment thought that a person's rational consciousness is an inner process—referring to or encircled by ideas—through which everyday practices and values are engaged, adjudged, and chosen from, and overall coherently arranged. Even though the idealistic liberal assumption of unfettered rationality constitutes the central problematic of poststructuralist and postmodern theories, approaches to rational choice stemming from these internal challenges to Western modernity remain deadlocked in one of two ways—either they only delineate the problem or/and they seek ideal alternatives. They are unable to conceptualize that *rational historical agency itself could be uneven and compromised at the same time so that it becomes cumulative* in its evaluation and correction of dominant norms.

We begin to account for the unevenness and contradictions in an activist individual's reasoning if we take a materialist approach. In this vein, it is helpful to view language as a practical activity wherein reasoning is embodied in the processes of relating to people and nature, satisfying wants, and also in communicating social relations. If we assume in this vein that a consciousness *textualized in language* refers to socioeconomic structures and allied media, then we are in a position to take into account that that consciousness, together with the structures mediating it, typically is permeated by conflicting interests and value judgements.

Authors in the World: Language, Imperfection, and Responsible Evaluation

V.N. Volosinov stresses that each linguistic unit or 'utterance', verbalized and internal, is potentially a 'multiaccentual' arena of social struggle.[44] Herein, voices mutually 'infiltrate',[45] evaluate, and retort to others' judgemental views of the world. In an unequal world, textual relations are bound to be hierarchical. The Orientalist accents we find in Tagore's defense against his dismissive British critics stemmed from his temporary transformation into an exotic Eastern poet-seer right around the time of his Nobel award for literature in 1913. It has been widely noted that Tagore strove with anxiety and frustration to fit his English voice and communicative style into the racialized romantic image his Western supporters sought—in the words of W.B. Yeats and Haldor Laxness, the image of a 'strange' and dreamlike spiritual seer essentially different from materialistic Westerners.[46] At this time Tagore was trying to gather not only cultural capital in the international literary circuit, but also financial capital. His publications and lectures in Europe and America were to support his educational projects at Shantiniketan and Sriniketan.[47] Overall, Tagore's rivalrous nationalism—which he intones through an exoticized self-pity for 'inarticulate Asia'—refers to the antagonistic practices and identity theories prevailing across a globe wherein some industrialized European nations had acquired the status of commercial world powers through their control both of material resources and of communicative channels.[48] In the latter regard, note that Tagore had even received the Nobel Prize in the first place as a tacit recognition from Europe that one native writer had imbibed civilized influence through the spread of British colonization and Christianity, according to the Nobel Committee's records.[49]

Since they were similarly located within specific historical congeries of power and underprivilege, such European activist intellectuals as Percy Shelley, John Locke, or Jean Jacques Rousseau also spoke in the biased accents of the racist and elitist colonizer or the patriarchal and property-owning social theorist (in such landmark humanist works on social justice or education as Locke's *Letter Concerning Toleration,* or Rousseau's *Social Contract* and *Emile,* for example). While such hierarchical voices as these do manifest in works of imagination, they do not necessarily exhaust the multiple accents and retorts. As overlapping social arenas of evaluation and critique, linguistic texts at the same time can reveal emancipatory trends against injustices.

These emancipatory trends, which heighten in times of social crises and change,[50] constitute an author's attempt to gain a perspective on his/her experiences of the social world in the light of coercions and violations. Tagore's 'darkest … dismay' at the power politics driving both nation-state formation and the peace-making League of Nations, carries this retort to social disturbance. Similar trends are at work behind such European humanist texts as John Locke's *Letter Concerning Toleration*—which conceives of life, liberty, and an inequitable distribution of property and goods[51] in the midst of religious violence and bloodshed—as pointed out by Kwame Anthony Appiah.[52] Mary Wollstonecraft's *Vindication of the Rights of Women* is another dialectical humanist text which retorts to the 'social tyranny of men',[53] upheld in her context by the seemingly egalitarian theories of human rights propounded by patriarchs. By striving to take 'responsibility' for what they say, such activist authors as these retain in their utterances a vibrant multi-accentuality rather than, as Volosinov puts it, turn the utterances into inert 'things' comprising *only* biased opinions.[54] We are able to further parse this notion of responsible multi-vocality through drawing on another concept advanced by the Bakhtin school—the notion of 'two-sided answerability'[55] or the doubling of frames of reference.

Adapting Kant's ethic to the Marxian dialectic, Bakhtin states in *Toward a Philosophy of the Act* that every linguistic act has the potential to be two-sided in its reference (p. 3). At the same time that it refers or 'answers' to a 'special' historical context and its unique norms (and hierarchies), it could gesture at a 'moral'[56] or transhistorical frame of reference. Bakhtin sees moral answerability not, like Kant, as an a priori propensity of human reason but rather as a potential only that could be realized through struggles against self-serving bias. Answerability constitutes a sustained endeavour on the part of the author/artist to remain fully accountable for her/his utterance.[57] The struggle facing activist agents situated amidst historical hierarchies is to keep alive this doubled—historical and provisionally ethical—meaning of every linguistic act. This is what constitutes responsible textuality.

Texts that explore provisional ethical norms for collective improvement, beyond one's narrow historical interests, fold back to evaluate and to retort upon the 'teleology of [salient] authorial contexts'[58] from marginalized perspectives. In its rigorously scrupulous form, this ethical doubling of frames of reference resonates with what Gayatri Spivak delineates as an activist author's or reader's textual struggles to achieve a substantial 'mind-change'—a process of writing and reading mobilized through being persuaded from below, with the socially 'compromised other as teacher'.[59] In the contexts of empire and capital I study, the 'below' is of course multiple and overlapping. It includes the compromised positions at once of such elite-marginalized persons as Tagore himself and of the many cast onto the margins of Indian society vis-à-vis bourgeois high-caste men such as Tagore. Accepting a dialectical materialist notion of the individual consciousness, Spivak goes on to reiterate that the activist intellectual's self-critical education about patterns of social dominance and oppression goes hand-in-hand with developing more inclusive notions about what one needs to be 'human'[60]. Yet this process of knowing is always imperfect, partially mired in power. We are able to delineate the slow textual struggles for knowledgeable mind-change by focusing on 'that part of the [author/reader] subject which takes on the intellectual's function'.[61] Focusing on the doubled narrative strands in the subaltern-activist fiction of Mahasweta Devi, Spivak points to a reading of tensions between the framing 'webs' of fiction and the 'weaving' in of conceptual and rhetorical spaces.[62]

Materialist readings of responsible agency such as these help us to elaborate in what ways and why its nature could be conflicting, yet cumulative. It helps us, in other words, to unravel the imperfections in an individual aesthetic agent's normative evaluations as well as discern how objective evaluations accumulate and widen humanist scope with reference to the agent's intellectual engagements with the world. For the purposes of the present study, we must now consider how we decipher the ways responsible normativity works in contexts where multiple cultural worlds and social arrangements intersect. In the discussion to follow, I do not claim that conceptions and practices of activist agency are better, in the sense of being less biased, at cultural crossroads. Instead my point is to find a way to discern how intellectual agency alters as we turn from monocultural and monolingual contexts to overlaps, and how we could read concepts coming together or disaggregating at such crossroads.

Pursuing the materialist view that culture and language are not idealistic inner processes but rather fields of social activity made and changed by human agents, Satya Mohanty proposes a helpful approach to cross-cultural norm development. He points out that '(rational) agency is a basic capacity shared by all humans across cultures'.[63] Our capacity for 'second-degree'[64] reasoning permits us not only to think about the 'political or moral world'[65] but also to evaluate how the status quo could be changed. That this second-order capacity to evaluate the world and formulate knowledge is universally shared makes sense once we accept Mohanty's conception of 'oppositional knowledge'.[66] On this view, knowledge ought not to be seen only as teleological abstraction, in the idealistic tradition of the Enlightenment. Instead, we ought to expand the broad Enlightenment idea of the self-cognizing subject to encompass a person's 'confused feelings',[67] 'vaguely felt ethical judgements', as well as 'more developed normative theories of right and wrong'.[68] As my subsequent contextual studies will show, Mohanty's flexible model of ethical knowledge proves especially helpful for unravelling the many thoughtful and emotional evaluations of good and bad that emerge within various forms of associative life, whether in modernizing or in advanced conditions of global capital. Moreover, this realist view of knowledge resonates with V.N. Volosinov's notion of affective reasoning in artistic evaluations. The latter maintains that we must not look to content alone but rather notice how various verbal and expressive modes of rational and affective appeal combine or conflict within the scope of a text. In this way, we could explore the author's/artist's analytical interactions with the worldly content being described and with potential audiences out there.[69] For the purposes of my multi-media study, these modes would include genre, style, intonation, imagery, the performative body, colour, sound, light, and allied expressive means.

On this referential view of knowledge, universality emphatically does not mean homogeneity. Instead, as Mohanty stresses, second-order thought (whether social or aesthetic) is bound to be 'elaborated'[70] in 'incommensurable'[71] ways by people situated in different historical contexts. For the very ways in which people exist in the world, make or change value judgements about human existence, could radically 'disagree'[72] between cultures. People could disagree upon what it means for one to be rational or social, to function in time and space, or to relate to nature and the cosmos, time and space. Moreover, the very way an individual understands one or more of these features within the same society could also vary depending on the social location of this thinking agent *and* of the specific community she claims for herself.

The following chapters will show that whereas the elite nationalist male intellectual Rabindranath Tagore wants to reject the possessive and territorial aspects of Western individualism, such marginalized public women of the same society as Monomohini or Binodini find it imperative to claim for themselves the new notion of property right and immunity. Yet in contexts where cultures overlap, such as the ones I study, a responsible agent's *trans*cultural self-evaluations of power and mystification could well be cumulative both across cultures and within the hierarchal positions ascribed in the same culture. The 'information' s/he garners from differing social cultures (practices and suppositions) could enable more precise and corrective readings of the 'relations of power and privilege'.[73] Chapter 1 demonstrates that in life-writings by marginalized public women in colonial Bengal, self-property and self-immunity are indeed claimed as constituents of the individual. Yet these transcultural margin-narratives 'inform' us about incorporating another constitutive element as an equally crucial property of the autonomous woman—a lived capacity to forge corporeal and familial bonds with other vulnerable people who co-habit on the peripheries of modern high-caste patriarchal societies. We will also see variations in the communicative mode—the prose and imagistic genres in actress-prostitute Binodini's autobiography vary in accord with her addresses to the centred or the marginal in society.

All in all, we are able to read textualization of transcultural ethical agency through the following steps. To begin with, we must consider how artistic thinkers at cultural crossroads experience and process the respective suppositions about personal and collective existence. The point to note is the conditions under which these experiences are hierarchical and what brings about a level ground of epistemic evaluation and selection. This means that in studying personhood within such hierarchical contexts as a capitalist colony or nation-state, we should be attentive about the extent to which an author/artist struggles through texts to be responsibly transcultural: to attempt a doubled or dialectical textual framework. We should read along the following lines: (a) consider in what ways different cultural images, tonalities, and suppositions are being put together; (b) discern where the antitheses and the retorts between them lie; (c) analyse what the ethical implications may be of intertextual disagreements; and (d) demystify the self-oriented biases of the author or artist through attention to how textual accents work against the doubled frames of reference and instead conform to dominant historical standards.

Along these lines, Tagore's conflict-ridden texts are readable at the crossing of multiple frames of reference comprising the unequal material cultures and discursive patterns traversed by the author. These include the racialized Euro-American and Indian-bourgeois-nationalist routes he treaded; the everyday rural routes and homes he encountered in his trips around the villages his landowning family held; and the elite upper-caste Tagore home in colonial Calcutta wherein learned and popular, European and indigenous traditions were simultaneously nurtured. The Tagore home brought under the same roof Sanskrit and Western-educated male and (some) female members; Bangla-educated elderly female members, as well as rural servants and itinerant performers and peddlers. We are able to unpack in what ways his texts refer to these disparate realities as their ethical transcultural struggles if we take account of aesthetic interactions within Tagore's works.

Analysing Tagore's aesthetic-ethical struggles against the imperial samprotik (contemporary), Sankha Ghosh astutely observes that the diverse material groundings of Tagore's works are better manifested through the 'experiential images' (*chitrajato abhigyata*) of everyday life in his work than through their more conventional verbal mode. His use of language trends becomes complicit with the cultural disintegrations (and defensive reactions) happening at many social levels in his colonized context.[74] My reading above of Tagore's commentary on *Red Oleanders* should illustrate that only by prying out the tension between his dominant Orientalist vocabulary and his oppositional gender imagery are we able to discern the imperfect yet complex transcultural amalgam of self-critique and self-surrender in Tagore's conception of the 'individual person'. Through diachronic and synchronic readings, Chapter 2 delineates that Tagore's gendered ethic of the 'individual person' likewise grows cumulatively complex in the way it grapples with his elite-male-oriented biases and revises them. As he grows to be more 'informed' both ethically and intellectually through his encounters with nationalist filiative orders, on the one hand, and with Western and indigenous feminist movements, on the other, his works begin to retort against seeing woman only as a pressure point on 'desolate' masculine identities. In the late woman-centred aesthetical experiments—dance dramas, poetry, prose—he begins to argue for respecting her as a *byektibishesh* (distinct person) with needs and capabilities distinct from male historical structures.

That said, Chapter 2 will stress as well that we should approach diachronic reading with a caveat in mind. Diachronic textualizations of justice ought not to be mistaken for a teleological accumulation of ethical knowledge. Note that Tagore's passage above, limited by his sexual politics of resistance, is drawn also from this late phase. This leads me to conclude that at some conjunctures of information, media, and 'socioeconomic circumstances',[75] it may be harder than at others to retrieve different and critical frames of reference. Imperial or defensive interests may become more persuasive for critical thinkers through some material experiences (or opportunities) than through others. Tagore himself self-critically insisted on the inconsistencies in his thought, arguing that you cannot distill one philosophy from his works.[76] To keep these specificities of material experience in view also means that we must be attentive to how cultures and languages overlap in such non-Western contexts as Tagore's or the rest of the authors/artists in this study. It is important that we read textual ethics at once through a transcultural and a translingual lens, as well as with diachronic and synchronic emphases.

Autonomy in the Eras of Empire: Culture, Economy, and Feminist Transcultural Individuation

So far, then, this chapter has argued that once we take a materialist approach, rather than one bounded by Enlightenment idealism, we are able to conceptualize how the liberal notion of the autonomous person is embraced and reconceived by transcultural activists in their struggles for decolonization. As also noted, transcultural practices of choice could significantly change shape on the basis of alterations in material culture. These alterations occur simultaneously in the various realms of culture: financial, social, and communicative (the processes of telling, learning, persuasion, debate). At all times, the interaction of persons with material culture encompasses, according to Raymond Williams, 'complex interrelations of movements and tendencies both with and beyond a specific and effective dominance'.[77] 'Residual' elements of earlier social arrangements can entwine with 'emergent ... meanings and values' at the same time that social residues are congealing into 'archaic' and revivalist forms. A look at the past and present of Indian humanism reveals that such cultural interrelations may be more open-ended and dialectical under some material conditions than others.

The extent of dialectic is inversely proportional, in my view, to the degree to which cultural relations are *economized*, managed, controlled,[78] and uni-directed. In the domain of aesthetics, we must consider to what extent artistic modes of describing human interactions with the world are being economized by dominant media. In this regard, a significant transformation has occurred between the two global eras of humanism I study. This is the transformation in technologies of communicating self-description.

Chapter 3 describes a neoliberal globalized world technologically advanced and largely self-governed. I consider that in transnationalizing Bengal and India, norms of personal and group autonomy, on the one hand are tailored to a wider social spectrum than ever before—channels of audiovisual and digital communication appeal to unequal persons and social groups; they represent and aestheticize myriad people's wants, and they debate gender issues and encourage democratic interconnections. Through careful readings of television, theatre, and the internet in Bengal and selected Indian diasporas, the chapter demonstrates that, on the other hand, these new technologies of aesthetic cohesively network with dominant self-images and resource structures. As media thinkers emphasize, the technological medium (visual technology, in particular) exerts a control unprecedented in communication history over the 'scale and form of human association and action'.[79] It precipitates the convergence of all social sectors into consumerist structures for it flexibly adapts to 'increasing variability and miscellaneity' at the same time that it produces iterative 'sequences'[80] of pleasure and profit. Along these lines, I analyse how transnational neoliberal media economize our recognition of Indian women who are autonomous and self-helpful or (dichotomously) choiceless and intransigent. They also uphold a temporal hierarchy of autonomy or backwardness through pleasing images that reinforce sexual divisions. While Chapter 3 specifies how notions of women's autonomy alter within different transnational formations of labour, race, and communalist nationalism, respectively in Bengal and the nation-state as against bourgeois Indian diasporas in the US, it also discerns a filiative economy of intent connecting the various iterations of autonomous womanhood (see also my discussion of the filiative order of imperialist nationalism in the Preface).

In view of today's flexible neohumanist imperialism, I am compelled to reconsider the implications of my foregoing conception of ethical individuation. For it seems that dominant images of choice and lack pleasingly mediate the emergent consciousnesses of all artists and intellectuals today. The imagery constrains their ethical choices regarding what is autonomous and it potentially compromises the capacity to learn from residual or marginalized cultures. In what form might transhistorical aesthetic agency endure under these circumstances, and how do we read it? In particular, how does an activist-aesthete keep alive a doubled frame of reference under the prevailing structures of visual mediation? In light of these concerns and questions, Chapter 4 explores in detail the feminist dance theatre of Manjusri Chaki-Sircar and Ranjabati Sircar and also films by Aparna Sen. In the remainder of this Introduction I consider a way to extend my conception of transcultural individuation to a reading of feminist autonomy under the visual networks of neoliberal empire. The lens for my discussion is filmmaker Aparna Sen's anti-war film, *Yuganto* (*What the Sea Said*, 1995).

Made in reference to the first Gulf War, *Yuganto* wants to make all individuals accountable for the worldwide violence against persons and nature. It seeks to make every person confront that violence is perpetrated in our world both globally, through the militarization of world commerce, and microscopically, through everyday forms of social, financial, and environmental imperialism. The film extends the scope of the humanist critique of international violence we encounter in Tagore's passage above. It connects violence and exploitation with the transnational mediatization of war itself and seemingly peaceful everyday life. The work portrays a top-level advertising executive called Deepak (Anjan Dutta) and an acclaimed dancer Anusua (Rupa Ganguli) attempting to reclaim a conjugal relationship fractured by the atomistic pursuit of careers, upward mobility, and fame. They return to a fishing village which holds youthful memories of their conjugal bonds. Flashbacks link the tale of their estrangement to such pushes and pulls as patriarchal coercions at the domestic and state levels, the devastation of marginal lives and environments under transnational expansion, and the marketability of merits in capitalist democracies at home and abroad.

On one level, the film reveals an analytical framework more inclusive than Tagore's, elaborating through dialectics of narrative and expressive codes. To begin with, it appears that men are commanding the (sexist) voice of analysis whereas the woman protagonist is being held responsible for compromising her own values and therewith the feminine principle of regeneration and nurturing by becoming captive to 'self-love'[81] and instrumental reason. A rapid succession of opening shots show moving railroad tracks to the accompaniment of the man Deepak's voice-over: he describes the woman Anusua's meteoric rise to international fame as a dancer and ends upon the question, does she not feel 'tired' of pursuing success? We learn at the close that Deepak himself has finally defied compromise by quitting his prestigious managing director's position in the hope of resettling with Anusua and writing novels. This modern man's voice of criticism, that goes hand-in-hand with his apparent ability to discard instrumental reason, overlaps with at least two other voices of male wisdom. One, quoted from the Hindu scriptures in the film's epigraph, is the saying of Sage Vedbyash that when the feminine earth has lost her *bigatoyauvana* (youthful prime), *pap* (crimes) are bound to proliferate; the other is the voice of a wise elder of the fisherpeople (Subrata Nandy) narrating a Hindu myth of re-creation while also foretelling destruction. In a work seething with irony these intertwined masculine accounts that idealize and objectify feminine nature with reference to a male-dominant worldview (in the vein of Tagore's idealistic accents) do not, however, exhaust the critical analysis. An alternative gendered explanation is implied through a visual linkage of Anusua's self-serving choices to male violence.

An acerbic Anusua and an aggrieved Deepak are shown on the balcony of their seaside guesthouse discussing their childlessness (an implied cause not only of their estrangement but of Anusua's loss of nurturing energies, in Deepak's analysis). The camera jump cuts to that fateful day on which Anusua had decided to abort a pregnancy. Following around an Anusua who is beseeching Deepak to drive her to the railway station for her dance tour, the camera reveals a home milling with Deepak's colleagues. As usual, these men and women claim that space to create advertisements while taking for granted Anusua's hospitable services, exactly as her husband does. In contrast to the heightening frenzy of Anusua's movements, Deepak's gestures show comfort in this space and command of its people. He flippantly ignores Anusua's entreaties by strumming a song to his 'gallery' of supporters, having dictated that she must not go lest she risk the pregnancy, and soon after violently blocks her exit by locking the gate (while some drunken male colleagues enjoy the sensational spectacle). Only after Anusua is driven by her spouse's emotional and verbal abuse to attempt a suicidal abortion (by swallowing pills in the only space she finds of her own—the bathroom) does Deepak patronizingly concede to sending away his 'guests' to soothe her nerves. Throughout the episode, medium shots merge the woman with her blatantly public home, underscoring how fully both her space and her (nurturing) habits are exposed to instrumental use while being governed by the patriarch's interests of family and career-making. It is evident that the woman is deprived of any autonomous space wherein she could have discussed and developed her life choices together with another independent yet companionate decision-maker.

Following this, Anusua claims a form of control of her body and talents that is both instrumental and atomized in its rationale. She summarily goes through an abortion so she is able after all to fly out for her dance programme. She also commodifies her creative work as cultural capital for an oppressive state by colluding with a corrupt official in order to accrue resources for her dance academy. She displaces her social and environmental critique to the global arena (creating a prescient dance number on the military and eco-violence of the Gulf War) while eliding local oppressions in the constituency of the government official who promises financial aid to her dance academy (these oppressions include a famine caused in local villages by a dam built by the state government). Furthermore, Anusua defends her tactical negotiations of activism and success by contending that through her (acclaimed and well-funded) critical art she is able to heighten public awareness of at least some sociopolitical issues if not all. Yet if this woman protagonist far more than her male counterpart seems ready to allow her choices to be compromised by dominant codes—as much of social critique as of social profit—it is eminently clear that she is more coerced than he in her choices. Delving into the liberal notion of individual privacy, *Yuganto* considers which of the two—man or woman—commands more privacy in choosing a life-plan. It clarifies that neither the public nor the domestic domain affords the woman a space that is ethically 'private' or protected from interference[82] by institutions of social behaviour and belonging.

Aparna Sen's work does not, however, stop at analysing gender oppression with primary (self-) reference to a bourgeois woman's burdens. In the vein of Tagore from the earlier era it draws on the Enlightenment view of the human monad responsible for enacting a common history. *Yuganto* casts both the woman and the man as insiders in a history of global networks, and it holds both accountable. On her part, Aparna Sen has stated that she considers this (relatively unpopular) film about 'compromises' to be her best work,[83] adding that she has a bit of both Anusua and Deepak in herself.[84] Playing on various aspects of Economic, Utilitarian, and Romantic individualism, filmic codes diagnose how the self-loves and competitive self-interests[85] of the two are heightened by the technologies of self-seeing that encircle people's existence today. We are alerted to how these tools encourage one to package the world in a specular way with reference to how one would like to see oneself in it.

For example, one suggestive shot shows Anusua enrapt in the disciplined movements of dance practice next to a television screen showing CNN coverage of B2 bombers over the Gulf (Figure 1). This parallelism of aesthetic and commercial media semiotically interlinks with two earlier shots, first, of a television screen portraying oil-drenched seagulls struggling out of a polluted sea (the oil spillage being linked to the Gulf War in the film), and thereafter, of Anusua's dancing body creating the intense pathos of the birds in struggle within the pastoral seclusion of a tree-enclosed yard at her elite dance academy. These interlinked visual codes guide us in reading the overlaps: activist performance art and commercial television converge in processing violent world events into 'miniatures'.[86] Both package affective rationales (of righteous anger or resistant pity) for various local and global consumers. Put in another way, Anusua's pleasing miniatures of activist thought network with the instrumentality of a mass culture that 'decontextualize[s] and distantiate[s]' imagination from the 'sociomoral pressures'[87] of confronting power and violence. Yet another shot underscores the way the artist adores herself in this miniaturist role. Through a camera held

Figure 1 Miniatures of Activism—Dancer and TV Screen
Courtesy: National Film Development Corporation of India

behind her, Anusua is portrayed to be gazing with possessive narcissism upon her pristine tree-circled space of individual creation (as sustained by national and global capital).

By contrast Deepak's growth in Romantic self-awareness at first glance appears to present a *telos* of moral intransigence alternative to Anusua's of possessive selfhood. Not only has he given up his prior pursuit of upward mobility and commodity fetish (as an advertising executive), he now strives hard to think through the 'unbounded' nature of global violence across ecological and social systems. It is also Deepak who seems inclined to look across cultural boundaries and to learn attitudes for a more sustainable existence from the residual culture of the fisherpeople, embattled as that culture is through ecological imperialism. Nonetheless, this Romantic individual's evaluation of residual and marginal people turns out to be curiously similar to the Utilitarian's mediation in respect of the economy of scale. Both in the novel he is writing in extremely erudite Bangla about working-class lives and in the nostalgic gaze he turns upon the fisherpeople through the lens of his expensive camera, Deepak too consistently miniaturizes and distantiates the margins—and that with the aid of the mechanical and conceptual technologies he has acquired from his upwardly mobile life. He takes symbolic possession of what the marginal and residual mean in his self-preserving pictures of global violence by eliding his own violence upon Anusua's emotions and her womb. Indeed, the filmic camera itself occasionally overlaps with Deepak's territorial camera: on occasion it comes to possess as nostalgic fetish the unconstrained labours and joys of the nature-enclosed fisherpeople.[88]

Even though Aparna Sen's work shares Tagore's humanist vision of accountability, then, it diverges in a number of ways. First, it is more counter-normative in its emphasis on how individuals today strike compromises with dominant institutions and reward structures. This implies, for our purposes, that it is especially difficult for any individual today to sustain a transhistorical or doubled moral frame of reference since all such activist dialectics tend to be reduced to conformity. In place of Tagore's transcultural interweave of ethical selves, this film gestures at a multicultural capitalism which utilizes yet miniaturizes all differences and conflicts. And then, with a somewhat self-indulgent specular slant, *Yuganto* appears to embrace a distinctly postrevolutionary and counter-humanist position. In this respect, Aparna Sen's bourgeois humanist aesthetic is at odds with the webs and weaves of rhetoricity Spivak detects in the subaltern-activist writing of Mahasweta Devi. Indeed, the film drives the point home by portraying the death of the one truly ethical individual who had struck out on the path of normative revolution. Anusua's activist cousin Bhaiya (Kunal Mitra)—who abandoned the prestigious career of a barrister to live and work for famine-stricken villagers and mobilize against local eco-violence—is slaughtered by gangs deployed by the very government official who funds Anusua's academy of activist dance. Certainly, through this demise of the avowed activist hand-in-hand with the compromises struck by the protagonists, the primary narrative appears to settle for a post-modern demystification of dominant individualisms, and a limited demystification at that. Yet there is more to reading this film than the primary linear narrative. Conflicting strands of story and imagery embark on a minimal trans-historical critique. They seek to reclaim an ethic of autonomy while taking feminist account of the autonomous agent's networked status. To parse the reclamation, we must be attentive to the various elements of artistic debate within the filmic text: description, juxtaposition, and retort.

The storyline closes with a surreal rupture of the status quo of normal and peaceful realities. Unmasking the unbounded nature of the violations, at once of ecosystems and social systems across the globe, the film shows the sea rising up in flames (from a torch unwittingly thrown into oil-polluted water by a drunken fisherman). What is significant for our purposes is that rather than leave spectators with the nihilistic image, final shots depict close-ups of the frenzied face of the woman. She stands completely alone confronting the spectacular consequences of destruction on a global scale (Figure 2). Despite the power of analytics they have previously held over the woman, all men are tellingly absent from these shots of confrontation. Prior shots have shown Deepak to be striding away into dark sea waters in an apparent bid to fulfil his Romantic death-wish and mark a heroic closure to his masculine existential angst; he has been provoked to ultimate disillusion by Anusua's lack of appreciation for his decision to give up his job in order to repair conjugal relations and his own creativity.

As such the woman's solitary confrontation of a global violence to which *both* their choices and pleasures have contributed, on the one hand, poses a striking visual retort to the (specular) heroic man's escape from historical agency. It serves as an indirect reminder that 'she' even more than 'he' is encircled by violent relations. As flashbacks of Deepak's abusive self-love have already suggested, a return to conjugal living would not guarantee Anusua freedom from masculine demands. What her confrontation with the landscape of violence implies is the call for a more global change. On the other hand, Anusua's solitary unrelenting

Figure 2 The Woman Confronts Violence
Courtesy: National Film Development Corporation of India

stance on the edge of widespread annihilation curiously juxtaposes with another image of an enduring corporeal entity presented earlier at the same spot. This is the gigantic female turtle of the elderly fisherman's re-creation myth which appeared moments ago on the same beach, being first exposed (through another surreal shot) to the wondering eyes of the woman Anusua. By Aparna Sen's testimony the film itself and its Bengali title *Yuganto* (End of an Age) were inspired by a Hindu myth of re-creation.[89] The version Sen draws on is not, however, the androcentric creation legend of dominant Hindu mythography. Here the turtle is not God Vishnu but Goddess Lakshmi in her maternal incarnation, called upon by the Creator-god to generate new humankind upon the end of a cycle of time and decadence. That this mythic image of maternity is at the same time juxtaposed with the antithetical image of the childless woman—and one who had protested patriarchal control over her womb, albeit through a self-violating abortion—implies a further direction of reading. This antithetical assemblage of mythic and human femininities prompts us to read in opposite ways. We disentangle the notion of woman-as-creator from masculine ideals of fertility, whether inherited from androcentric Hindu myths or recultivated within modern capitalism. At the same time, we note a quality of maternal nurturance in the childless woman, against the grain of the aggression attributed to her earlier in the narrative. Aparna Sen follows Tagore and other modern Bengali thinkers in reinventing pre-secular concepts within history.

Thus the dialectical imagery of feminine creativity leads us to a fresh normative notion of feminist ethical autonomy. The implication seems to be that in order to claim historical autonomy, the feminist must re-create human progress: She/he must destroy substantial components of existing masculine empires at the same time that she nurtures some radically new approaches to human independence and mutuality. If only in germinal form, this closing directionality retorts against what earlier had appeared to be the liberal woman's inexorable telos under masculine networks that invariably she must compete with and improve upon masculine possessive identities. Through diachronic readings of recent films (*Paromitar Ek Din* [*House of Memories*], *Mr. and Mrs. Iyer*, *15 Park Avenue*), Chapter 4 studies how this minimal norm of *feminist temporal agency* is being further explored by Aparna Sen. Her cinema grows increasingly self-reflexive about dominant standards of feminist autonomy, showing Aparna Sen's ongoing engagement with her own status inside capitalism and empire.

Along the lines laid out in this chapter, the contextual studies to follow (Chapters 1 through 4) are contrapuntally organized. They juxtapose and contrast humanist Indian voices from colonial and contemporary eras of empire. My point overall is to demonstrate that processes of transcultural individuation reappear in somewhat different forms in the two eras of humanist Indian aesthetics, being shaped differently in relation to the respective imperialist conditions. Nonetheless, all critical thinkers in question converge in embracing the monistic premises of European humanism. They seek to mobilize against the differentiated and divided identities of imperialist times. With imperfect objectivity, they are striving to imagine a person who is independent of dominant dictates and, therewith, the agent of progressive human independence. My Conclusion situate these contextual studies of the transcultural autonomous self within the current debate on humanism between liberal and poststructuralist/postmodern feminist thinkers. Speaking to this debate, I maintain that the challenge facing all activist thinkers today is to cultivate a principled transcultural eye—an eye to evaluate how some of the more pleasing choices we make in our lives cause human solidarities to disintegrate around us and also beyond our narrow confines. Meeting this challenge, I conclude, should be an important collaborative goal of feminist activism for an equitable world.

PART ONE

COLONIAL CONFLICTS

1

OWNERSHIP ON SEXUAL MARGINS

Bodies, National Media, and Autobiography

Sukumar Sen records that the practice of life-writing burgeoned in Bengali from the mid-nineteenth century. According to him, this corpus included extended autobiographies and biographies, as well as such commentaries on daily living as episodic memoirs, diaries, and personal letters.[1] We should add to this list self-reflexive poetry. Quite correctly, critics see in this trend a radical shift in the indigenous consciousness of personhood.[2] The cultural departure here, as Sudipta Kaviraj notes, is not simply a reflexive turn in self-consciousness. The reflexive realization that lives can and ought to be narrated, pre-dates the nineteenth century chronologically. Bengali, as well as other languages in the subcontinent, nurtured long-standing traditions of exemplary life-narratives that held up 'social principles' for various communities stratified by caste, occupation, and trade.[3] The departure is that myriad, apparently non-consequential lives suddenly became narration-worthy because a radically new self-awareness had begun to prevail. Everyone, irrespective of the person's status in society, was perceived to be able to 'grasp'[4] her/

his life in a narrative. I begin my exploration of individuality in activist aesthetics by looking at self-writing at this onset of literary humanism in Bengali culture.

Conscious self-activism is, of course, at the crux of the new personhood whose elements we find here. Charles Taylor notes that this 'individual' person is marked by the capacity to know her/his life as a story with a unique meaning that the events of life come to 'manifest or illustrate';[5] hence, s/he is able to actively chalk out a future as well as to choose a new direction in order to revise and change the life to come.[6] Self-narration, in other words, inaugurates the Enlightenment's subject of social change. Resources for this self-making are independent of revealed truth (whether divine or social), lying instead in the inward recesses of the mind. And choosing and changing one's life-path also rests on the specifically modern capacity to observe one's own attributes and experiences from a 'disengaged' perspective.[7] In effect, the new individual self comes to *own* her/his qualities and activities such that these may be selectively taken possession of, re-classified, or discarded in the course of telling and of doing. However, this also means that the narratable self could well be at odds with self-engagement in ethical activism. As I have been developing the concept in this book, ethical activism constitutes an ongoing critique of dominant knowledge aiming for radical social-epistemic change. In contrast, the actively narrated self is typically the 'possessive individual' who constitutes, according to C.B. Macpherson's argument, the 'central difficulty' in Western moral history.[8] This type of person is poised to be 'calculative' in his/her interests[9]—that is, driven by instrumental reason in making choices and therewith self-bounded by dominant interests rather than self-yielding and community-oriented. This possessive individual lies at the core of empire, wherein proprietorship 'acquires an element of political domination [over the person of the native] as well as of territoriality [over land and resources]'.[10]

Macpherson speaks of metropolitan Europe. Conditions in colonial Bengal differed in at least two significant ways. On the one hand, colonial capitalism would not permit a full development of such Western liberal-capitalist norms as the self-as-proprietor and contractual exchange. Without a doubt, pre-existing life-arrangements had been significantly disrupted and so had non-subjective traditions of self-reflection and self-performance. As yet however, they had not been completely re-structured. Ranajit Guha reminds us that substantial parts of indigenous 'civil society ... had not been assimilated to the [colonial] state'.[11] On the other hand, the reflexive subject emerged in the colonial state with reference not to the monistic ideal of the right-bearing citizen but rather to a notion of separate and unequal territories (of civilization, race, sexuality). Thus on these grounds, self-writing joined in a drive for civilizational change in which the reflexive self was expected to be an instrument of higher historical aims. The drive itself, I will argue, was uneven and contradictory. The formulated aim, however, was historiographical. The aim of narrating a particular life was to systematically present growth and development and to discern the moral difference between past and present conditions. The push overall was to determine a set of national characteristics unique enough to rival and to supersede colonizers and invaders (British and Muslim). I detail below that the conventions of autobiography prevailing in Bengali literature of the colonial period required that only those qualities of the author be developed that illustrate common national interests. Personal attributes, narrated self-reflexively by a particular author, were expected to project the overarching collective's calculated choices regarding its own uniqueness and superiority, in other words, to present generic possessions. Invariably, these burgeoning genres of national peoplehood came to be inflected by empire even as the imperialist categories of racial superiority and inferiority were being harnessed to indigenous corporeal knowledge. In the authors' self-reflexive attempts to hone the ideal attributes of 'Bharatiya' (Bengali/Indian) femininity and masculinity, we discern the growth of a *filiative order* of national family poised to evolve along the path of its unique cultural-racial history. Hand-in-hand with national historical consciousness, Victorian Social Darwinism had begun to infiltrate into pre-existing divisions of caste and society and to vertically order their parameters.[12]

In this group-oriented instrumentality of particular selves, the *new technologies* of mediation and communication necessarily played a central role. In nineteenth-century Bengal, these mediating agencies included structures of literacy and education governed by an influential caste of Hindu teachers and mentors, as well as by male transcribers and editors of women's life-stories (in instances where women authors were illiterate or sequestered, and/or without financial and communicative resources). They also encompassed print media and various other communicative traditions of visualization and performance which, in this period, were altering at a rapid rate. Changes in visual culture from the mid-nineteenth century onwards are especially significant. Cartesian points of view came in with technologies of photography and illusionist proscenium stagecraft. Sensory perceptions of the *habitus* began to be reduced and homogenized, resolving contradictory forms of quotidian embodiment into singular sights of 'truth'.[13] Therewith, ideals of identity and alienness, pure or despicable human attributes also tended to 'mortify'[14] into antagonistic forms. In this context, the homogenous trends were of course less than pervasive. Point-of-view photography or etiological prose, for example, had to negotiate oral and performative traditions of associative life and collective memory.

As such, there was a counteractive side to this pursuit of a collective goal. The very assumption that every self-writer is personally committed to a collectivist project constituted a common reference point. Underlying this common framework was a new presupposition that people from all strata of indigenous life are coming together through a natural affinity of inclination, that they want to change and improve their country. The personalized task of setting a common direction gathered steam from at least two very different processes—from the deep disruptions occurring in inherited life-worlds within the vortex of modernization and urbanization; and from the discourse of humanism filtering into urban Bengali sensibility through various channels of European learning. To these I return below. For the moment, I stress that the various processes of change created grounds for the germination of another 'community of experience [or] ... structure of feeling', a new structure of affective reasoning upon which, to use the words of Raymond Williams, 'communication' and 'community' would begin to depend.[15] The counteractive structure of associative life, which fought for birth in the volatile public realm of modernizing Bengal, was assuming the possibility of reciprocal communication between community members—that is, for communication sans authoritative representation. Persons committed to the project of narrating their lives and re-developing attributes sometimes wanted to point out which actions and inclinations did not fit the collective tracks of knowledge and of sight and to persuade about where the disagreements lay. In these disagreements, disparate traditions of telling life-stories and textualizing reality came into play.

Recent studies have shown that selected autobiographies born of colonial modernity did break away from dominant parameters of reason.[16] Expanding on that line of argument, this chapter goes on to explore instances of *subjective* reflexivity—points at which self stories chose to diverge from prevailing historical conventions of autobiography. I argue that at junctures such as these the narrating self sought to communicate and build community in ways uncensored by group calculations. Herein, we see the emergence on colonial grounds of what I call in this book transcultural individuation.

I show that while these divergent narrative choices appeared in bourgeois self-presentations, they take provocative turns in works by narrators who were marginal to the moral economy of anti-colonial nationalism. In some works by sexually 'aberrant' women, for example, we encounter in vestigial form a profoundly radical engagement with the Enlightenment vocabulary. These women's self-stories grasp and re-tell precisely the problematic concept of the individual-as-proprietor; at the same time, they vocalize the concept in transcultural terms. The chapter rounds out by looking closely at two such works. The first is a self-focused letter written in 1869 by one Monomohini Dasi, advocating the rights of prostitutes such as herself in a context that denied legal subjecthood to women classified as unchaste. The second is the autobiography by renowned actress-prostitute Binodini Dasi— *Amar Katha* (*My Story*, 1912–13)—which grapples with the antagonism found in visual culture between the chaste and the fallen woman. These marginal narratives invoke in different idioms such key aspects of the language of proprietorship as the right to own one's person, the right to own physical goods and comforts ('indolency' according to John Locke's formulation),[17] and the demand for contractual exchange. Yet they make these proprietary claims in curiously anomalous terms. The claims not only emphasize personal benefit and immunity in the habitual Western way,[18] they also call for the immunity of vulnerable marginalized communities. If self-immunity is seen as a property of the individual, corporeal bonds are claimed to be another such core property of the self. The latter constitutes a natural capability for forging non-instrumental familial ties within the bare processes of survival. Therein, the filiative order of family, so widely propagated by patriarchal nationalist thought in this context, also comes to be sidelined. To get to this recalcitrant form of auto-writing, we must first take account of several processes: how the self was narrated in nineteenth-century Bengal, how conventions were set by the new elite, why conventions shifted within bourgeois contexts, and what new forms mediation and communication took in the course of shifts and variations.

Autobiography, National History, and Empire

An advertisement posted in the first decade of the twentieth century presents an accurate picture of the conventional view of autobiographical writing in this context. The advertisement was posted by Harendralal Roy, elder brother of dramatist D.L. Roy, for the publication of their father's autobiography. In Harendralal's words, '*Even though* this life-writing relates to a *bishishto byekti*'s (specific/eminent person's) character, thoughts, and activities, in this is portrayed a seventy-five-year-long *samajik itihas* (social history) of Bengal' (emphasis mine).[19] To publicize the work, Harendralal finds it necessary to insert an explicit disclaimer regarding the individuation (of eminence) depicted by the narrative. He calls on the reader to attend instead to the historical relevance of the work to be published. A glance through autobiographical pieces of this era reveals that a disclaimer such as this does not indicate any fundamental departure from the type of self-disengagement Charles Taylor diagnoses in the modern narratable self. In fact, we encounter an element of radical disengagement in the very first full-length autobiography in Bengali, *Itibritta* (*Annals*), now attributed to poet Krishnachandra Majumdar (1868).[20] While invoking certain conventions of a pre-modern moral exemplar, the anonymous narrator of *Itibritta* does look at his own activities and inner inclinations as if from a distance. If only rather awkwardly, he evaluates these attributes against social prescriptions of virtue and vice, industriousness and laziness, and so forth. In effect, he claims ownership of his culpable self, taking possession of attributes such that he can disengage from them and strive to revise himself.

What Harendralal Roy's disclaimer regarding individualist narration captures, on the other hand, is a convention being used in this era to grapple with the new awareness that one can write oneself as a story. The practice being followed here is to disengage from the individual narrator's activities, outwardly and inwardly, such that the person's life can be told in terms of a collective history. Whereas narrative individuation in the metropolitan West is characterized by inward development, here that inwardness is made categorically social. All other aspects of self-reflexivity ('thought' in Harendralal's words)—regardless of their particular eminence—are classed as irrelevant to a necessarily collective process of growth. *Subjectivism*, in other words, is *systematically withheld* as a matter not only of rhetorical but of moral approach. When Sukumar Sen's *History of Bengali Literature* classifies early Bengali autobiography and biography as variations of history-writing, then, it reiterates the nineteenth-century convention of self-narration.

Early autobiographies were framed in a number of different ways by the awareness of self-admitting into time and collective development.

First, many were surprisingly accurate in plotting the temporal and spatial coordinates of a given personal life. Indeed, a notion of the narrator moving along a historical timeline marked by calendars and public events brought a new linearity into prose, compensating for otherwise fragmentary or generic composition styles, in literary mode. Patterns of spatiotemporal coherence hold together, for example, the otherwise colloquial or uneven prose of some early women writers. A case in point is Kailashbashini Debi's *Janaika Grihabadur Diary* (*Diary of a Certain Housewife*, written between 1846 and 1873).[21] The piece is remarkable for the precision with which it connects life occurrences to dates, places, and historical events such as the Sepoy Uprising. Another in fact is Binodini's *Amar Katha*. While substantial parts of this narrative are written in the stock poetic prose of the pre-modern genre of *bedona gatha* (song of lamentation), the generic authorial voice is regularly interjected by a subjective author addressing and directing specific occurrences in her personal life and the theatre. To the latter, I return below.

Second, life stories were conventionally presented by authors themselves (sometimes anonymously) and also marketed and read as first-hand accounts of how women and men from all corners of customary society were contributing to social change. The rhetoric was that all authors willingly partook in society's choice of new directions. Since reforms of the Hindu home and sexual codes were the central issues of change and social anxiety, women's voices led the trend. One early example of the drive to be included in this pursuit is an anonymous autobiographical letter to the editor published in the name of one Amuki Debi (literally, That Lady) by the periodical *Sambad Kaumudi* (1831). The letter seizes the tide of the first wave of reform, which was driven by a new awareness of equal rights and women's subordination.[22]

Addressing the movement under way in the city of Kolkata against the Hindu *kulin* (a clan amongst Brahmins) practice of polygamy, Amuki Debi presents her own life experience of victimage as a kulin bride. Victim portrayals of this sort, of oppressive Hindu marital customs or women's seclusion and illiteracy, were legitimizing the drives by Western-educated Bengali men, colonial legislators, and British missionaries to seek reform in everyday practice and in law. Another willing self-narrative, written in a later phase of nationalist mobilization, demonstrates how women were recombining reform and custom in order to evolve uniquely national codes of gender practice and sexual virtue that superseded Westernization. Nistarini Debi's *Sekele Katha* (1913) balances her potentially reformist tales of the oddities of kulin polygamy, and women's devaluation therein, with a telling contrast. She pits the authentic selfless devotion of her grandmother, an illiterate *patibrata* (austerely devoted to husband-serving) Hindu wife of the past, against the un-austere and unauthentic *pati*-service of present-day educated Hindu women versed in plays and novels.[23]

Posed by an educated woman from an 'enlightened' family (comprising Christian and Brahmo men),[24] this contrast implicitly sketches a new feminine selfhood addressing the conflicted temporalities of sexual reform and anti-colonial nationalism. Nistarini Debi does admit that at least some modern women attempt to practice appropriate wifely devotion. Her real points of contention are the distractions brought upon present-day women (a membership that includes herself) by unregulated social change. These vectors of change include the self-centred romanticism promoted by *nataks* (plays) and novels, as well as nuclear families and disposable income. The latter catalyses in women an instrumental craving to acquire jewellery from the husband through a connivance of devotion. Thus, Nistarini Debi does not imply that women's lives ought not to alter and reform but that the reform should aim always for an *amalgam of attributes* wherein temporalities of femininity are selectively brought together. The new educated woman ought to recall the high-caste Hindu legacy of devoted wifely service and to re-possess its surrendering sense of self-gratification[25] (*nijeke kritartha jnan*). The evolutionary goal here is to redirect *strisvabhava* (licentious feminine nature) towards dharma (social and religious orderliness). Underlying this goal is the assumption that a woman's natural inclination for licentious behaviour is unleashed by education, consumerism, and public orientation of Westernization.[26] Nistarini Debi's goal ought to be read in the light of contemporary male nationalist debates on *strisiksha* (women's education) as well as of their immediate provocation, allegations by imperialist European commentators that Hindu 'superstitions'.[27] and degeneracy were to be blamed for women's illiteracy and subordination. We find in Nistarini's reflection elements of a solution proposed by nationalists to the supposed moral danger of unbridling strisvabhava by providing education for women. The solution, paradoxically enough, is to evolve backwards into the virtues of a purer Hindu-Aryan femininity; the European Orientalist view of Hindu civilization is an unmistakable influence.[28]

A misogynist association of uncontrolled sexuality with publicness underlay concerns such as Nistarini's with modernizing women. This misogyny was bred at the intersection of indigenous and European imperialist sexual prejudices. On the one side lay a belief ingrained in the Hindu caste system that the bodies of women and lower-caste people were relatively 'open' and prone to pollution, in comparison to the bodies of high-caste Hindu men.[29] On the other lay a bourgeois Victorian dichotomy pitting the chastened and angelic homemaker opposite the public whore. While this dichotomy is foundational to the Judeo-Christian view of female sexuality, it acquired racial meanings in the course of Europe's expansionist phases (exploration, colonization, and slavery).[30] The dichotomy circulated widely amidst the new Bengali intelligentsia through English education, travels in Europe, and, not least, through missionaries and other educators of the native elite.[31] At the intersection, indigenous sexual biases regarding pollutable bodies of women and the lower born were hardening into a binary racial framework. Obviously, the misogyny was especially burdensome for openly public and *itar* (low-born) women such as Binodini. For these women stood outside the sexual protection and the proprietorship, on the one hand, of high-caste Hindu *kula* (patrilines) and on the other, of the growing cult of enlightened or *bhadra* (elite) Hindu domesticity. Hence, such women as these were catching head-on the sociobiological conflicts of imperialist nationalism.

Through an imperialistic sexual lens, it was especially prohibitive that they partake in writing the gender history of the civilized nation being 'imagined'[32] by the bhadra (elite) folk. Through the nationalist lens, on the other hand, it was important that the public and the low-born be embraced by the historical storyline of inclusion and reformation. Some public women were of course being brought into the bourgeois fold by necessity since they were acting as substitutes for the respectably sequestered elite *bhadramahila*s in nationalist experiments such as the public theatre. But at a deeper conceptual level, it was necessary to uncover all existing forms of sexual embodiment so that these could be placed in various categories within the unfolding history of the nation, with the subject's consent. In the next chapter, we will see how a self-critical male nationalist struggled responsibly to engage dominant nationalist categories of female sexuality. Rabindranath Tagore's depiction of the outcaste *chandal* girl's desire through his two versions of *Chandalika*, inscribes the struggles of an elite male intellectual to communicate in a reciprocal (non-coercive) way with sexually marginalized women. For the moment, let us return to nineteenth-century autobiographical writing.

A convention for resolving the prohibition against the public woman's self-narration was also developed in this context. It appears in the memoirs of the actress-prostitute Tinkari Dasi, collected and possibly transcribed by the Sanskrit scholar and theatre-historian Upendranath Bidyabhushan.[33] Tinkari's autobiography presents an evolutionary narrative paralleling and complementing that of an elite high-caste lady or bhadramahila, such as Nistarini Debi. It tells of how Tinkari's life-choices helped to sexually reform and civilize the public space she operated in, as against the domestic space centering the elite patibrata wife. Predictably, her choices rest on the same moral premises as the bhadramahila's, namely, sexual orderliness and the pursuit of a *brata* (austere religious rite) defined by patriarchs. The narrative portrays how an innate (implicitly *dharmic*/reformist) urge drove Tinkari to reject the luxury of residential prostitution offered by two profligate dandies. Instead, she learned to embrace the austere pursuit of high Western dramatic art (no less than Shakespeare's *Macbeth*) under the tutelage of the visionary of national theatre—Girish Ghosh. Time and again she is depicted as prostrating herself at the feet of her guide and patriarch in profound gratitude for the enlightenment she receives.

Such conventions of selective self-narration as these, while withholding assertions of unique agency or individual eminence, opened the space for a third textual practice. Works especially by elite men narrated the very process of inclusion and collectivization and told how self-consciousness needs to be adjusted with others' viewpoints and choices. A good example is the approach taken by the well-known political leader Surendranath Banerjea in an autobiography appropriately titled after the common cause *A Nation in the Making: Reminiscences of Fifty Years of Public Life* (1925). The preface presents the work as a fraternal project: 'I have been encouraged in the idea by some of my friends (and I share their view) that they [his reminiscences] may throw light on some of the most interesting chapters in our current history ....'[34] The language, as we see, is pointedly placing in parenthesis the author's unitary perspective upon the said historical chapters, suggesting instead that personal choices have been willingly subordinated to a collective interpretation. The same rhetorical gesture is deployed to frame an aspect of self-development that is unquestionably unique rather than shared.

The book concludes with the story of how Banerjea has kept up his body as a 'machine, working with precision' and 'co-operating with the moral' development of his mind such that his disciplined habits supersede even the British regimen of healthy routine (we are told that no less than Lord Chelmsford deferred respectfully to his needs).[35] This narrative of developing a uniquely disciplined self-attribute is introduced, however, with the caveat that it was fraternally conceived—his friends requested that he 'record' for posterity what he considers to be the 'secret' of his exemplary physical and mental health. Hence, the storyline is somewhat open as well to adjusting to his brethren's preferences and goals regarding what the ideal attributes of Indian manhood ought to be; we hear, for example, a self-ironic little narrative about how Banerjea disregarded his puritanical regimen to attend a late-night play at the London theatre with his friend Gokhale.[36]

Predictably, self-adjustability went only so far. Inclusion in the collective storytelling could as well radically stratify narrators, tracking them to develop only in selected social roles. Especially revealing in this regard is where Banerjea's father is positioned within his textual space. While Banerjea's storyline embraces the father as an embodiment of originary humanistic virtues ('sympathy for the poor', 'abhorrence of sordid means'), at the same time it defends against a possible misreading by the European of the father-son bond as an instance of 'high-strung sentiments'.[37] Banerjea notes that their father-son sentiments should be read as 'filial piety ... one of the cardinal virtues of the Hindu', and that these should be seen as representing (in romantic-humanist terms) a 'spontaneous outflow of the soul'.[38] Yet the one obvious illustration of 'high-strung' sentimentality—uncontrollable, potentially hysterical, and effeminate—appears in the portrayal not of Banerjea's own emotions but of his father's. We hear of his father's unquenchably tearful demeanour as he stands clad in a 'simple' customary dhoti[39] bidding farewell to the son voyaging out for Europe.

In the final reckoning, Hindu-humanist properties attributed to the father and those acquired by the metropolitan son and his enlightened fraternity present categories of time and gender that mutually interrelate yet alienate. Even though high-caste Hindu paternity contributes the natural basis—the biological and moral genealogies—for the evolution of a new national fraternity, father-figures occupy an 'anachronistic'[40] sexual space vis-à-vis enlightened and self-controlled Indian manhood. Put in another way, an unmistakable temporal tension, deriving from imperialistic categories of the convergent and the anachronistic, subtly invade the 'tender ties' between father and son.[41] At the same time, these ties are also being reasserted with anxious nostalgia on the face of changing and disintegrating family life. The configuration we find here of an enlightened bourgeois masculinity complements and balances the more visible endeavour by Bengali nationalists of this period—male and female—to cultivate hyper-manhood.[42] Both figures of masculine growth spawned off of British commentaries on the effeminate or emasculated Bengali babu. The figure of the hyper-man and its indigenized counterpart—the virile Hindu ascetic—outright suppressed the threat of emasculation. This figure of the enlightened man instead displaces that threat onto the bygone generation, while also claiming that high-caste ancestry for the evolution of a modern Indian fraternity. Chapter 2 will discuss how Rabindranath Tagore wrestled with these various anti-colonial configurations of manhood in light of their repercussions on women.

I have dwelt at some length on the key conventions of autobiographical writing in colonial Bengal. My point is to emphasize several key features. First, while the narratable self develops in the subcontinental colony quite differently from the classic imperialistic autobiographer of the metropolitan West, this alternative selfhood subsumes the personal to collective reflexive agency. In the post-Enlightenment tradition of self-writing, 'individual autonomy [is realized] within a narrative so exclusive that it becomes the legitimation of an irreducible heteronomy'.[43] Since all narratives of social identity are measured against an ideal set of attributes and a unitary path of development, they universally uphold 'an imperial Man whose destiny is always the same'.[44] We see above that in colonial Bengal, on the other hand, the rhetoric of narration was to reduce self-particularity and self-eminence and instead to defer to the inclusion of voices and preferences regarding personal development. However, this rhetoric of inclusive-self-making also required that narrators take responsibility for self-developing along stratified social tracks in order that they co-create and balance a hierarchal collective.[45] We have seen that even though actress-prostitute Tinkari claims the essential feminine virtues, in order to be included in the collective narrative, her track for developing these qualities has to be distinct from and beneath the high-caste lady's.

Second, the difference between autobiographical selves born respectively in the metropole and in the colony has to do with historical variance. As I briefly suggested at the start of this chapter, the traditional unitary individual of metropolitan autobiography was (and is) based on the liberal-capitalist state and on its homogenous notion of right-bearing citizenship. The colonized, on the other hand, received subjecthood (through processes of modernization), but were denied both citizenship and market freedom by the colonial state.[46] The Preface noted that the metropolitan logic of individualism, on one level, was displaced in the Indian colony by an order of empire that complemented individualism in British thought of this period—that of universal filiation or the family of mankind. Elaborating the displacement, Purnima Bose helpfully argues that colonial individualism from within came to be 'not conceived of as a system of exchange between free individuals', but rather as a web of relations 'founded on a notion of radical inequality' based in interlocked race and caste prejudices.[47] These relations were governed and tracked by colonial policies of education, law, census, and property settlement (notably the Permanent Settlement policy instituted in Bengal). Entwined in these structures of colonial governance were the more volatile drives of nationalist self-consciousness within indigenous language and practice.

What I have demonstrated in this section so far is the drive to include all walks of life visible to the urban eye in creating the new women and men of Bengal and *Bharatbarsha* (India). In this drive to historicize an inclusive new community/nation we do find 'residues'[48] of pre-colonial rural and urban arrangements that typically sustained contiguous and partially permeable life-worlds as well as accepted sociobiological hierarchies of bodily purity and pollution. What we also encounter full-force is the burden of an *anti-colonial* nationalism that was enframed by the radical—rather than contiguous—stratifications of modern empire. The burden of anti-colonial nationalism was to turn quotidian pre-colonial practices of value into the coherent value system of a superior national history. Norms for national morality were formulated in terms of such community-facing values as 'love, kinship, austerity, sacrifice',[49] and these values were consciously pitted against territorial formations of civilization and civilized personhood. The accountability demanded of every narrator was to affirm these kin filiations from a specified social stratum.

Yet this very call to every person to build (national) kin relations, rather than just inherit them, was also bound to have an *enabling and oppositional* momentum. The third feature of autobiographical writing

I wish to highlight is this oppositional trend. In the next section, I explore subjective self-reflections that migrated away from historical conventions.

Indigenous Grounds, Subjective Interventions

The oppositional momentum gained in at least two ways. First, on quotidian indigenous grounds, pre-existing and newfound structures of 'feeling',[50] of associating, and of textualizing relationships, quite simply, clashed with one another. And then, some subjects of self-stories assumed that they would be able to and they ought to narrate the clashes and, accordingly, re-evaluate the collective *telos* of change.

As noted at the start of this chapter, a structure of feeling and association different from the communitarian was also infusing minds and actions through transnational circuits of European ideas and travels. These were the principles of humanism. From the early decades of the nineteenth century, European humanist texts—circulating widely amidst educated Bengali men and (some) women—were being read in the original where possible and also being translated into Bengali and enacted in vernacular genres. Further, reformist periodicals were in step with the social and literary movements under way in Europe. Giuseppe Mazzini, Tom Paine, Ernest Renan, Immanuel Kant, John Stuart Mill, Mary Wollstonecraft, George Eliot, and the British Romantic poets comprise but a handful of the names we encounter in conversations of this era.[51] Within the daily conjunctures of material and ideological change, an *indigenous humanist* framework of feeling and association was struggling to take shape. On the colonial grounds of the subcontinent, this framework *would not allow* the assumption that the individual *was bounded* by his/her interests, separate from larger social relations. What it did breed, however, was a germinal supposition that persons committed to national community could engage in *free and mutual communication* regarding life conditions and conflicts. The premise of any such communicative ethic as this is the core humanist assumption of 'two-sided' referentiality—that it is possible to narrate particular lives and aspirations at once from within 'special' historical frameworks and also from positions of *partial* objectivity.[52]

Born of a vortex of changes, personal stories about life arrangements had a tendency to make *subjective choices* regarding what to bring in. Narrators wanted to include the various 'discoordinated'[53] temporalities riddling their lives and, quite simply, to attempt thinking these through. Moreover, different habits of textualizing and transmitting life stories, including oral traditions, came into play in these attempts. On occasions, these personal evaluations could openly disagree with the agenda that collectivity is to be narrated while subjective understanding is subsumed. Arguing against the homogenous historical drive, Rabindranath Tagore wanted to account for the 'historicality' of everyday joys and sorrows[54] on the discoordinated grounds of colony. Chapter 2 will look closely at Tagore's activist ethics. For the moment I wish to examine some pressure points at which self-stories were grasping lives differently from the conventional mould. They were choosing what to emphasize, omit, or rethink. At these liminal points we discern autonomous attempts on the part of narrators to think against historical inclusion, stratification, and self-censorship. Jnanadanandini Debi, wife of the well-known social reformer and civil servant Satyendranath Tagore, concludes her *Katha* (Story) with an apology for its fragmentary nature. She regrets that having grown old, partially blind, and weak in memory, she has been unable to tell a chronological story. Instead she has narrated in unregulated and 'abrupt bits and pieces' (*khapcchara bhabe*), largely because her daughter persists and she keeps answering the questions.[55] This does not mean that a telos of enlightenment is completely missing from her Katha. We hear of how Jnanadanandini progressed from her life as a nearly-illiterate little girl in an East-Bengal village, through marriage into the eminent urban Tagore family, to travels in England and life with a highly educated and cosmopolitan elite. True, her sketch of self-development shows some glaring omissions. It omits, for example Jnanadanandini's own well-known contribution to the women's reform movement, notably her agency in developing for the new Bengali woman a virtuous public attire in line with the 'moral-sartorial dream' of male reformist family members.[56] Nonetheless, her narrative presents a consistent teleological thread. Also encompassed in this thread is the development of her companionate relationship with a Westernized husband.

We hear that at first Jnanadanandini was unable to talk directly to her husband. Her initial silence is represented in conventional nationalist language as a surfeit of respectable feminine modesty or *lajja*. It also appears from the narrative sequence, however, that the young village girl is simply at odds with the kind of association demanded of her by her reformist and Anglicized husband, namely, a companionate heterosexual commitment between two romantically inclined persons. For we hear that Satyendranath, in fact, had to engage his young bride in a kind of childlike game by offering the bribe of a watch before she was prepared to give in and speak. The narrative also suggests that the initial gap between their respective forms of association and feeling eventually gave way to companionate intimacy. Since the intimate sphere was conventionally withheld from nationalist representations of ideal Hindu domesticity in this context,[57] we are 'told' of this development of companionship through a veiled signifier only—that Satyendranath began privately to call her by the diminutive name of 'Jneni'. That a new attribute of personal emotional commitment has grown within Jnanadanandini as well is decisively narrated through an anecdote about her romantic inclination. On the eve of Satyendranath's departure for higher education in England, she is seized with the *sakh* (happy whim) to pen a song of parting. No doubt, the general cultivation in the Tagore family of ideas of companionate marriage also drove this appropriate development of emotion.

All Jnanadanandini is able to turn out, however, are two lines. The first imitates stock Vaishnava lyricism on *viraha* or lovelorn separation. The second line, on the other hand, is an odd departure from the previous teleology of companionship. It directly charges her husband that he will shortly be going off happily along with his friends (*tumi to jabe anande, sangigan laye sange*). The implication is that she will be cast behind him as he moves onward on his homosocial international journey. The story goes on that after Jnanadanandini had abandoned her literary enterprise and left the room her husband found the poem and composed it in full. While Satyendranath's polished production retains the appropriate first line of his wife's composition, it rewrites the troublesome second to blend into the rest of the poem. We get a stylized romantic ditty avowing his lovelorn companionate loyalty towards her (no matter whither he goes). The little anecdote has a telling conclusion. Jnanadanandini refrains from commenting directly on the way her little couplet was altered by her husband. Instead, she rounds out with a laconic remark that her husband was well versed in song-writing as he frequently wrote devotional *Brahmosangeets* and had wanted to be a Brahmo preacher. As I see it, Jananadanandini's assessment is that the song her husband wrote was not about their relationship at all, rather the abstract output of a literary expert and resonant with his own public interests.

The multiple and conflicting accents of this anecdote capture the scattered growth of Jnanadanandini's autonomous voice, at odds with her history of self-development. The original verse line she had penned had minimally exposed her disengagement from her own expression of companionate feeling. Moreover, it implicitly measured

Satyendranath's humanistic construction of companionship against the real lack of coordination yawning between their respective spaces of association and agency. Her final words only confirm her awareness of this discoordination. They suggest that such concepts as companionate relationship are for him matters not so much for quotidian personal cultivation but rather for theoretical cultivation in the homosocial public domain of national enlightenment (not unlike his cultivation of the Brahmo faith). Seen in another way, Jnanadanandini's words reveal a doubled frame of evaluation. They place life-writing against national history and they explore the disconnections in-between while keeping in view an overarching goal of social change. That is, they refuse *to compliantly resolve* the discrepancies on the ground into a conventional teleology for Bengal's social history (of companionate marriage, in this instance). The anecdote stands as a telling example of how self-remembering can constitute an imaginative space for suppressed voices. The space enables 'struggle and contestation about reality itself' through a rethinking of 'lived relations as a basis for knowledge'.[58]

What Jnanadanandini's *Katha* registers are two crucial aspects of communicative politics in this context. First, the khapcchara and contestatory narrative captures the down-to-earth rhythms of women's talk within the home. Second, this entwining of women's orality with printed text reveals that in this context appropriate resources could enable a woman narrator to communicate her contestatory reality in a relatively unencumbered way. These resources included access to public media and, where needed, to appropriate mediators who could help with the access without imposing conventions. On the latter score, the credit in this instance goes perhaps to the intimate ear of Jnanadanandini's educated daughter and transcriber Indira Debi Chaudhurani. Through Indira Debi's sensitive transcription, we get to hear the differing and khapcchara voices in Jnanadanandini's thickly layered life story and we also learn to accept her silences and her glaring omissions. We see here in a minimal form how a woman-to-woman community could permit subjective re-communications and deeper self-knowledge. In instances where such enabling agents or mutual mediators were impossible to reach, subjective approaches to conventional autobiography necessarily differed.

For women narrators outside the privileged fold, conventions of narration and mediation constituted a double-bind. On the one hand, these narrators could not very well refuse to comply with the dominant narratives produced by national history and its media. Precisely their conventions of inclusion and reformation were giving the low-born a narrative outlet in the first place. On the other hand, these very conventions of narration and mediation were decisively robbing low-born women narrators of the possibility of subjective reflection. As we saw in the instance of Tinkari Dasi above, such narrators instead were being made instruments of vicarious reflexivity. They could reflect only upon how their changing lives contributed to the reform of sexual and social attributes in the imagined nation; they could not narrate and 'own' themselves or their actions in any other way. In self-narratives by public women of this era, we also encounter certain subjective strategies for intervening in their own instrumental voices. One typical strategy was to draw on the historical convention of compliance as only a ploy for breaking through dominant structures of knowledge and media. The endeavour was to make autonomous points regarding their own lives vis-à-vis collective goals. Down this line, authors sought to intervene in historiographical self-narration at a deeper level. They attempted to *re-own* their personal needs at the same time that they were re-orienting the futures of vulnerable marginal communities such as theirs.

Self-Owning on Sexual Margins:
Mediators and Subjective Communication

In an autobiographical letter written to the editor of the periodical *Somprakash* (1869), one Monomohini Dasi pleads for the institution of physical exams for male customers of prostitutes.[59] On its face, this letter regarding a personal issue is not unlike Tinkari Dasi's memoirs in the way it is framed by conventions of style and content. To begin with, it presents a cohesive argument in polished prose. Further, its content fits with historical narratives regarding prostitution and chastity that were prevalent both in Bengal and in the metropole at this time. Hence, at first glance, it might seem that a male reformer took on a woman's voice to write the letter in a progressive periodical known to publish social controversies.[60] The practice of reformist ventriloquism was not uncommon in this period. In fact, the authenticity of this letter has been under debate in Bengali language criticism.

Romakrishna Moitra has alleged that it was in fact written by an elite man versed in English literature. Rebutting Moitra's position, feminist critic Sutapa Bhattacharya points out that the prostitute writer herself could have been an educated woman. For a government report, published in 1853, records that a large number of prostitutes living at this time in the Sonagacchi red-light area of Kolkata were educated

Brahmin women who had fallen from caste and status.[61] While I do side with Sutapa Bhattacharya's basic point, that the letter was written at least primarily by a prostitute woman, I will show that there is some weight on both sides of this debate. On the one hand, the letter is embedded in prevalent bourgeois narratives regarding sexual chastity, pollution, health, and contagious disease. On the other, however, it is not mired in the convention public women adopted to write for the bourgeois nationalist media. As I demonstrate above through my discussion of actress Tinkari Dasi's conventional autobiography, the public woman as life-narrator was expected to take on a historiographic task commensurate with her social position. She was supposed to objectify her public body through narrating how she complies with the vision of national moral development by reforming and chastening her polluted ways. Instead, we find here a significantly subjective authorial voice. To a substantial extent, Monomohini is invoking narrative content and convention as an introductory ploy for carving out another textual space. This other space comes to be filled, at the core, with an autonomous perspective regarding her personal corporeal conditions and the new direction they ought to take.

Monomohini begins with the claim that she has a *parameswardatta* (god-given) nature in common with all others of the *strijati* (feminine race). We saw earlier the claim of a feminine essence was also invoked by actress-prostitute Tinkari Dasi. Monomohini takes the claim much further, however. On the basis of her feminine essence she identifies, first, with the core attribute of womanly virtue accorded by male nationalism—lajja. Himani Bannerji has argued that the discourse of lajja in colonial Bengal was crucial to appropriately fashioning the sexuality of the gentlewoman—at once to highlight and to cover up 'sexual potentialities'.[62] By grasping and coming to possess this god-given lajja within herself, Monomohini blends herself into the essence of the bhadramahila. Beyond this, Monomohini stakes potential commonality with elite women of a very different capacity. Later in the letter, she contends that had women numbered among the lawmakers, the health plight of prostitutes such as herself would have been addressed.

This point about legislative representation is a striking oddity in this context of reform because, quite simply, 'unchaste' women were denied legal subjecthood. While legal reforms were being targeted to alleviating the so-called barbaric subordination of lajja-draped Hindu homemakers, the public woman was deprived of redress both by colonial law and by popular media. Then and in the decades to come of escalating nationalism, even violence on 'unchaste' women was not deemed criminal in the eye of law.[63] And on the side of nationalist publicity, supposedly honour-enhancing violence of this kind was in fact applauded at all levels—in *bhadralok* authors' farcical plays, in *pathapustika* or 'street literature' put out by inexpensive Battala presses, and even in urban-folk art such as scroll painting by Kalighat *patuas*.[64] In these legal politics of chastity, the racial patriarchy of the colonial state meshed with anti-colonial misogynist nationalism.

Monomohini's aspiration for legal mobilization, on the other hand, is intertextual with the feminist agitation burgeoning in Britain at this precise moment against the Contagious Diseases Act of 1864.[65] Such leading voices of the movement as Josephine Butler were in fact making a humanist argument not dissimilar to Monomohini's, that women of all strata ought to see themselves as implicated in the Act rather than settle for 'private respectability'.[66] No doubt information about these agitations trickled into Bengal via the reformist vernacular press. In her claim of affinity with a potential cast of feminist legal advocates on her behalf, then, Monomohini (and/or perhaps a reformist co-writer of the letter) is drawing on an argument from contemporaneous British feminism. For a woman such as Monomohini, the import of staking this affinity with feminist legal activists is that, on this basis, she is able to imagine legal individualism for herself. In other words, she is able to claim the universal right to a healthy life irrespective of the non-normative (unchaste) sexual status she has in her own repressive context.

The complication is that Monomohini upholds only two categories of women as ideals for all women—the category of the lajja-embracing woman and that of the feminist legislative advocate, respectively. Thus, the letter ends up narrowing down the range of reference. By presenting only these two types of women to be appropriate synecdoches of the strijati at large, it falls into the conventional vein of exclusive humanism. The dark irony here is that neither ideal permits reference to Monomohini's individual body or life condition. Clearly, a prostitute such as herself stands alienated from the virtuously lajja-draped, aesthetically chastened bhadramahila of the inner home because the prostituted body (Monomohini's body) has been publicly exposed and sexually utilized. Her position is equally at odds with legal subjecthood. This caste-based and male-dominant context was supported and strengthened at the higher strata by colonial and nationalist patriarchies. In this context, the theory of the self-sacrificing and desire-abstaining maternal body of the gentlewoman constituted a polemical tool against the self-interest-driven and sexually aggressive bodies of colonizers and invaders (including Muslim invaders of the pre-British past). I will detail these polemics in Chapter 2. Suffice to say for now that within these sexual politics of nationalism, Monomohini's aspiration for legal mobilization on her behalf by liberal feminist advocates was at best a utopian dream. By positing these synecdochal ideals of femininity, then, Monomohini's voice in effect retreats into the convention of upholding the ideal attributes of national femininity, be these Hindu traditionalist or Westernized reformist. And through the very process of narrating the ideals, she also eclipses herself as an autonomous entity. If her affinity with the lajja-draped bhadramahila eclipses her narration of issues on her own terms, rather than on vicarious terms, her imagined commonality with the feminist advocate and potential ally fizzles out to a 'what if'. Both ways she reaffirms that her lot is only as a woman doing *kuthsith karma*[67] (ugly work), exactly in the vein of Tinkari Dasi. Therewith, she sets herself up for describing that she does in the public space what the civilized homemaker is doing in her respectably draped domain— differentiate between civilized and unclean male activity—and thereby vicariously enable masculine upliftment through clarifying the moral categories.

As I see it, however, the core import of Monomohini's letter is otherwise.

Her little self-tale refuses to settle for her ascribed lot. And precisely in that refusal, I hear the struggles of an oppositional subjective voice. The endeavour of this authorial voice is to deploy histories and conventions of narration only so as to create a different textual space. Thus the endeavour is also to wrest the *medium of communication and persuasion* for her needs. This printed word tells of her *personal indigenous* life condition rather than serve as a media compelling the narrator to settle for self-instrumentation—that is, for use by national historical constructions of value and by historiographers of an indigenized modern value system.

The letter grasps through narration the body of the female prostitute— the narrator's own body—as an autonomous corporeal entity. In the course of the narration, Monomohini comes to *re-own* her bodily needs by way of disengaging from the various qualities, interests, and movements of men and women in vanguard positions. Monomohini emphasizes that many prostitutes have already died from contracting illness from men, and that those (such as her) who are well will also soon be contaminated by sick men. To prevent this from happening, the law must cease to be *pakshapati* (favouritist) towards men.[68]

Thus, the letter makes bodies of prostitutes worthy of narration, in sickness and in health. No longer does Monomohini depend on any mediating structure, whether of knowledge or of persuasive style. Her point of reference, instead, is her own vulnerable body placed within an unregulated and unprotected system of livelihood. This reference point is irreducible to any mode of generalization, native or foreign.

One related social condition requires this emphatic self-referentiality. As public women were denied legal subjecthood by (because of) colonial, national and legal reforms, they were as yet unselfconscious as a class of women workers. The growth of a working-class consciousness, as E.P. Thompson reminds us, depends on the articulation by working people of a common 'identity' of interests as 'different from (and usually opposed to)' that of others; it occurs as much in the form of institutions as at the level of 'human relationships'.[69] Hence the emphatic consciousness here that the prostitute's person and body are her own property—a socially viable product ready for exchange—has to come across as an irreducible self-reference rather than as referential to an articulated set of judgements and differentiations regarding these workers. What this referential argument also flagrantly exposes is that, in this context, there is a severe discoordination between humanist national and colonial agendas and the misogynist violations propagating on the grounds of indigenous marginal lives. The argument is also a public reminder that these reformist domains enforce 'patriarchal right' because they are controlled by racialized fraternities (colonial administrators, Orientalist and Anglicist educators, high-caste Hindu men invested in the Aryan discourse, and so on).[70]

Yet, for our purposes, one final point Monomohini makes is indispensable. While her frame of reference begins with her own body as an autonomous (rather than mediated and instrumental) entity, it neither separates her body from other prostitutes in her community, nor does it attack the goals of the larger Bengali collective with a view to her prostituted community. The future she chalks out and the legal change she demands refers not only to her own bodily status and its allied community of vulnerable prostituted women, they also prophetically direct a change of sexual attitude at the national level. Thus in tandem with the growth of the modern reflexive self, we see here the germs of a worker-consciousness based on a common ground of needs and vulnerabilities. This consciousness, in contrast to the British context E.P. Thompson studies, is not being articulated as an 'identity' of interests set against different interests; nor is it demanding to institutionalize these antagonistic terms. Instead, the consciousness being narrated here is based on daily need and violation and refers to an indigenous culture of neighbourly relations. Monomohini's narrative grasps these excluded grounds of Bengali gender-culture, even though this grasp is imperfect. As we have seen, the multi-accented narrative is decidedly two-sided in its reference as it does also reaffirm the exclusion on an idealistic level. Yet, at a deeper subjective level it rethinks the overarching goals and calls for attitudinal change within the national collective.

All in all, this autonomous voice of Monomohini Dasi is a remarkable assertion of the ethical idea of transcultural individuation that I am developing in this book. It underscores the individual as the 'substantial entity' from which all 'collective categories'[71] are derived. To this end, it wrests the individual from various mediating categories of knowledge. In the process of persuasion, it also puts the medium (printed word in this case) to new use. Along these lines, Monomohini's narrative re-communicates the prostituted individual on her own terms, as a corporeal entity grounded in her indigenous needs, violations, and practices of reparation. And in so doing, her narrative invokes the cultural terms in which she is *indigenously accustomed to feel and to rationalize her life conditions*—in the terms not of a separate individual but of one who is bound on a daily basis to her marginalized neighbours and co-workers. On these transcultural terms of a specific need-bearing community of workers, she then intratextually disagrees with the national-historical framework of collectivism. The point of this disagreement is both to criticize the narrowness of the framework and to correct the narrowness by making vulnerable persons and communities participatory, rather than mediated, members of the collective project of modern change. And it is in these battles with mediating frameworks of self-reflection that Monomohini's little personal letter overlaps with the textual politics of communication in actress-prostitute Binodini Dasi's full-length autobiography *Amar Katha*.

Despite the fact that both pieces are self-focused reflections by prostitutes of colonial Calcutta, *Amar Katha* shows some striking contrasts to Monomohini's letter. It is not simply that one is an argumentative letter whereas the other is a relatively long autobiography written largely in the genre of a pre-modern bedona gatha or song of lamentation. At odds with the subjective pull in Monomohini's letter,

Binodini apparently embraces dominant patronage and media. She is eager to accrue whatever opportunities come her way from fitting into her track. As Gayatri Spivak puts it, Binodini's narrative memory is 'unemphatically at ease with the pragmatic patriarchal culture that thwarted her.'[72] In grasping herself and her social relations as aesthetic objects, her narrative is always poised to deploy the exploitations and misogyny of this culture as instruments by which to delineate the acquisition and the exchange of properties (of her own person as well as of physical goods and comforts) for higher personal benefits. As such, Binodini decidedly is *not* a subject of 'subaltern' narrative; instead, she wants to establish a 'line of communication' between her own self and the new 'circuits of [bourgeois national] institutionality'[73] and her narrative is embroiled in the frustrations of her pursuit.

This contrast between Monomohini and Binodini in their respective aesthetics of self-attribution refers, in my view, to the 'extra-verbal pragmatic'[74] conditions of differing marginal lives. It reveals how sexual borders shifted for women on the ground in response to altering needs of national representation. As I see it, Binodini's easy and opportunistic embrace of patriarchal exploitation is driven by two factors. The more obvious factor is that she was a displaced and isolated subject-on-the-move: such actresses as she and Tinkari were among a handful of marginal women who had been dislodged from habitual and possible support groups of similar status and launched on a path of embourgeoisement on account of their capacities for self-change. Identified as one with exceptional physical and emotional merits, Binodini herself was surrounded on one side by Western-educated mentors who schooled her in transforming her natural ways according to tasteful *jukti* or analytical logic,[75] not unlike the vein of David Garrick's theory of acting (indeed, Girish Ghosh was famed as Bengal's Garrick);[76] on another, she was kept by a series of wealthy aristocrats and beaus. Hence, she had none but the bourgeois framework to refer to for self-sustenance and self-development. Yet, it is not simply that she was bemused by the language of meritocracy and exceptionalism surrounding her within the growing entertainment industry at the turn of the century. The less obvious factor driving her easy adjustment to available structures of bourgeois patriarchy was the promising use to which it seemed that she could put her merits.

In her capacity as an actress on the nationalist stage, Binodini was involved in the experiments underway with performance and allied visual media (painting and still photography). In different ways, these nationalist experiments were seeking to transform people's habits of perceiving the real. They tried to cultivate new ways to see and interpret the seen. The goal was to resist the subjugated present—to improve conditions or to transcend subordination. As a meritorious subject at the leading edge of the experiments, Binodini worked upon an assumption of self-revision and perfectibility—that through cultivating new physical and spiritual attributes (whether in performance, print, or photography) she could alter how respectable people perceived who she really was and could become, as against the way her birth and genealogy had situated her. In the Preface he had initially written for her autobiography, her mentor Girish Ghosh says that a life story such as hers could hold up a social telos to other unfortunate fallen women. If well-narrated, Binodini's story could tell such other women that by dedicating mind and body to the theatre and austerely pursuing the command of theatrical roles, they could overcome their 'despicable birth' and gain fame and acceptance as important contributors to respectable society (and nation).[77]

However, Girish Ghosh's preface itself was at first rejected by Binodini on the charge that it was omitting many 'true events'.[78] What it did include is Ghosh's disapproval that Binodini had narrated her life ineptly. Ghosh charges that instead of detailing the processes of self-transformation that had enabled her contributions to the national theatre, and brought commensurate fame and acceptance amidst native and foreign bourgeoisie, Binodini had exposed the many disappointments and rejections of her life. In other words, she had failed in the *kaushal* (technique) of autobiographical narration.[79] She had brought in materials both redundant and damaging to the history of her particular contribution to the national goal—the history of how she was transforming herself into her ascribed roles. Several critics have noted Binodini's allegations regarding her betrayals by the male-dominant bourgeois society and the imagined nation; as noted by Girish Ghosh, a most grievous sense of betrayal arose in Binodini from her failure to get her daughter admitted to a respectable school on account of her own marginal social status.[80] For our purposes, I find it useful to focus on another form of male bourgeois treachery Binodini narrates, one that hitherto has not been discussed. She identifies a treachery foundational in the nationalist aesthetic of communicating self-transformations in the requisite way. Binodini delineates that while, as an aesthetic worker, she immerses in embodying new notions of the beautiful, pleasurable, and good, at the same time, she finds these bourgeois notions to be unreliable. Moreover, her multivocal narrative does not stop at resistance. It weaves into her resistive storyline of treacheries divergent strands of persuasion regarding self-change and community.

Aesthetic Authorship, New Media, and the Reflexive Narrator

Binodini's *Amar Katha* is framed by a paradox of communication. From the opening and closing compositions, we are led to believe that her life-story is at once incommunicable to her readership yet, conditionally, transparent. A closer look reveals that the two sides of the paradox complement each other. Together, they point up the treacherous forms of mediation and mediatization faced by such public women as Binodini when they attempt to vindicate self-change. Binodini prefaces *Amar Katha* by lamenting that, in writing down her story of pain, she is wasting ink and paper.[81] No one will listen to her with kindness and want to know of the pain in her heart because she is a fallen person, a *ghrinita barnari*[82] (a despicable public woman). Binodini closes her narrative with a similar lamentation about her incommunicable pain, bemoaning that all that people will see in her is a *mahapataki* (an extremely viceful woman) from whom they must immediately turn their eyes in order to re-purify themselves in the name of their god or goddess (by chanting '*hari, hari*' or '*durga, durga*').[83] Against this apprehended failure of self-communication, Binodini pits another framing image—that she is a Galatea being constructed and enlivened in society by bhadralok (elite male) Pygmalions. She depicts that as their creation she has been eminently viable and visible in elite spaces, both public and domestic. Despite the fact that she relies heavily in her closing composition on the non-subjective tropic structure of the bedona gatha—evocative of the *rasa* (taste) of pain and of connecting with the outflow of *karuna* or compassion in the audience—Binodini's logical resolution of her paradoxical status is clear. The implication of (and implied allegation behind) her self-portrayal as simultaneously transparent and incommunicable is that in order to retain viability as a socially legitimate person and as an autobiographical author, she must be made and guarded by elite male Pygmalions.

Binodini identifies two principal aesthetic progenitors, as well as other minor figures in their lines. The first, appearing in an introductory composition, is her Pygmalion-*hridaydebota* (god of her heart), the unnamed aristocrat who kept her as his mistress for thirty-one years, after she prematurely quit the stage, and accorded her the status of a family member. Through an appropriate recasting of stock phrases of the *prem gatha* (song of love) in human-companionate terms, Binodini presents his 'tender love' (*snehamoy bhalobasha*) for her as born of the cosmic 'enchanting force' (*mahamayar mohini shakti*) coursing through human life.[84] The force of the divine-human love of her hridaydebota, she says, had brought her to life from stone. The second Pygmalion, named in the closing composition titled 'The Last Two Words of Volume One', is her dramaturge and eminent mentor Girish Ghosh. We hear that he called her the '*sajeeb protima*' (live statue) he had moulded.[85] As sculpted by these two loving artists, Binodini posits herself as paradoxically transparent and opaque.

From the closing narrative I described earlier, it appears that Binodini's principal barrier to communicating her difficult life to an accepting audience is that no one wants to *see her* for who she is nor for what she had made of her person through appropriate moulding. The crucial problem she faces, in other words, is one of a negative visualization of her femininity. This focus of Binodini on sight and the visual dimension is directly intertextual with Girish Ghosh's treatise on ways of seeing the public actress. More broadly, it is referential to the altering visual culture of this time. A few years prior to Binodini's publication of her autobiography in 1913, Girish Ghosh had mounted a spirited defense of prostitute-actresses on the public stage (1910). In his view, the fault lay in the eye of male spectators looking upon actresses who had been appropriately cast and disciplined within their roles. Ghosh was defending against the charge that prostitute-actresses are prone to *apanga nikshep* (throw leering glances) at spectators, thereby disturbing the tasteful *bhava* of spectation.[86] The point to note here is that the image of the leering public woman was appearing not only in popular theatre criticism, at the time it was being widely visualized through the new technologies of urban-folk art.

Jyotindra Jain has shown that many such images of voluptuous public women with seductive looks were circulating in late-nineteenth-century Calcutta through Kalighat scroll paintings. A number of these images were of celebrated heroines from the public stage. While these drew on the Sanskritic aesthetic of the *nayika* or entertainment woman, they also often depicted the uplifted screen of the newfound proscenium arch.[87] What we find here are products of new humanized notions of the image and sight. Both Jain himself as well as Ashish Rajadhyaksha have insightfully argued that with the onset of Western humanist influence on art and other factors of social change (such as urbanization), the non-subjective 'frontal address'[88] and cosmic storylines of Indian iconography significantly altered. Instead, the 'characters began to look out into the camera ... [and] to flirt with the onlooker'.[89] These changes in painting were allied to transformations in theatre art, specifically the displacement of the non-illusionist folk play or *jatra* in favour of the proscenium stage. Inaugurating new notions of the human perspective, the reconfigurations enabled the eye of the voyeur off-screen and off-stage. The masculine Cartesian eye began venturing across space and time, on an imperialistic track. It was roving away from the civilized and respectable quarters of chaste women to the more primitive margins of national culture that offered sexually low-down, open, and seductive women. Put another way, we encounter in the repetitive imagery of leering public women, whether in the Kalighat *pats* or in verbal reproductions of the image in contemporary theatre criticism, the initial tendencies to expose and to 'mortify'[90] marginal bodies in the national gaze.

The solution posed by Girish Ghosh to the problem—of forbidden 'communion'[91] between degraded sexual object and predatory voyeur—was also eminently modern and revisionary. In the same essay on actresses, Ghosh suggests that the path is to return and reform the communion between the gazer and the gazed. The implication is that the visualized communion ought to be given a self-conscious ethico-temporal 'directionality'[92] that *approximates* the cosmic directionality revealed in the timeless frontal address of religious iconography. To begin with, this path of *sangsodhan* (reform) is to be pursued by parties at both ends. At his end, the onus on the male spectator is to cull the *hladini shakti* (feminine delighting power, in the vein of Vaishnava aesthetics) from the 'superior actress'.[93] He must see the *madhurya* (divine sweetness) and the *gambhirya* (natural sobriety) in actresses who were embodying appropriately chastened roles.[94] Digging into the taboos and anxieties of the respectable voyeur, Girish Ghosh goes on to echo his guru, the Hindu saint Ramakrishna's caution against the degraded tendencies of the contemporary age of *kaliyuga*.[95] Ghosh notes that to look otherwise than this at the maternal beauty of (disciplined) actresses is to commit an incestuous act. In his words, as in Ramakrishna's, the men who do so also fear to call their own mothers beautiful.[96] At her end, the prostitute-actress was required by Ghosh to take on the onerous charge of fitting herself into her appropriate form within the visual fabric of the civilized national family/society—that of a *madhur* (sweet) woman who vicariously embodies chaste maternity. As delineated elsewhere by Girish Ghosh, the onus on the actress was to self-reform through an austere disciplining of comportment, voice, and look in front of a mirror (whose reflections, in the prostitute's case, served as a self-chastising measure of failure and success).[97]

Yet Ghosh also emphasizes that neither party need take on their respective charge of image-reform autonomously. Instead, they should be led by an authoritative idealizer. Predictably self-centred in its frame of reference, Ghosh's pathfinder and ideal mediator of the reformed gaze is none other than an elite male or bhadra aesthete—the quintessential progenitor and worshipper of feminine *madhuri* (sweetness).[98] Girish Ghosh rounds out his essay on the chastening of the gaze with the story of one such sweet-beauty-worshipper. He narrates how a painter transformed a prostitute and her beau into iconic figures eliciting pious meditation.[99] Once again we meet this madhuri-worshipping artist in Girish Ghosh's musical play *Mohini Protima*, an appropriation of the Pygmalion-Galatea myth that Binodini herself invokes.[100] This Pygmalion-artist's model and the enabler of his idealism is the prostitute Sahana, in whose role Binodini was frequently cast. Sahana is depicted in somewhat provocative language and was played in accompanying poses.

Figure 1 is a photograph of Binodini posing as Sahana for Pygmalion-Hemanta, with her body held at an inviting erotic angle. The image itself reveals how still photography and camera angle came to strengthen the voyeuristic communion between gazer and gazed born of theatrical illusionism and allied painting. Note also that Binodini's pose as Sahana differs from the stiffness of figuration typical of photographs of the new gentlewoman in public attire that virtuously draped her 'sexual potentialities'.[101]

Figure 1 *Mohini Protima*—An Erotic Galatea
Courtesy: Devajit Bandopadhyay, Kolkata

As against the elements of depth and movement we find in this Sahana, the stiffness in artistic configurations of high-status women 'resisted potentially disruptive perspective forcelines ... [or] a conventional "point of entry" for the [voyeur's] eye'.[102]

Notwithstanding the aspect of titillation in Sahana's words and comportment, she is also presented as eminently transformable through artist Hemanta's elevated imagination. Yet the embodiment of the artist's elevated telos turns out not to be the prostitute model after all. Instead, the Galatea whom Sahana eventually delivers before Hemanta in the form of a perfectly pleasing statue is none other than his patribrata wife whom he had previously ignored. The unmistakable source of Girish Ghosh's imagery of the Pygmalion aesthete is the sexual mythification prevailing on the contemporary Victorian stage, and embodied in such actresses as Ellen Terry whom he had also presented to Binodini as a role model for acting and *sajsajja* (costuming).[103] Victorian theatrical commentaries of this period routinely demanded a classicist aesthetic of statuesque femininity in which the actress was expected to look 'beautiful [but] not to disfigure her face by distortions'.[104] Ellen Terry had gained popular acclaim by presenting herself as a 'demure domesticated statue',[105] while her configurations constituted the 'major experiment' of her Pygmalion-like costumer Edward Godwin.[106]

Binodini reflexively processes how treacherous conditions devolved on herself from Galatea-like transformations, especially because she was identified as a meritorious and compliant learner. The first strand of her argument is that on various accounts of the elite Pygmalions giving her shape(s), whether in the public moral realm or the private emotional realm, she had been identified as having exceptional qualities for sublimating the customary feminine binary portrayed in *Mohini Protima*, which fell between the fallen public model and the chastened domestic ideal. As such, she embodied the national aims of spiritual progress and reform and was also corroborated by shape-givers in these new capacities. Along these lines, she also embraced the stiff figuration of a high-status bhadramahila as her non-theatrical everyday look, using one such photo as the frontispiece of the first edition of *Amar Katha*. Figure 2 reveals that Binodini accents the stiffness of her embourgeoised virtuous look by consciously turning her gaze away from the camera and its potential voyeurism.

Through disengaged narratives of her perfectly transparent interiority Binodini depicts how mesmerically she had internalized the *suruchi sanjukto* (tasteful) lessons given by august mentors (such as Vaishnavite

Sisirkumar Ghosh) about how to embody pious roles like that of Saint Chaitanya in Girish Ghosh's *Chaitan-yaleela*.[107] As Binodini puts it, her eyes would completely turn away from external sight to her ecstatic inner recesses wherein she saw the 'lotusfeet' of God Chaitanya while she was hearing and mouthing the chant of '*gourhari*'.[108] Through these ecstatic rehearsals of cancelling the cognitive eye/I (*ami-jnan*) she was poised to embody,[109] in other words, the theatre of *bhakti* as defined by Ramakrishna. Its goal was to lead the spectator's

Figure 2 Binodini the Gentlewoman
Courtesy: Devajit Bandopadhyay, Kolkata

eye away from *bahirmukh* (external materiality) into *samadhistha* (an inner state of enrapt meditation).[110] In the general eye, Binodini had succeeded in the ecstatic transformation of her *heena* (lowly) fallen self,[111] in the vein of the low-caste transcendental visionaries whose names she lists elsewhere in the narrative (Guhak the Chandal, Haridas).[112] Her performative transformation had been vindicated by the benediction she received for her role as Chaitanya from Ramakrishna himself.[113]

Her principal mentor-artist Girish Ghosh corroborated that Binodini was transformed enough to be fulfilling the larger civilizational goal of bhakti nationalism. Describing Binodini's performance as the love-lorn chaste wife in his play *Buddhadebcharit*, Ghosh argues that (far from distracting the spectatorship with the leers of a fallen woman) the performance had so enrapt spectators in pious meditation that it had impressed upon the Orientalist observer Edwin Arnold how superior a level of spiritual progress the Hindus had achieved.[114] In the context of the rivalry of bhakti nationalism with imperialist sexuality, Ghosh's accolade was especially significant. In effect, he is suggesting that in achieving this enrapt spiritual communion with spectators, Binodini embodies a form of self-alienation and sublimation sought for by the male-national collective at large. She is discarding the seductive *kamini* both within herself and, by extension, in the temptations all around. And she reincarnates in various forms, as the chaste and pious woman (in *Buddhadebcharit*) or the feminized saintly man (in *Chaitanyaleela*). Within the 'gynophobic' parlance of the bhakti movement,[115] the lusts for *kaminikanchan* or woman-and-gold had come to represent 'the economic and political subordination of the male householder in colonial Calcutta'.[116] The sublimation of sexual-financial lust through the 'unreason' of devotional ecstasy, on the other hand, constituted a gendered spiritual triumph; this victory was over the lustful materialism of the ostensibly responsible heterosexual Victorian man, enslaved to clock-time and work-routine.[117] Binodini's spectacular alienation of her kamini-self (both lusted-for and lustful) implied for Ghosh a triumph of precisely the male Hindu spectatorship in communion with her aesthetic reincarnation. This pious communion not only presented national spiritual progress for the approval of the Western male observer, it implied a triumph of Hindu national identity over that Western man's materialistic/sexual propensities. In the process, Binodini's own self-transformation into new attributes was institutionally ratified.

Despite the fact that Binodini's *Amar Katha* draws on a variety of pre-modern genres of Bengali poetry and song that are constitutively non-subjective and untemporized, as I noted earlier, it follows some timelines. It not only contains a linear story of her involvement in the theatre, but with anxious narcissism, it returns to her idealistic telos of chastened and alienated selves, as in the portrayal of her transcendence of ami-jnan described earlier. This teleological trend reappears in her narrative memory of quotidian life and personal relations. We hear that even as a little girl living in a red-light neighbourhood, Binodini inwardly alienated the animalistic behaviour patterns she saw around her, vowing to herself never to stoop to this *ghrinito* (despicable) and tasteless behaviour.[118] Similar nostalgia surfaces in Binodini's memories of the *ramoniyo cchabi* (pleasantly delightful picture) of herself running around on the banks of the Ganga at breaks from rehearsal, or of her palpable *gharmakto* (sweating) body as she, a child from a poor family, faced the glitter of the lighted theatre.[119] These vivid verbal pictures of the ideal purity of a humble child are at once intertextual with the parables of childlike humble people to be found in contemporary bhakti literature (as against the lustful glitters of modernization),[120] and with the Romantic aestheticization of innocent nature in the line of Rousseau (which Binodini derived from Western-educated writers and mentors). And pictures such as these lay the groundwork also for a more radical strand of argument. Binodini claims that notwithstanding her necessary outwardly prostituted and public existence, she *personally* maintained serially monogamous, chaste, and loyal commitments in her various social relations—with the men she cohabited with as well as the theatrical 'families' she cleaved to. The most vivid delineations of her pure (potentially divine) interior surface in the stories of her commitment to her god-like companion and keeper for thirty-one years—the hridaydebota of high kula for whom she had abandoned all other sukhsaubhagya (happiness and luck) and become bound by a mutual humanistic commitment to *satya* (truth).[121]

The argument Binodini emphatically returns to is that none of these promises and pursuits of self-transformation lasted. At the end, all that is left in the grasp of narrative is her body heaped over her hridaydebota's funeral pyre—none other than that of a fallen woman exposed and mortified by the morality of the respectable eye.[122] The logic of her betrayed condition, in practice and in narrative, is simple enough. Her status in all walks of life—personal, public, authorial—is designed, enabled, and also *disabled* by the creative and revisionary new men of the nation. In a flamboyant ironic metaphor of her possessed and exchangeable moulds, Binodini says in her 'dedication' that in writing down her life she is giving back to her Pygmalion-hridaydebota the *jinish* (thing) he had made.[123] While the irony resists her objectification by bourgeois men, at the same time it folds back and defeats itself. It reaffirms Binodini's 'easy'[124] acceptance of the various patriarchal ideals of feeling and association (narrative, performative, visual) which instrumentalize her individual agency. Noteworthy, however, are the strands of logical voice that escape these historical folds of narrative irony and style. I round off the chapter by looking at the 'two-sided'[125] reflexivity in the content and style of *Amar Katha*.

Self-writing and Community in the Folds

Rimli Bhattacharya rightly notes that Binodini's autobiography *Amar Katha* differs in style from the other narrative she published two years later, *My Life as an Actress* (1914–15). In comparison to the latter, it comprises 'discontinuous, multiple texts' written and edited at different times.[126] I wish to expand this insight regarding prosaic fragmentation by calling attention to conflicts in style that occur both across the different vignettes of composition but also within them. The vignettes of *gatha* are composed in the conventional flowery and repetitive style; they frequently incorporate as well a spectacular visual quality that makes words themselves into a 'locus' of her desires[127] for compliant self-transformation. In between, we *also* encounter vignettes in *chalit* (colloquial) prose (the editors of the Bengali *Amar Katha* note her narrative to be an early example of fluent chalit style).[128] These not only depict realistic details, but sometimes they register or imply uncompromising references to alternative possibilities for self-development and for narrative development, even though the author might go on to compromising with the dominant nationalist bind described above. At her points of refusing compromise, Binodini's delineations of her personal properties vis-à-vis collectivity turn radically different from compliance.

For one, Binodini seeks just benefits and immunities in exchange for being an untiring and highly productive worker under the very unstable conditions of the theatre industry of late nineteenth-century Calcutta. On occasion, the emphasis of her storyline is decidedly not on *achieved* self-transformations into bourgeois male scripts. Rather, as Rimli Bhattacharya also notes,[129] Binodini's point of reference is the body of an adept woman worker subjected to *harbhanga mehanath*[130] (unrelenting bone-crunching labour). Whether explicitly or implicitly, this referential framework is irreducible to the family-like structures of patriarchal association and feeling she comes up against.

It appears that the tutelage of a competitive and ambitious master has inducted Binodini into a similarly competitive sense of self-interest, but that at great cost. On the promise that the theatre alone could constitute the ladder to her development (*unnatir sopan*),[131] Girish Ghosh keeps her under so much pressure to learn and perform new plays and pantomimes that for a while she falls seriously ill.[132] Upon return from the only fifteen-day rest Ghosh would allow her, she faces another exploitative male attitude, that of her Marwari theatre-proprietor who refuses her paid leave.[133] In protest she quits that theatre and resolves henceforth to labour only for higher wages agreed upon under a *chukti* or contract.[134] That is, she resolutely grasps through the narrative the changes in self-understanding afforded by an altering legal landscape. She claims for her own immunity the emergent discourse of self-proprietorship, civil liberty, and of commonality as a rational 'coalition' rather than a hierarchy of wills.[135] Her grasp of these concepts does seem to be no more than momentary, though. We soon hear that she was dissuaded from her demand for equal contractual relations with potential employers by her bhadra Bengali mentors and cohorts and once again re-tracked in patriarchal relations. In the larger interest of her theatrical 'family', she is induced to pawn her body to another Marwari entrepreneur such that her troupe can obtain capital to erect a theatre of their own. And in the course of her retraction, Binodini yet is again thwarted (in her realizing her love for self-merit, in this instance) by her bourgeois Bengali male associates. They do not fulfil their promise of enshrining her exceptional talent by naming the theatre after her.

Despite these portrayals of Binodini's capitulation to patriarchal compulsion, the episodic narratives of her work experiences have a tendency to reach back to her claims for legal autonomy. Noteworthy in this regard is another curiously tentative depiction of her compliance with familial hierarchy. The new Marwari theater-owner and her keeper, Gurumukh Rai, wants to rectify what he considers to be Binodini's unjustly subordinate status in the company by endowing her with the *swattwa* (part-proprietorship)of the new playhouse.[136] Once again Binodini capitulates, this time to a decision asserted by her mother but dictated by Girish Ghosh. She declines the offer of proprietary right in exchange for her contributions. Yet this time around, her accord is narrated in uncharacteristically impersonal terms. In contrast to her pronounced self-focus throughout most of her autobiography, Binodini pointedly withdraws her own agency from her portrayal of the decision, noting that since her mother was deeply respectful of Ghosh, in no way did she (mother) want to disobey his direction.[137] The impersonal and abrupt tone of her comment leaves a germ of doubt about whether her subjective preference differed.

The emphasis we encounter in these episodes on the labour and just rewards of a woman-worker of humble origins such as Binodini is constitutively at odds with the bhakti logic we found in other vignettes of *Amar Katha*. In Ramakrishna's *Kathamrita*, for example, the 'labours of artisans, peasants, and women become a parable of perseverance and devotion'[138] held up as a moral/aesthetic standard against the dreary labour of Westernized male materialism. Resistance to the latter is what Girish Ghosh invokes in his argument to Binodini's mother against Gurumukh Rai's offer of swattwa. As quoted by Binodini, Ghosh contends that 'donkeys' should be left to carry *bojha* (loads)— of ownership and materialistic transactions—while they (that is, Bengali theatre practitioners) concentrate on the 'work',[139] no doubt of enlightenment. Clearly, the depletion of Bengali commercial ventures from 1840 onwards in the face of Marwari mercantile capitalism[140] was a ground for this thinly veiled ethnic imperialism in Ghosh's elitist parable.

That Binodini might disagree with Ghosh's approach and with the moral aesthetic of bhakti nationalism in this vein, is implied elsewhere. She suggests that the possession of a theatre through her own agency in kind (that is, proprietary right) and/or in name will permit her family a steady income and herself immunity against exploitations (as prostitute and as actress).[141] Her minimal notion of herself as a right-bearing subject, as we saw, is grasped and explicated through her story of demand for a chukti. The material change allowing these self-conceptions was the institution of the Indian Evidence Act and the Indian Contract Act in 1872. The new statutes established the 'figure of ... the interested subject ... as a legal subject', confirming a 'century-long shift from a physiocratic model of political economy focused on land as a source of revenue and wealth....'[142] Still, colonial legislation inhibited the temporal transition to be found in Western Europe from *Gemeinschaft* to *Gesellschaft*, status to contract, by imposing on all ethnic domains of vernacular capitalism the 'Anglo-Indian legal construct [of the] Hindu Undivided Family';[143] the Marwaris, comprising a number of immigrant groups from different parts of Western India, through their business practices by and large 'affirmed the patriarchal authority of the joint family, religious orthodoxy, and the currency of culture'.[144] Binodini's memory of Gurumukh Rai, on the other hand, suggests more eclectic explorations of the notions of property and contractual equality at the level of quotidian interpersonal relations within this transitional world of commerce and law. It also suggests that in the course of these transitions, mutually respectful and egalitarian relationships might have been forged across patriarchal and ethnic lines.

As such, Binodini's narratives seeking legal-commercial individualism demonstrate a larger argument of this book. They show that subjects positioned in different social strata on indigenous grounds appropriate and understand the Enlightenment vocabulary quite differently. Binodini's appropriation of possessive individualism, for example, stands strikingly at odds with the male nationalist intellectual Rabindranath Tagore's critiques. This distinction of position and self-understanding will become clear in the next chapter. For the moment, we must return to the point that despite her germinal awareness of individual rights, Binodini willingly returns to narrating how she voluntarily gave up her individualist demands in favour of her familial relationships, both personal and theatrical.

However, her narratives of *voluntary* familial submission differ from her more idealistic and spectacular stories of self-submitting to her

Pygmalion artists and their family ties. The contrast lies in the narration of a peculiarly corporeal form of personal commitment, irreducible to abstract hierarchical logic. In certain familial stories, *bodies and their interrelations* are the focal points of communication. Words function as inconspicuous aids to this presentness of form, rather than as sites of immanent desire. Some of the most memorable passages of *Amar Katha* present corporeal attachment as a crucial property of the self-as-survivor. Partially violating the taboo of genteel nationalist literature against physical heterosexual intimacy, these moments of narrative depict mutual care-giving in health and in sickness. For our purposes, it is also important that these narrative moments *dismantle the dominant filiative or paternalistic national order of family life* and instead reinforce the (theatrical) family as a site of nurturance. They discard authoritative patriarchal figures as such, or turn the men into care-needy and mutual bodies. In closing I paraphrase one such passage, attempting to retain its cryptic tone and fast yet unemphatic movement of detail.

As a young actress with the Bengal Theatre, Binodini was once travelling with her troupe to Chuadanga for a performance. At a stopping point, some of the men disembarked to buy some food from the railway station. When one Umichand did not get back on board in time, his relative, the theatre-patriarch Sharatchandra Ghosh, started to look around and call his name with much anxiety. As the train was pulling out, Umichand did reappear and jump back on board, only to collapse the moment after. Fearing that he was coming down with a heatstroke, Sharatchandra himself and other men of the troupe called out for some water and started to fan Umichand in the hope of cooling down the fever. Yet such was the ill turn of fate that none at all in that entire compartment had even one *gondush* (handful) of water to quench the thirst of this *mrityu mukhe patito*[145] (on the brink of death). The actress Bhuni had just joined Bengal Theatre. Finding no *upay* (other means), Bhuni, herself a lactating mother at the time, took breast milk in a *jhinuk* (feeding shell) and put it to his mouth. He was dead the moment after and all within a span of ten or fifteen minutes. Everyone in the compartment was *bhaye bhabonay mujjhyoman* (stupefied with fear and anxiety); and, with his face on Umichand's breast, Sharatchandra himself started to weep like a little boy.[146]

The narrative poses a down-to-earth aesthetic allowing for a brief yet equal attention to each spontaneous action and every autonomous actor in this tragic episode. Nobody nor any bhava or mood is focused upon, emphasized, or spectacularly adorned. The point is none other than to depict a resourceless collective's emotional-corporeal struggles for life and around death. After finishing up the story with a few quick details about how the death was reported and the body taken for cremation, Binodini rounds out her narrative with an unexpected remark. She notes with apparent regret that had the tragic event been portrayed by some able writer (*yogya lekhak*), the terrible picture might have been clarified to some extent—*se bhishan cchabi katak parimane parisphuto haito.*[147] The comment is anomalous in at least two ways. Binodini is not repeating here her general complaint that she wastes ink and paper all along because she will not get a readership amidst the respectable literate public. Her point, made with deliberate reflexivity, is that she is not in command of the language and style of the yogya lekhak necessary to represent the event. In light of this argument, the second anomaly I find here is that Binodini has shown ample command elsewhere in *Amar Katha* over the conventional language she needs to spectacularize an event such as this. A language readily available to her through her professional and personal immersion in nationalist discourse, as noted earlier, is the language of mother-worship. That language would have been most appropriate for aestheticizing Bhuni's action within the conventional register.

Why Binodini does not invoke that language and rationale, in my view, is a matter of conscious critical discernment. Her omission of that language, coupled with her rhetorical move of calling the reader's attention to that subtle choice, has to do with her minimal rational grasp of the discoordinated times and spaces she straddles. The historical idealism of mother-worship or, for that matter, its sexual teleologies of the spiritual maternal aesthetic quite simply contradict her communicative needs of this moment. Their idealistic structures of collectivism—of knowing and seeing—would gloss over these uneven personal commitments to community shown by working people on the ground. Moreover, Binodini's own reflexive statement reinforcing these discoordinations of experience and of aesthetic, which envelop her life, also enables the reader to grasp the difference. It alerts the reader to start evaluating Binodini's *other aesthetic voice*. This voice is attentive to some of those indigenous practices of autonomy vis-à-vis community which emerge from different personal struggles for survival amidst uneven change.

2

NATION AND INDIVIDUATION

Manhood and the Aesthetics of Womanly Desire

The previous chapter focused largely on voices that were marginal to anti-colonial nationalist discourse or, at the least, were diverging from its assumptions of gender behaviour. Does this mean that the elite mainstream of nationalist thought was as hegemonic as earlier sections of Chapter 1 made it out to be? Far from it. As noted in previous chapters, recent studies have been exploring the many diverse and contradictory strands of nationalist modernity in Bengal itself and elsewhere in the India of this era. I round out my own reading of gender politics in colonial India by focusing on one powerful conflicting strand which arose from the heart of reformist nationalism in early twentieth-century Bengal. My emphasis in this chapter is on the late works of Rabindranath Tagore. This focus helps the purposes of this book for a number of reasons. First, Tagore was the foremost thinker of this era to challenge the dual processes of empire and resistant nationalism on the bases of humanist premises. Second, he was attempting to take responsibility for what he considered to be at the masculine core of the territorial and reverse-possessive attitudes of his time—in Europe and in India—the manipulation of femininity and desire. And third, as primarily an aesthetic thinker, Tagore was deeply concerned with the role *imagination* was playing in these pervasive sexual-territorial politics. In particular, his late humanist works struggled against the grain of dominant textualizations of gender virtue, trying to re-imagine woman's autonomous growth and responsible sexual relations in other pleasing ways.

My reading of aesthetic nationalism in the previous chapter may have already suggested that I agree with one part of Dipesh Chakrabarty's argument regarding Bengali nationalism. I concur that the nationalist 'refusal' of the values of European civil society constituted an aesthetic response encompassing 'contesting desires' and imaginations.[1] My concern is that, to substantiate his larger theoretical position, Chakrabarty emphasizes some aspects of nationalist aesthetics while he ignores other critical strands. Chakrabarty suggests that gendered anti-colonial politics rejected autonomous individualism through reviving pre-modern domestic practices in secular form. Foremost of these was an aestheticization of the 'pleasantness' of Bengali patriarchal family ideals and allied values of the larger patrilineal clan or kula.[2] In his estimation, nationalism's refusal of Western individualism, in other words, went hand-in-hand with the consolidation of an indigenous filiative order eclectically combining patriarchal and caste biases with Victorian disciplinary codes. Chakrabarty goes on to stress that herein lay 'a crucial difference between the ideology of Bengali modernity and some of the critical assumptions of patriarchal liberalism in Europe'.[3] The import of Chakrabarty's analysis is that nationalism's refusal of Western individualism went hand-in-hand with the hardening of a native order of filiation based on patriarchy and caste. He also clarifies that he is not 'defend[ing]' the Bengali patriarchal ideals.[4] Rather, his academic objective, undoubtedly an important one, is to present a postmodern model for historical analyses more nuanced than the homogenous practices of modernist Western historiography.[5] As already discussed in the Preface and Introduction, Chakrabarty's broader goal is to consider differences from Enlightenment modernity. The implication of what in turn becomes Chakrabarty's own homogenous emphasis on (multi-) cultural difference should also have been implied by my readings in prior chapters. Chakrabarty's model is applicable to selected aspects of Bengali nationalism—specifically to the more orthodox and territorial voices of nationalist resistance, or to those strands of intertexuality that bind the more critical voices (such as Binodini's) to the orthodox standards. While it encourages this lens of selection, Dipesh Chakrabarty's model forecloses our alertness to how contestatory aesthetical desires on grounds of empire came to be logically textualized and in what ways cultural territories were criss-crossed and re-twined in the course of cumulative textual critique.

The point of the present chapter is to parse the struggles of affective cognition faced in his individuated critique by one such aesthetic activist. Rabindranath Tagore sought to critique his own nationalist tendencies to idealize pleasant maternity and to pit self-giving femininity against the aggressive masculinities born of empire and urban capital. In the wake of the First World War in Europe and anti-colonial militancy at home, Tagore could no longer rest satisfied with these binary sexual politics of Indian nationalism. His overarching endeavour was for a transnational 'cooperation between people' as against 'isolation',[6] territoriality, or reverse-possessive nationalism. Hence he struggled self-critically to think through the roots of separatist aggression here and there; in that process, he tenaciously revisited and rethought the sexual bases of sociopolitical aggression. In some of his woman-centred productions late in life, Tagore was striving for what I described in the previous chapter as a counteractive drive for associative life—the drive against dominant male agendas in general and for a reciprocal 'community of experience'[7] which communicates and negotiates about what a common future might be. That he was especially interested in these works also to experiment with the tools of communication—language itself and the expressive forms of song and dance—is far from accidental. He and his team were experimenting with cooperative ways to communicate pleasure and goodness by drawing on an eclectic body of aesthetic practices and philosophies. These draw as much from everyday folk forms of India as from the other parts of Asia and Europe which Tagore traversed and intellectually explored in this phase of his life. Tagore's endeavour was to be and to see in ethically dialectical ways. He wanted to evaluate formations of separatism and filiation which were zigzagging through his globe—rank-ordering families and nations—and manipulating sexuality in the process.

As already discussed in the Introduction, Tagore's dialectical vision of gender, like other activists' dialectical struggles, was constrained and unconcluded. It did remain partially limited by the theories it sought to challenge, especially when it came to sexuality in relation to caste-location and social status. My objective in this chapter, then, by no means is to stake an ontological faith in Tagore's exceptional capacity to transcend bias. It is a modest attempt, focusing on a few late woman-centered works out of Tagore's vast oeuvre, to read the trajectory of a principled exploration of anti-possessive aesthetics.

Gender, Imagination, and Classification in Tagore's Thought

In 1928, Rabindranath Tagore wrote a commentary on the status of women which I consider to be a key to understanding his exploration of femininity in relation to male imagination. Originally written by Tagore as a letter to a family member, the piece was later published in his collected works as an essay titled *Narir Manusatya* (The Humanness of Woman).[8] The piece begins on a paternalistic polemical note and one which resurfaces off and on throughout the essay. At the same time, paternalism and patriarchal logic are internally displaced and rethought.

Tagore begins by complaining about some of the excited and burning (full of *uttejana* and *daha*) rather than enlightened (with *alok)* feminist voices he hears in the writing of his day. In his early life, Tagore himself had faced challenges from a burgeoning Bengali feminist press for his investment in orthodox gender-nationalism. Noteworthy is a rebuttal written in *Bharati O Balak* by his older sister Swarnakumari Debi[9] to young Tagore's misogynist attack upon the famed Marathi feminist Pandita Ramabai's call for gender equality (both published in the same periodical in 1888);[10] Tagore had based his attack on a staunch belief that woman's dependent status is what maintains *samanjasya* (peaceful equilibrium) in the household.[11] Also to be noted is that Tagore's affirmation of women's liberty many years later in *Narir Manusatya* substantially overlaps with reformist voices both in Bengal and in Britain. His affirmative view is intertextual with feminist positions such as the moderate Swarnakumari Debi's and also that of the more radical Krishnabhabini Das, who had meticulously contended for the intellectual strides all women were able to take once given the opportunity.[12] Among male thinkers, precedents are to be found in the early argument against women's *adhin* or subordinate position in quotidian Bengal levelled by Rammohan Roy,[13] and also the argument for independent judgement in sexual relations mounted by Tagore's reformist brother Satyendranath in the course of the Age of Consent debates over child marriage (among others).[14] There is little doubt that British gender thinkers such as Mary

Wollstonecraft, John Stuart Mill, and George Eliot (mentioned by Swarnakumari in her rebuttal) were basic influences on these Bengali reformist debates.

Yet the point of account here is not the simple one that Rabindranath Tagore rethought his own early conservatism through imbibing influence from reformist voices and progressive intellectual traditions, although those undoubtedly must have been factors. What we ought to take account of in *Narir Manusatya* are more basic evaluative processes—at least two, in my view. First, far beyond a reformist agenda, Tagore is attempting to rethink the founding assumptions of gender division in his contemporary historical contexts and he is relating them to causal structures that include the political, the economic, and the aesthetic. And then, quite consistently, he is using the first person mode of address, the pronoun *amra* or we, to describe the causality.

Sudipta Kaviraj has helpfully pointed out that even though the first person pronoun—the singular ami and the plural amra—existed in pre-modern Bengali, it took on an entirely new inflection with the onset of modern consciousness in nineteenth-century Bengal. The person acquired a new 'feeling of self-responsibility', an urge to make an identity in secular time.[15] Kaviraj goes on to consider in what way Rabindranath Tagore's reflexive poetic use of ami deviates from Western 'esthetic individualism',[16] indigenizing selected premises such that 'atomistic individualism'[17] is thoroughly challenged.

Extending Kaviraj's insight, I emphasize that the picture is even more complex when gendered pressure points enter Tagore's textual processes of self-making. In these textual spaces, Tagore's scrupulous self-responsible onus is to critique the filiative territories produced by the dualities of empire and resistant nationalism. In the essay at hand, Tagore thinks against these global processes, and he speculates upon an irreducible individuality. He calls this *byektimulak acharan* or autonomy-impelled behaviour against the grain of *srenimulak* or classified behaviour.[18] Since paternalistic and status-based polemics are invariably intertwined, it is necessary that we read Tagore's self-responsible textualizations of gender justice with an eye to their conflicting affective logical strands. Note also that, written as a letter to a family member, this piece is thickly layered with reflections rather than more neatly arranged in the form of a public debate as are many other essays by Tagore. By his own testimony, the letter began as a little fountain and became a swelling river, giving release to katha or many words that hitherto had been frozen static in his head.[19]

Our challenge in reading this piece is to follow the many bends in his outflowing idea-centric words.

The basic argument of his letter/essay *Narir Manusatya* is common to liberal feminists of Tagore's day. It is that even though nature creates sexual difference, it does not ascribe *swatantra jagat* (an exclusive world) to either sex, rather, it places both on a common ground.[20] There is, in other words, *sadharan manush* (a common human being) in both sexed people;[21] when released from gendered social boundaries, each and both are poised to contribute to human history in *nijer bhabe* (her or his own way).[22] Inevitably, this argument gets embroiled in self-oriented tension regarding which gendered differences could be overcome by women and which not; women's inclinations for maternity and against abstract thought are seen as obdurate. This rather tedious polemical strand of the essay need not detain us, however, because other deliberations internally engage the patriarchal logic.

Tagore deliberates upon what stands in the way of the emergence of the 'human' woman into history. He discusses two broad structures of male dominance impeding the emergence. In England, women have been confined to *bishesh o shankirno byabohar* (limited and specified patterns of behaviour) in the same way that land expanses are fenced in to be utilized as *shikarstan* (hunting grounds) or consumed as *bilash aranya* (luxury forests) by aristocrats, whereas the arable land ought to have been opened up for common agricultural use.[23] Tagore detects a not dissimilar arrangement of *adhikar* (male proprietary right) in his own subcontinent. Therein the colonized man perceives his wife to be his only territory of control, the larger patriarchal family treats the girl child as a burden,[24] and male nationalists in general tend to erect an 'abstract' notion of national *heet* (well-being) to whose end *byekti* (individuals) are mercilessly sacrificed.[25] The root of this ubiquity of masculine proprietorship in his day, despite the historical variations, according to Tagore is not natural difference. Rather, it constitutes heightened discursive framings of the difference, not only in *sanskar* (traditions of society), but even more accentually in *kalpana* (traditions of aesthetic imagination).[26] English literary productions routinely attach to portrayals of feminine nature such ornamental (like *alankar*) exaggerations of weakness as *kakukti* (supplication), *murccha* (fainting), and *lajjaraktimata* (blushing).[27] Contemporary Bengali men, on their part, view women through another mediating aesthetic of objectification in that they encrypt woman in the same *kotha* (category/column) as *kanchan* (gold), as if to untie a purse and empty it out is all that it takes to give *mulya* (value) to a woman.[28] Tagore is referring, of course, to the systematic denunciation of kaminikanchan to be found in the masculinist bhakti nationalism of his Bengal, as discussed in Chapter 1.

With a compelling insight into the gendered bases of such attitudes as these of empire and cultural capital—that is, proprietorship and objectification—Tagore goes on to conclude that at the root of these territorial mentalities lies a binary approach to the gendered being (identity). In his view, the various social practices and imaginations of his world converge to cast people into *ekanto kore sreni baddha* (excessively aligned) formations—reducing autonomous behaviour and instead conciliating all into a *kathamo* or structure of hostile *bhed* or difference.[29] Tagore's point of this conclusion, however, is not simply to accept the prevalence of gender antagonism even while he dismantles its structural bases. As an activist intellectual, he looks urgently for alternative human agency. Written from the heart of the misogynist Hindu nationalist context of early twentieth-century Bengal, these reflections on antagonistic identity show a tenacious urgency to envision betterment. Indeed, this piece on women well illustrates Abu Sayeed Ayyub's observation that Tagore's late writings are propelled by an activist consciousness of time and needful social change (see my discussion in the Introduction). The essay goes on to point to a *tritiya jati* (an ensemble of third people), those who are metaphorically born not in the home but on the road.[30] These are people who interject khapcchara *baichitra* (incoherent variety) into the human race.[31]

Tagore brings up these third people directly after reiterating one more time his own complicity with binary thought, namely, the maternal drive in woman versus the work-oriented public drive in man. In the very next paragraph, he is soundly undermining the binary through an affirmation that the third people of the road are propelled from within by a force of autonomy—*swatantra shakti*—to stray from the flock (become *juthabhrashta*).[32] Note further that this intratextual displacement of the chaste maternal ideal of domesticity and nationalism—of image proliferating in the misogynist Hindu aesthetic—is not an accidental transgression in Tagore's gender writing of this phase. It has intertextual longevity. As we will see below, precisely this displacement is dramatized in Tagore's performative retelling of the Hindu epic story of princess Chitrangada—the woman leader and nurturing protector of her people who strays from the kathamo of maternal national governance when she feels and knows desire. Such intratextual and intertextual debates as these over humanism permit (partial) rectifications of complicity with the antagonistic and territorial human. And these forms of textual debate and dialectic are also what get erased by postcolonial models which take the anti-Enlightenment position to be a solid foundation for all readings of the Indian modern self.

Our next case in point, with regard to Tagore's view of maternal femininity, is Ashis Nandy's lens. Nandy reads in Tagore's aesthetical explorations of femininity an invariable vertical arrangement that places over and above women's 'conjugal selves or sexuality ... maternal selves'; the latter uphold 'the authenticity and authority of the feminine self which serves as an organizing principle of the Indic civilization'.[33] This vertical view constitutes Nandy's critique of 'values embedded in the masculinized world of nationalism and nation-state ... what could be called the principle of egalitarian patriarchy ...'.[34] Seen in light of the larger postcolonial engagement with masculine individualism and historicist reason, the implication of Nandy's reading is that Tagore's gender thought basically did not disagree with the prevalent Hindu nationalist symbolism of self-surrendering maternity and sexual chastity (abstinence from pleasure). Tagore embraced this principle for challenging imperial hypermasculine individualism which, in contemporary Victorian patriarchal contexts, was coming to be rationalized as the egalitarian bourgeois family man. We saw in Chapter 1 that this maternal symbolist critique of Victorian masculinity was widespread in the bhakti nationalism of colonial Bengal.

No doubt Nandy is careful to distinguish between the overtly 'masculinized' voices of mother-privileging nationalism and more discerning thinkers, such as Tagore and Gandhi, who drew upon Indic civilizational principles to rebut modern masculinism. Nonetheless, by emphasizing the maternal in Tagore's imagination, and by endorsing this element as the authentically 'Indic' aspect of Tagore's thought, Nandy's model compels us to ignore what we find in *Narir Manusatya*, as well as subsequent feminist works by Tagore (as discussed below). This activist male intellectual attempts to think transnationally against different historical coercions of women's desires and sexual relations (imperialist and resistant nationalist), while trying as well to learn in a self-responsible way from different gender cultures. By presupposing Tagore's rejection of the Enlightenment with regard to gender thought, Nandy's model forecloses all the ways Tagore invoked autonomy to engage the organizing filiative principle of dominant modernities, a principle that invariably requires the subordination of women and sexuality. We have noted above that in this connection, Tagore seriously objected to the current Indian trend of sacrificing the autonomy of individuals to abstract ideals of 'well-being' for the national family. More broadly speaking, Tagore's ways of appropriating and indigenizing the Enlightenment individual vindicate an insight offered by a different postcolonial thinker. According to Kwame Anthony Appiah, as European humanist concepts 'root themselves' in disparate historical contexts, they are opened up to robust forms of 'deliberation ... [and] argument'.[35] Precisely along these lines, Enlightenment ideas were and are being appropriated and re-rooted in South Asian thought by generations of activist thinkers; these thinkers deliberate upon what fits with 'Indic' frames of reference and also how these frameworks themselves might have to adapt to change. Chapter 4 will discuss in what ways feminist thinkers of our own day are engaging in such deliberations. Not to conceive of the Indic or the South Asian in this way as an altering civilizational space—one open to critiques and restorations from different social standpoints—is to reduce the constitutive dynamism of the subcontinental civilization to a coherent theoretical framework.

That said, it may appear that I am making more of Tagore's meaning than there is to it. For if his earlier comments were oscillating between an affirmation of sexual division and a negation of sexual hierarchy, in reference to a common *manush*, these later comments on the autonomous 'third people' could be seen as tilting towards another kind of stratification. It may seem that we are hearing a Romanticist celebration, in the vein of John Stuart Mill, of the spontaneity of 'individual power and development'[36] as against the 'common modes of thinking'[37] which befit 'customary characters'.[38] All Tagore could be doing is to pit past 'custom' against future-oriented 'choice'.[39] As a matter of fact, he goes on to explicitly temporize thirdness. Tagore says that the distinctive third people are poised to spearhead historical change, even though he throws in a caveat that some amongst them are rendered quite ineffective or even chaotic under the burden of social codes.[40] All in all, these comments on history and the *atiparimito* 'bound-surpassing' self-creator[41] could well come across as yet another high-modernist celebration of exceptionalism/genius and a self-referential one at that. However, a closer read tells us that whereas inflections of Romanticist thought are unmistakable in the passage, they are diverging from European Utilitarian-Romanticism such as espoused by John Stuart Mill. Tagore is dialectically rethinking the temporal binary of custom-versus-individuality and reinterpreting in the indigenous context.

In at least two ways, Tagore's 'third' autonomy refuses a self-oriented endorsement of non-conformism in the vein of what Marshall Berman describes to be the 'whirlwind' of modernity as a 'dialectic motion'— the push against customary social structures to be found in nineteenth-century Europe.[42] First, Tagore's dialectic of history and the individual is an affirmation neither of the teleology (of pushing back custom) nor of the atomization (of the person pushing away from society) assumed to constitute modern progress in the European version of the Enlightenment. The key to this teleological and atomizing nature of the European modernist dialectic is to be found in John Stuart Mill's use of the word 'development' in the quote above. We learn from Charles Taylor that, at the core, 'development' assumes 'the demise of a traditional society'[43]—individuals self-develop by detaching from prior social relations. Moreover, the philosophical convention of linking developmental enlightenment to demise leads to a further assumption which we also detect in Mill's formulation. The assumption is that exceptional individuals are able to *perfect* a progress discontinuous with earlier and other selves. This approach to individual perfectibility seen on a temporal scale is what constitutes Tagore's second point of disagreement with the dialectic of individualism in its European conception.

To begin with, the thirdness of Tagore's notion of swatantra shakti or force of autonomy lies precisely in that it constitutes a corrective/ normative drive against antagonistic classifications of social behaviour and imagination; in other words, it is a principled interrogation of binary formations in general which would include the teleological binarism of pitting a non-conformist individual against all customary behaviour. More specifically, neither customary behaviour nor autonomous behaviour for Tagore is temporally stratified. He notes that in Bharat's/ India's middle ages many such atiparimito individuals emerged out of the lower-born strata as cultivators of *adhyatyatwatta* (metaphysical/ intellectual truth), despite the fact that people of these strata had been systematically excluded from the institutional cultivation of religion and knowledge.[44] And more germane to the topic of gender at hand, Tagore goes on to affirm human autonomy in women at the same time that he takes a nuanced view of how gendered domination stands in the way of this instantiation of autonomous agency. Tagore hastens to stress that when human autonomy wants to overcome women's specified packaging (*bisesh morok*) of the mother or the homemaker (*mata ba grihini*)—packaging which mediates their social recognition (*tader parichay*) as women—it tends either to go unacknowledged (*aswikrito*) or to be slandered (*nindito*).[45] One needs only to recall the short story *Streer Patra* (Letter from a Wife, 1914)—widely recognized to be one of his finest feminist creations—to realize that here Tagore speaks from an inter-temporal view. He links packaged and autonomous women then and now while, as we saw above, he also recognizes that the packaging differs by time and by geographic location. The protagonist of *Streer Patra*, homemaker Mrinal, is shown to be inspired in her struggles against patriarchal classification through remembering the sixteenth-century woman mystic Mirabai (neither of them is a mother).[46] Indeed, this endorsement by Tagore of women's autonomy, resting on a critique of their domestic packaging, not merely inveighs against his defensive masculine rhetoric earlier in the essay. It implies a scrupulous rejection of anti-modernist abstractions, such as Ashis Nandy's in our day, with an eye to the possible impact such 'abstract' theories could have on Indian women's lives (impacts by way of entwined social imagination and practice).

Beyond this are the intertextual politics of the metaphor of the 'road' Tagore invokes in conceptualizing the autonomous third. As elaborated through this and several other late writings, the road metaphor constitutes Tagore's implicit disagreement with a European notion of self-development such as John Stuart Mill's—the notion that one is able to self-develop to perfection along a homogenous historical timeline. Tagore's road is decisively not this teleological symbol of freedom from gendered classifications of power. Rather, it is a flexible metaphor of 'unfinished' self-movement, to use the potent term Abu Sayeed Ayyub brings up in another context.[47] This is a self at once personal and placed in relation to collective 'cooperation'.[48] As Sankha Ghosh presciently argues, Tagore's metaphor of the road pursued by an unfinished individual is broken up by structural impediments produced by modernization (as seen in the allegorical play *Muktadhara*, for example)[49] at the same time that it encompasses the remnants of Bengali agrarian communities.[50] As such Tagore's road at once constitutes the site of material and of conceptual struggle: it forks through barriers both of social power as well as of *chittapat* [51] (mental picture). As we delve further into this key metaphor of imperfect autonomy later in the chapter, we will see that in

Tagore's woman-centred works this road of struggle must fork through the historical kathamo/structure of the masculinist home and the filiated family (at once nationalist and imperialist).

Having engaged in these various practical and metaphorical explorations, Tagore closes the letter/essay with a thundering endorsement of Enlightenment modernity. He applauds the *jugantakaler bhumikampa* (epochal earthquake) underway in the West,[52] looking to how social movement is rocking gendered society down the middle, hurling both man and woman outside the *gandi* (boundary).[53] Yet my discussion of this piece thus far, and supporting quotations, should have revealed that Tagore is at the same time entering into robust 'arguments'[54] with Enlightenment thought. Quite simply, he is attempting, on the one hand, to rescue the framework of self-reflexivity and progress from the imperial man and atomistic teleology; on the other, he is embracing what he sees in Enlightenment humanism as an unprecedented radical possibility of *bhanga-gara* (breaking-and-rebuilding) socio-imaginative premises. Most notable among these is the breakdown of *probhu-daser samparka*[55] (master-slave relations), various gendered forms of which Tagore earlier identified both in European imperialism and in native nationalism. In view of his deep concern with the obduracy of these gendered crypts of social alignment (*samajik srenigata kuthori*), Tagore avers that the most radical social movement in this regard is the women's movement in the West.

Despite the emphasis on women, Tagore's focus throughout the essay is on male self-responsibility. And through this focus, his reflections to an extent get embroiled as well in the defensive posturing I record above. After all, Tagore was writing in a completely male-dominant context, and one in which an independent women's movement was being stymied by the broader collective goal of national liberation.[56] Tagore ends the essay by saying that once woman attains her fully dignified stature as a byektibisesh or distinctive person, man too will attain his *purnata*[57] (human fullness). These elements of self-reference and conflict persist through his creative works and they require textual readings, as detailed below. At the same time, Tagore's searing attack on the antagonistic core of the transnational sexual politics of his day strives for a critically self-responsible position. This position wants to take, to use Gayatri Spivak's powerful characterization, 'disgrace in its stride'.[58] And in this regard, Tagore's self-responsible critique is of a radical order quite at odds with reformist modern men's at both ends of the cultural spectrum he examines.

By Way of a Clarification: Modernity, Reform, and Radical Gender Critique

We have seen earlier that Tagore diverges from the liberalism of a John Stuart Mill. He breaks away from Mill's atomistic and self-aggrandizing telos of individuality pitted in binary contrast to backward custom. Tagore is diverging as well from social reformers in his own Bengali context who are discussing gender. His difference with the latter is that they fail to radically critique the premises of historical domination even though they may be arguing against various dominant conditions. To round up the discussion above, it is helpful to clarify where and how Tagore's approach to the woman question differs by looking briefly at two contrasting voices from the latter group.

A rather obvious contrast to Rabindranath Tagore's interrogative approach to transnational gender history appears in the position on women's history presented by a modernist reformer such as Jyotirindranath Tagore, Rabindranath's older sibling. In an essay titled 'Sekaler Inraj Stree' (The English Wife of the Past), published in the periodical *Bharati O Balak* in 1888, Jyotirindranath poses a stark temporal binary between *sekal* (the feudal past) and the modern *ekal*. He notes that both in the legal and in the common parlance of feudal England, women were characteristically subordinated and enslaved to the husband (made *adhin* and *golam*), while femininity itself was characterized as *mithyabadi, dhurta, ekgune* (lying, conniving, and stubborn).[59] On these grounds, Jyotirindranath wholeheartedly embraces the demise of the sexist feudal traditions in the works of such modern English thinkers as John Milton and John Stuart Mill.[60] That is, Jyotirindranath argues in the vein of a typical modern reformer. He is not probing in any radical way into the premises of sex domination or hierarchal social relations. Therefore, he is unable to analyse two limitations in his espousal of women's cause: first, that he is affirming a new enlightened patriarchy in the place of the feudal one and second, that alternatives to dominant sexual relations could be discerned in both past and present contexts. On both these scores, Rabindranath Tagore's radical exploration sharply diverges from the reformist teleology we find in Jyotirindranath's essay. Rabindranath pries out the gendered premises of historical domination and his probing rests on a refusal of modernity as development and discontinuity.

If Jyotirindranath's modern reformist voice derives from the mental empire spread by colonial education—a form of empire analysed by Gauri Viswanathan and Tejaswini Niranjana, among others[61]—so do some voices which speak for tradition. A more complex contrast to Rabindranath Tagore's critical humanist position—one dependent not on a telos of temporality but a reversal—appears in the observations on women by the renowned traditionalist reformer of nineteenth-century Bengal, Vivekananda (or Narendranath Datta, to use his family name).

Even though he invokes humanism, Vivekananda upfront diverges from Rabindranath Tagore in one crucial way. In place of Tagore's monistic approach, he takes a cultural relativist position. In a speech he gave in the US on 'Women of India', Vivekananda begins with an even-handed argument that even though all people ought to look speculatively towards 'a common humanity', it is indisputable that 'perfect human nature ... is working only in parts, here and there'.[62] Delineating these relative racial lines of human evolution, he goes on to identify India's 'ideal woman' as the mother and the West's as the wife.[63] He explains further that the core of the Indian 'all-suffering' and 'all-forbearing'[64] maternal ideal is realized through the obligatory pre-natal fasts and prayers pursued by both the [high-caste] mother and the father such that their child could be 'born through prayer'; this is the code of Aryan childbirth laid down by the 'law-giver' of the 'socialistic'[65] Hindu caste society, Manu.[66] Yet exactly in examining the moral sexual core of racial progeny, Vivekananda's even-handed relativism also gives way to a vertical order of civilizations. Setting India's austere maternal code clearly above the Western wife-centred pursuit of companionate heterosexual relationship, he avers that at its core the 'individualistic' tenet of personal satisfaction promotes a relative lack of (racial/national) responsibility in the West.[67] For girls can easily fall in love with aberrant people (drunkards, lunatics, consumptives, deformed) and devalue the human progeny.[68] This also means that the onus of keeping the human racial womb pure lies on the girl, although subsequently, both parents of the ideal non-conjugal marriage are responsible for purifying childbirth through austere spiritual practice. Along this line, Vivekananda goes on to exhort American mothers to rethink their ways and embrace the humble path of prayer.[69]

In this speech delivered to an American audience, Vivekananda unilaterally reverses the Social Darwinist history of the family of man such that he can pose the filiative order of the Hindu Aryan past as the model for human evolution as a whole. By contrast, writings addressed to Indian audiences are less polarized in assessing modern time and space. In his essay titled 'The East and the West', Vivekananda is not unlike Tagore in his alertness to the volatile landscape of his contemporary

India, which has been subjected to drastic change, poverty, and difficulty, as well as to the social uprooting imposed by a dominant foreign culture.[70] The upshot of his assessment of India's future, however, turns out to be little else than a more comprehensive and clarified version of the sexually inflected view of racial history he presents in his American speech on women. Drawing on the prevailing Orientalist discourse of a decaying ancient Hindu/Aryan civilization, Vivekananda deplores the fact that while 'national virtues' are gradually disappearing, the new virtues of 'regularity, method, and cleanliness' that allow Western people to prosper are not being acquired.[71] Vivekananda's eagerness to imbibe the prosperous West's disciplines demonstrates that at the core of his view of the Hindu-Aryan past is a developmental notion of modernity. His overall argument is simple. Only through the demise of the unmethodical and impure traditions of a decadent present hand-in-hand with the appropriation of Western disciplines, in a non-individualist way, will the robust regularity of the Hindu-Aryan progeny be reinstated at the forefront of human history. The roles at once of the chastened mother and the ascetic patriarch-householder (tokenized in the praying father-to-be in Vivekananda's narrative above) are crucial to instating this filiative order of human history. At the same time, the woman carries the obligations of spiritualizing sexuality and preserving caste/race purity— by keeping within caste practice and not indulging in aberrant love— whereas the purified patriarch attains apotheosis in the abstinence of the male ascetic. That the ascetic acquires exemplary status in Vivekananda's order of nationalism reveals his self-referential imagination (as a celibate ascetic himself). As noted by Indira Chowdhury, the various debates underway in Vivekananda's Bengal on Hindu marital customs (such as the Age of Consent controversy over child marriage, debates on the Restitution of Conjugal Rights and the Marriage of Widows) form the context of Vivekananda's traditionalist approach to sexual reform.[72]

While taking account of the specifics of historical content in these Bengali reformist views of women and sexuality, I want to stay a bit longer on the role played by image and form in the respective gender politics of male reform. Despite their disparate angles, both these texts on femininity present women's social labour to be inextricable from available semiotic codes of recognizing and communicating femininity in various societies—that is, from the social and imaginative signs of learning and of persuading about what is pleasant and virtuous or vile in womanliness. Dealing directly with literature, Jyotirindranath Tagore discusses that women's social behaviour—such as being *swamir ajnanubarti* (obedient to husband)—works and alters hand-in-hand with social and literary *adarsha* (ideals).[73] On his part, Vivekananda establishes a circular cause-effect relationship between the eroticized aesthetic of worshipping the virtuous mother as a goddess—a practice pervading religious, social, and literary imagination in his Bengal—and women's quotidian hardships of self-purification (fasting, prayer, and so on).[74] Because both thinkers readily accept that a *transparent relation* exists between women's daily practice and prevailing representational codes, they are able to offer seamless justifications for exploitation by interpreting these practices in terms of dominant imaginations of beauty and virtue.

As we saw above, Rabindrananth Tagore's *Narir Manusatya* is trying to rip apart precisely this transparency in the communicating of femininity. It unravels the imbrication of discursive theories with material practices of subordination and objectification by maintaining that male *kalpana* (imagination) is the mediating factor bringing about practices which subordinate and objectify women worldwide. Perhaps the most subtle yet crucially radical aspect of Tagore's critique of sexual empire, in my view, is this attempt of his to confront this problem of dominant male imagination. As I discuss further below, Tagore was quite keenly aware of how available communicative media—language itself, traditions of song, bodily movement, and dance—were tending to be commodified by the new technologies of imagination in his colonial Bengal. His conceptual experimentation with aesthetical imagery and media arose from this awareness. Even though the experiments remained limited to bourgeois space and invariably constrained by allied bias, the radical philosophical import of these late works on gender ought not to be overlooked.

Male Imagination, Women's Desires, and the Aesthetics of Ethical Communication

Three years after his interrogation of feminine representations in British literature, Tagore turned his critique homeward. In the polyphonic poem *Sadharan Meye* (Ordinary Girl, 1932), he took issue with Bengali nationalist men's authorship of women's life-stories.[75] At first glance, the critique appears to be limited to the novelist Saratchandra Chatterjee, whose fictional depictions of Hindu women had wide currency in early twentieth-century Bengal. Although Chatterjee was ostensibly far more liberal in his approach to women than a Hindu nationalist such as Vivekananda, his portrayals forged subtler links between Hindu and

Victorian patriarchal ideals. Stating his thesis on Indian women in an essay appropriately entitled *Narir Mulya* (The Value of Woman, 1928), Saratchandra Chatterjee had severely criticized women's oppression in native and foreign contexts while stressing that alternative ways to value women are to be derived both from ancient Hindu civilization as well as from progressive Victorian thinkers; he found especially appealing Herbert Spencer's emphasis on 'voluntary' rather than 'compulsory coop-eration' as the key to gender harmony.[76] *Sadharan Meye* undoubtedly revolves around an ironic rebuttal to Chatterjee's stereotypical imagery of the voluntarily long-suffering Hindu woman, constituting another attempt by Tagore to engage the sexual politics of Hindu nationalism in his Bengal. Yet it also pushes beyond to implicate in the irony male authors located in different times and spaces. And it brings into the intertextual compass the poet himself, Rabindranath Tagore.

Writing the polyphonic poem in colloquial Bengali, Tagore takes on the voice of a nondescript young woman living in *antahpur* or the secluded women's quarters. She has been abandoned by her love, a man who now studies and travels in England and, presumably, pursues European women. In bitter irony, the secluded Bengali girl pleads with Saratchandra Chatterjee to retell her life-story in a way that will help her to forget the sorrow. Yet as she speculates on how Chatterjee's *uccho mon* (elevated mind) might re-imagine her tale, the girl Malati apprehends that she will be turned into another 'abstract' national ideal (to use Tagore's own words above) in the mould of ancient Hindu heroines. For perhaps the novelist will lead her, like the Shakuntala of Kalidas's imagination, down a path of *dukkher charame* (extreme sorrow) and *tyag* (self-sacrifice). She implores her imaginary author to take pity and come down to her *samatale* (level) such that he could grant her the *asambhav bar* (impossible boon) for which she weeps every night.[77]

The 'ordinary girl' Malati wants instead to be represented as a woman on the path to success, commanding equal access to such socioeconomic resources as modern education, etiquette, and mobility such that she is able to compete with her liberated European rivals. Down this path, she stakes her claim to fulfilling her social and corporeal desires. In this vein, the poem's ironic repudiation of the ancient Hindu heroine Shakuntala's sacrificing femininity clears the space for a Westernized feminist articulation of the Bengali woman's autonomous desire. Whereas this quintessentially Western-liberal endorsement by Tagore of equal socioeconomic opportunities—that is, of an equality *blind* to gendered and racial difference—ought to be recognized as an important strand of this poem, it should not be grasped as the only narrative strand. For the poetic irony interweaves dialectic against the homogenous teleology of liberal democratic development. Note also that the teleological strand takes the liberated Western woman as its model at the same time that it appears to be even-handed and race-blind. Yet what 'ordinary' Malati is asserting in bitter irony is not only that this ideal of progress is unachievable for her at present but that it is nothing but an asambhav or impossible pipe-dream that cannot even be realized in fictional imagination, let alone in fact. The poem concludes with the abrupt termination of its protagonist's fantasy and a brief lament that the divine energy within women such as her is being uselessly expended—*bidhatar shaktir apabaye*.[78] Within the polyphony of feminist irony, Tagore's secular speculation upon a common 'divine' humanity is saying at least two things. First, it asserts that the woman shares a common human nature with all her immediate and possible authors, partaking in the same fount of human needs, wants, desires, and the will to choose life options accordingly. Second, it interrogates why none of these authors do or are likely to comprehend her human desires and claims. And in this pointedly untemporized and cross-spatial compass a whole range of masculine author-positions are included: native and foreign, pre-modern and modern.

To begin with, we encounter the challenge to Hindu/Victorian nationalist writer Saratchandra Chatterjee's representations of self-sacrificing Bengali women in the archaic vein of Kalidas's heroines. This in turn implicates at once the Sanskrit dramatist Kalidas's pre-modern version of the self-surrendering woman and the general modern Bengali nationalist trend of intertextually reviving and solidifying the ancient Hindu past in gendered ways. The deeper struggle upon which Tagore embarks through this critique of modern-traditionalist sexual politics is that of rethinking his own coercive representations of ideal self-sacrificing Bharatiya women. As I have noted elsewhere, the ironic image of Shakuntala in this poem implies a cumulative reconsideration on Tagore's part of his own idealization of the Sanskrit heroine in the early essay titled *Shakuntala* (published in 1902) for one.[79] While Tagore implies self-critique along this line, however, his staging of antithesis to masculine authorship is not confined to the national domain. As in the essay discussed above, Tagore stages as well a connection with transnational history, specifically with the imperialist division of representational capital from semiotic labour. For, *Sadharan Meye* also depicts, tongue-in-cheek, how this dark Oriental woman would have been received by Western people had she access and mobility; she would have been adulated for her exotic eyes that sparkle with the natural beauty of India's clouds and sunlit sky.[80] Perhaps this racialized portrayal of an Oriental in the Western international circuit was mediated by what we saw in the Introduction to be Tagore's own experience of having Western authors exoticize yet degrade his voice and perspective.

Yet neither the critique of Orientalism in the poem nor any other aspect can be reduced to only self-reference. For the poem's larger framework unrelentingly challenges the partial and possessive codifications of femininity endemic to masculinist languages across Tagore's world. Further, it seems to me that the poem is enjoining upon its entire cast of authors the acknowledgement that all such dominant attempts to represent woman and the feminized other are fundamentally *non-communicative*. They are mediated by the apparently transparent morok or packages of patriarchal and allied sociobiological perceptions (of race, caste, and so forth). Put in another way, the habit dominant authors have of reconciling portrayals of gender relations to patriarchal assumptions forecloses attention to cooperative or communicative forms of gendered associative life. For, as a result of the mediating categories, male writings ostensibly about women and intended for women audiences (Saratchandra Chatterjee's works certainly aimed for this appeal) end up ignoring how women and the marginalized deal with particular and altering socioeconomic circumstances and how their structures of feeling and of reasoning adapt thereto. In the multi-form dramatic works to which I turn next, Tagore is trying to grapple with this communicative problem and with how aesthetic imagination needs to be altered to address it.

Some observations Rabindranath Tagore made in earlier writings on aesthetic knowledge and power are relevant to this dramatic poem itself and the other late experimental works on women. Ranajit Guha has rightly characterized Tagore's approach to the 'creative process' as the way for a 'direct perception of the world'[81]—the way to grasping the world 'unmediated'[82] by dominant or 'statist narratives' of historiography.[83] With this in mind, we should turn to Tagore's groundbreaking essay *Viswasahitya* (Universal Literature, 1906) which names three impulses through which a person's inner world connects with the surroundings: the intellective, the needful, and the blissful. Demonstrating that the immediate referents for his literary psychology are historical narratives of empire and capital, Tagore places the first two in a group apart from the third. His reflections on knowledge in this essay forecast the later analyses of European and Indian nationalist representations of femininity in *Narir Manusatya.*

Tagore suggests that an individual's ratiocinative intellect connects to the world in an antagonistic way, like a hunter's to his *shikar* (prey), whereas the instrumental intellect looks upon the world and nature in a possessive way as *bina betaner chakar*[84] (wageless servants). As against these possessive and objectifying forms of cognition is a direct grasp of the world achievable through *ananda*[85] (bliss). Elsewhere, Tagore characterizes ananda-full knowledge as constituting the human tendency for *milan* or concord; he avers that since literature widely transmits this *pranarasa* or life-relish of concord the Sanskrit word for the literary is *sahitya* and its root the notion of *sahit* or being with.[86] Along these lines, literary creation is poised to encompass the vibrant variations of reciprocal communication enabling non-antagonistic community on (non-metropolitan) quotidian grounds: The 'unabated exchanges of embraces and whispers among human beings ... women gather[ing] at the waterside steps, friend run[ing] to friend, letters go[ing] to and fro ... meetings, arguments, disputes—even scuffles and skirmishes'.[87]

Without a doubt, Tagore's idea of the literary rasa of humanity is inflected both by the Sanskrit aesthetic theory of rasa and its indigenous eastern Indian appropriations in the course of the Vaishnava bhakti movement. Sanskrit aesthetics propound that the cultivation of artistic sensibilities (through various media of drama, dance, and poetic writing) enables a psycho-physiological intensification of human experience. Cultivated performers and participants alike experience the *sthayi bhavas* or 'permanent moods'—which potentially exist in all human beings— in the form of an 'actually relished state' (that is, a physical experience of tasting).[88] Underlying this psycho-aesthetic theory is the metaphysics that all such artistic intensifications of human experience aim for a 'mental repose' that 'approximates' deliverance from existential suffering of mundane life or *moksha*.[89] In learned and popular adaptations of rasa into the bhavas of the bhakti movement (or loving devotion to Krishna) the idea of deliverance from the mundane had taken on more coherent formulation.[90] Further, through new technologies of colonial Bengali popular culture, certain bhavas or transcendental moods were turning into mortified and separatist tools of sight and knowledge. We saw in Chapter 1 that the notion of the madhur bhava or feminine sweetness and pleasantness was yielding misogynist and caste-based representations of women.

That even in earlier days Tagore was thinking critically through these available aesthetic vocabularies is clear in at least three ways. First, he wanted to emphasize the human sensuality of rasa. In the essay *Sahitya O Saundarya* (Beauty and Literature, 1907), he stated that the literary *manab rasa* or human relish can enable *atmiyata* (kin feeling) between creator, audience, and created character because of the corporeal constitution of language itself—that it can act upon us erotically as an *indriyaswarup* or sensory perception.[91] Second, he wanted to be alert to the various ways rasa/aesthetical sensuality is deployed in this world and in the cause of antagonistic worldly politics. In the same essay on literary beauty, he attacks the tendency individual authors have to define the *utkarsha* (essence) of the aesthetic—of *saundarya* (beauty) and of *suchitā* (purity)—and he imputes the essentialism to *samprodayik* (sectarian) attitudes linked to class and race.[92] And third, Tagore refused to connect blissful knowledge to a transcendental deliverance from power and domination. His self-responsible exploration was for a this-worldly blissful literature aware of institutional codes of authorship. He saw in the authorial endeavour, a necessity to *sapinya dite* (deliver oneself) to the really small, weak, and insignificant.[93] Precisely this ethically charged aesthetical endeavour is what takes on sharply dialectical and transcultural inflections in Tagore's late writings on women and gender. As Sankha Ghosh notes, not only did the content of Tagore's late works show conflict and restlessness, so did the form.[94] Tagore was thinking with heightened awareness through linguistic and expressive codes and how to cultivate these in different ways. This self-critical endeavour of the male writer against antagonistic knowledge and for expressive reciprocity or sahit with his woman protagonist/audience, is what manifests in the pieces I have looked at so far: in the colorful ironic polyphony of the poem *Sadharan Meye* and also in the more restrained internal polemics of the prose piece, *Narir Manusatya*. These gendered works illustrate well Volosinov's position that so long as social contexts remain hierarchical, activist authors will be prone to address both their content and their potential audience in conflicting accents—at once as ruler to subject and also as comrade to comrade; formal elements such as genre, style, and intonation will be combined in these dialectical authorial interactions.[95] Dialectical experimentation toward a sensually imaginative sahit takes unprecedented directions in Tagore's woman-centered dance dramas.

In a letter he wrote in 1939 to his friend Amiya Chakravarty about his three dance dramas, Tagore maintains that he launched on these because he had developed *sanghsay* (uncertainty) regarding *bakyer sristi* (the creation of words); words tend to be judged upon *chalti kheyal* (many current and transient whims) such that it is not possible to discern the exemplary adarsha core behind the representation.[96] In his view, song offered a way out of the representational quandary because music lends to the human mind *duratwer pariphrekshani* (a perspective of distance).[97] In taking this position, Tagore no doubt shared in the general distrust of European Naturalism to be found in *swadeshi* nationalist aesthetics,[98] tilting instead toward the indigenous non-illusionist notion of intensified aesthetic experience or rasa. My discussion thus far in this book of Tagore's aesthetic practice should also suggest, however, that he was working beyond the nativist aesthetical inclination. In the letter at hand, he is critiquing contemporary sociopolitical practice—in this case, specifically current aesthetic trends vis-à-vis political economic change in his Bengal. In regard to drama, song, and dance, Tagore consistently criticized how the commercial Bengali stage (led by such dramaturges as Girish Ghosh and Sisirkumar Bhaduri) was commodifying folk forms of drama, song, and dance in a bid to compete with the prevalent folk theatre or jatra.[99] His concern had been with the technologies of illusionist stagecraft—in his view, an imitation of the European (Victorian) theatre which turned performance into a glittering *sphito padartha* or inflated object.[100] No doubt the larger ethical point of his aesthetical concern with contemporary drama lay in his general challenge to instrumental knowledge, as voiced in the essay *Viswasahitya*. While in the letter to Amiya Chakravarty Tagore asserts the need for artistic distance from these current social and aesthetical whims, paradoxically he goes on to aver that his three dance dramas are in no way *swapnobostu* (dream material); rather, they are verisimilar creations concerning *teebro sukhdukkho bhalomando*[101] (intense happiness and sorrow, good and bad). The key to the paradox of course is Tagore's life-long endeavour for a creative practice of direct perception, as noted by Ranajit Guha. Against mediating technologies of historical domination, Tagore sought to apprehend what he called *manab rasa*.

Together with his troupe Tagore sought to achieve a synergy of song and dance with drama which was to capture the multi-layering of communicative human motion. As put by his daughter-in-law and choreography-collaborator Protima Debi, the performative aim was to be alert that in the same way as human language finds an extra-lingual (*bhashateet*) expression in music/song, so the passion of the human heart finds expression for the rhetoricity of quotidian movement (*jagotik gotir sahaj alankarshastra*) in the rhythmic *talas* of dance.[102] Noteworthy here is that, despite a superficial resemblance to European conceptions of opera, the framework of the Tagore dance-drama significantly differed. In Tagore's emphasis on capturing the exemplary core of human life and in Protima Debi's on embodying quintessential human motion, we certainly hear resonances of Richard Wagner's postulate of the *Gesamtkunstwerk* or total art work (1851). Wagner's idea was that a combination of the pure and sensuous art form, music, with the poetic 'human voice [which is] the oldest, truest, most beautiful organ of music' produces the totality of expressive humanness.[103] Drawing on Schopenhauer's premise that the contemplative art of music could transfigure the degraded materialism of ordinary life through allowing 'an escape from the self and will',[104] Wagner pre-figured the Symbolist Theatre by delineating that through completely 'emotionaliz[ing] the intellect' the total musical theatre (combining 'dance, tone, poetry') could return to the original art form in which the human being per se is the subject.[105] Moreover, Tagore's earliest venture into operatic drama is known to have been inspired in part by Herbert Spencer's humanist theory of musical emotion.[106]

Nonetheless, the Tagore approach diverged in significant ways from the idealism of pre-Symbolist imagination of the Wagnerian variety and, moreover, from the Symbolist Drama that followed. We should, in general, be cautious about drawing one-on-one comparisons between Tagore's thought and that of Europeans of the Romantic, Symbolist, and Dialectical (Epic Theatre) schools who were also rejecting Naturalism (I find this lingering tendency in the otherwise profound scholarship of Abu Sayeed Ayyub and Sankha Ghosh, as well as other Tagore critics). In my view, it is crucial to consider in what ways Tagore's philosophical presuppositions conflicted, notably in respect of the Cartesian split of subject-and-world that in various ways was entrenched in all these European responses to Naturalism. More broadly speaking, it is important to take account of how philosophies and imaginations entwine with politico-economic formations such as empire, nation, capital, and labour. This is the general lesson I draw from one such as Tagore who struggled from the heart of empire to scrupulously imagine his world and also to openly communicate about the difficulties of perception.

To take our instance at hand, the Tagore conception reveals at least two points of departure from Wagner's Romanticist focus upon the perfectible contemplative individual. Rather than centre the work on an individual who looks upon the world with a remote and disembodied eye,

Tagore conceives the artistic production as a sahit-inducing endeavour enabling communities of individuated experience and their multiple rhythms of expression. Protima Debi's emphasis on the quotidian worldliness of their performative philosophy, as concretized in an eclectic admixture of folk forms in the dance dramas, evinces an awareness not unlike Kapila Vatsyayan's that the folk arts forge intimate connection with the 'functions of daily life' and environmental change.[107] Tagore's experiments with music complemented this philosophy. As with dance, Tagore's musical scores are eclectic admixtures of the classical ragas (Hindustani and South Indian) with popular and folk tunes drawn from local and translocal sources; the objective overall was to 'wed' semantic denotations and connotations with appropriate musical notations[108] so as to accentuate the rhythm of human drama. Stagecraft embodied the philosophy as a whole. On one side, Tagore drew from the participatory Bengali folk jatra,[109] and, on another, from Japanese *kabuki* theatre.[110] Performances typically avoided the proscenium arch and instead brought together a close-knit community of performers and audiences/participants. Figure 1 shows Shambhu Saha's photograph of a dance-drama performance such as this—being held indoors at Shantiniketan and including in its compass the dancers/singers, the spectators, and the creator himself.

Beyond this, the individuated community being performed in the Tagore dance drama is neither seamless nor a transparent expression of harmonious daily rhythm. Hence it does not, by any means, constitute an escape from the everyday tussle of wills in the vein of a Schopenhauer's philosophy of self-centric contemplative art. Tagore's explicit emphasis was on embodying dramatic *agon* through dance and song,[111] and the bases of his conception of dramatic tension were gendered forms of antagonistic and instrumental knowledge as criticized in such essays as *Vishwasahitya* and *Narir Manusatya*.

The Dancing Woman
and Self-responsible Male Imagination

In his two versions of *Chitrangada*—produced respectively in 1892 as a poetic play[112] and in 1935 as a dance drama[113]—Tagore retells a story from the Hindu epic Mahabharata in somewhat different ways. It is arguable that the alterations inflected Tagore to change positions on nationalism and gender together with a cumulative self-critique. Both versions follow the epic in narrating that whereas, at divine behest, Princess Chitrangada had been raised by her father as a boy and schooled

Figure 1 Tagore Dance-Drama—A Performing Community
Courtesy: Visva-Bharati University Press

in princely duties, she experiences desire after meeting the epic hero Arjun. She pursues an erotic relationship after breaking him away from his temporary ascetic pursuit of celibacy and eventually ends up as his wife. The 1892 depiction poses several telling contrasts to the dance drama to follow. Princess Chitraganda is portrayed as being on a solitary pursuit of the ascetic hero; as aided right from the outset on her path of heterosexual desire by the Hindu male godheads of erotica and sexual youth, Madan and Basanta; and as charting the telos of a feminine sexual self which develops from a state of abandoned desire (resonating with current masculine views of uncontrolled feminine nature or strisvabhava as discussed in Chapter 1) into the pleasant/balanced maturity of the potential chaste wife of epic hero Arjun. The dance drama version, on the other hand, shows that Chitrangada realizes her autonomous worth—sexually, emotionally, and intellectually—not through her relations with Arjun but on her own and amidst her same-sex companions or *sakhis*. More broadly, it suggests that to self-actualize in this pleasant way the woman must first exit male imaginations of all categories—

mythical/epical, sociopolitical, and personal—such that she is able to reclaim her status in society through rectifying the possessiveness and instrumentality in these categories. In conjunction with his dramatic team, Tagore was not only rethinking in the dance drama his own prior nationalist assumptions about women in the vein of *Narir Manusatya*, he was also rebutting contemporary Hindu nationalist misogyny and clarifying the difference in his approach.

Noteworthy among the latter was the attack dramatist D.L. Roy had levelled against Tagore's early version of *Chitrangada*. Roy's charge was that Tagore had misappropriated the Hindu epic through depicting the princess as a prostitute-like profligate woman self-indulging with her lover Arjun and therewith desecrating the virtuous chastity of daughter and wife depicted by the original epic (1916).[114] Consider also that, despite his avowed inclination for Westernized humanism (in such works as *Mebarpatan*), D.L. Roy's own portrayals of women were posing stark contrasts between the unbridled (sexualized) individualism of the alien woman and the self-surrendering tranquility of the chaste Hindu mother. His *Nurjahan* (1906), for example, poses the demoniacal power hunger of the Muslim princess Nurjahan opposite the goddess-like calm of Hindu queen Reba and it resolves the ethnic-sexual tension by showing that a repentant Nurjahan yields her self-love to maternal sentiment.[115] Within the larger gender politics of early twentieth-century Bengali nationalism, Roy tussled with Tagore over the current trend of celebrating cultural figureheads of masculinity or *birpuja*; whereas Tagore's early writing shared in the proclivity to glorify Indian male valour, his late works were fundamentally rethinking that glorification in the light of escalating communal-nationalist militancy.[116] The dance dramas *Chitrangada* and *Chandalika* were immersed in these intertextual politics of re-evaluating various nationalist positions on masculinity: D.L. Roy's as implied in his attack on *Chitrangada*, Vivekananda's in his explicit endorsement of celibate ascetic valour, and perhaps also M.K. Gandhi's in his politicized endorsement of male celibacy through experiments with abstinence.[117] As the dance dramas reveal, Tagore was concerned about the territorial implications of these male identity politics vis-à-vis women's autonomous desire. He sought for a more sahit-inducing or mutually communicative understanding of the beauty of autonomy in women's desires.

The dance drama *Chitrangada* was produced at a time when Tagore wrote explicitly *narider pakhya niye*[118] (from the side of women). The work begins by clarifying that sexual coercion is involved in the overlapping social and aesthetic filiations constituting the image of an epic Hindu heroine in the current nationalist context. The initial narrative sequence clarifies, in other words, some ways that conventional nationalist imagination of the epical Hindu woman wants to reinforce a transparent paternity and cohesive genealogy at once for religious-mythic, literary, and social notions of women. The drama opens with depictions of the manly woman Chitrangada out with her followers on a princely hunt, of her experience of being seen as a little boy and thus patronized by the adult hero Arjun, and thereafter, her new feeling of a feminine desire hitherto suppressed under male upbringing. This exposition of Chitrangada's new self-actualization unravels multiple ancient and contemporary Hindu hierarchies of heterosexual relations. It implies that hierarchy not only is immanent in the epic itself, it propagates through current nationalist literature and also through social texts that perceive women to be turning into secondary/infantile men if given strisiksha (education) and public mobility.[119] The larger point is that sociobiological coercion of women is endemic in a modern Indian filiative order that combines the Hindu tradition of glorifying high-caste patrilineage as divine descent (found in the notions of kula and *gotra*) with the Victorian-masculine tradition of glorifying the publicly active male adult (the ideal modern bir or valourous man). Subsequently, Chitrangada diverges from these social and aesthetic filiations by cultivating the rasa of desire not through dependent relations with Arjun but on her own and amidst her same-sex companions or sakhis.

The ensuing song-dance numbers strive for a 'blissful' rhetoricity of desire flourishing through same-sex support. Protima Debi notes that while the numbers combine a variety of Indian folk forms, they lean towards the Northeast-Indian Manipuri tradition.[120] Note that the Manipuri tradition casts Vaishnavite performances, such as the Raslila, into dance-drama versions.[121] Protima Debi also emphasizes that rather than stay within the typicality of native forms only, *Chitrangada* incorporates as well the dramatic accentuation and directionality of passion to be found in European dance practice.[122] These sakhi scenes present an eclectic transcultural aesthetic depicting the growth of pleasant desire in the body/mind of the woman. As such, they radically depart from the attribution of pleasantness to chaste maternity and its basis in objectified female desire. Since the Tagore troupe's performances far pre-date my time and *Rabindrik* dance traditions have altered in subsequent eras, I explore how choreographic and performative imaginations coalesce in the aesthetic by looking at selected song-lyrics; on Protima

Debi's testimony, these lyrics by Tagore formed the bulwark of their conceptualization of the dance dramas as a whole.[123] Noteworthy in regard to the aesthetic of autonomous feminine desire are two lyrics, the first turning inwards and the second embracing same-sex reciprocal support.

Soon after being attracted to Arjun and facing rejection in her first overtures, Chitrangada performs a solo as she heads to bathe in the river. The lyrics imply a dialectical choreographic design. Here and in subsequent discussions of dance I am drawing on Susan Leigh Foster's important position that innovations in choreography—that is, the organizing of performative space in complement with bodily movement—could go either way: from a bird's-eye historiographic view, they could impart to embodied space a 'stillness that masquerades as omniscience', or they could enable bodies to be critically ambulatory, to think and write themselves against the grain of historical narratives.[124] A form of ambulatory critique such as this is to be found in the bathing song. Mingling the erotic with critical analysis, the lyrics unpack the core assumptive framework that had 'bestilled'[125] Chitrangada's self-growth: the patriarchal home. Implying a constitutive sexual coercion in the patriarchal family and in allied social/aesthetic structures of domestication, the lyrics suggest that to plumb the depths of her desire the woman cannot do other than break away from the proprietary family home. Unmistakable here are resonances of Vaishnava bhakti literature portraying the love trysts of the self-surrendering feminine devotee— the one en route to *lila* or a sexual/spiritual love-play unmediated by domestic worldly interests (of property and dynasty).[126]

Time and time again do I hear in me
The beckoning of depthless waters,
My mood stays not, stays not at home
Restless is my mind.
On high tide will I float myself,
My worries I will wash away in a forgetful stream

[*Shuni khane khane, mane mane
Atala jalera aobhan.
Mano rayna rayna rayna ghare,
Chanchalo pran.
Bhasaye dibo aponare
Bhara joare,
Sakala bhabona-dubano dharay
Karibo snan*][127]

These words picture Chitrangada to be not only journeying away from her proprietary *ghar* or home but also to be sweeping aside the 'worries' of boundary-crossing; they seem to entwine the self-surrendering sexual/spiritual quest of bhakti with the self-centring individual's dialectical freedom from custom. While we should be alert to the overlaps, we cannot reduce Chitrangada's journey to either conceptual category. Neither is it an ideal quest for an androcentric divinity nor an atomistic telos of freedom from custom.

To begin with, even though subsequent lyrics continue in the Vaishnava vein to show how the love-lorn Chitrangada is collectively nurtured in her pleasant desire by same-sex companions, they also depart from that vein by presenting the collective feminine pursuit as andro-critical rather than androcentric (as in the Vaishnava tradition of bhakti). Her companions are shown to be responding to Chitrangada's call to adorn her anew such that she overcomes the lajja or shame of being discarded as an emaciated *shunya shakha* (bare branch) by the male hero.[128]

Let the restless dance of bliss vibrate you limb and limb,
Let it surge and surge.
Let youth discover its dignity,
In the desired union

[*Anandachanchal nritya ange ange bahe jak*
Hillole hillole,
Jaubana pak sanman
Bancchito sammelane][129]

Unmistakable in these lines is an emphasis on the corporeality of a flesh-and-blood woman who desires and who seeks reciprocity. The concreteness of imagery calls for a this-worldly choreography and performance—of an organizing of womanly bodies and desires such that they move with and 'alongside' one another[130] to actualize the rhythmic rhetoric of a women's support community. Note also that here Tagore's deployment of the word lajja implies a radical critique of the current bourgeois parlance on the bhadramahila's or gentlewoman's modest shame. As discussed in Chapter 1, the gentlewomanly lajja was tied to chastity, in other words, to metaphoric (and real) draping of woman's erotic sexuality. Chitrangada's lajja signifies not at all a modest draping of the woman's erotic/emotional potentiality, but rather her humiliation in not being recognized by the man as an erotic/emotional person in her own right. To redress this fundamental devaluation of corporeal humanity, her sakhis reciprocate Chitrangada's call for a renewed adornment with a song-and-dance invoking the pleasure of erotic bliss in her.

Beyond this, even though Chitrangada is thus enabled in corporeal-emotional autonomy through a radical departure from domestic/nationalist filiations—she becomes a 'third' self-straying down the road to self-actualization—her path leads not to free self-expression but back to masculine classifications. In other words, the woman's dialectic motion to freedom is shown to be invariably mediated and inconclusive. In this instance, Arjun's eye persists with conventions, as he fails to recognize beauty in the self-adorned Chitrangada and rejects her erotic advances on the plea of his celibate vow. This failure on Chitrangada's part to *communicate* to Arjun her same-sex-nurtured desire is what finally drives the woman to enter the masculine communicative aesthetic of heterosexual erotica in order to redeem her humiliated self-esteem. Pointedly resolving narrative antithesis for the moment, Tagore retracks his storyline into the original epic by showing that Chitrangada redecks herself with the aid of the male godhead of *eros* Madan, and thereby finally succeeds in seducing Arjun away from his dogmatic asceticism.

Even though Chitrangada appears to concede to the glittering seduction attributed to erotic womanhood in the prevalent nationalist parlance, Chitrangada's concession ought to be read as Tagore's rebuttal to nationalism, not acquiescence. One turn of the dialogue reveals that Tagore is in fact attacking the glorification of ascetic Indian valour, and he is denouncing the misogynist Bengali motto of kaminikanchantyag. We hear a sakhi reacting to Chitrangada's rejection by Arjun with a sharp prosaic retort, not sung but spoken. She asserts that the pursuit of celibate *bramhacharya* is a form of masculine *spardha* (arrogance)—self-defeating for womankind at large[131]—and, on that note, supplicates the male god Madan for his mediating hand. Through this mediation, Chitrangada's autonomous womanly desire has to be reconciled with Hindu masculine codes: epic, mythic, contemporary nationalist. Note also that throughout her subsequent erotic alliance with Arjun, Chitrangada is torn between an anxiety over her estranged and transient self and an abandonment of *male-dependent desire*. Underscoring the objectification in the latter, her self-sacrificial drive toward Arjun is imaged as an object to gratify the male-centric fire of desire: her drive is cast as an incendiary *ahuti* (homage) in fire-worship at the same time that it is depicted as the conventional feminine attribute of madhuri.[132] For his part, Arjun is shown to be basking in the *gaurab* (glory) of his recovered valorous manhood,[133] until he tires of private self-indulgence and looks again for vigorous public life.[134] It is then that, in his self-interest, he finally seeks out the legendary mother-king Chitrangada he has been hearing about.

On that trajectory also, it could well appear that Tagore's seemingly radical imagination is retrenching into the nationalist symbol for communicating strong femininity. He is presenting Chitrangada as a national mother, constructed and adulated by the male follower. Retraction into conventional Hindu imagery is further reinforced by a song of the sakhis which asks Arjun to look upon his bride-to-be as his *sevika* or care-giver.[135] There is little doubt in fact that these elements of compromise with nationalist representational hierarchy, based on the lingering sociobiological stratifications of gender role we find in Tagore's *Narir Manusatya*, do recur. They vindicate a reading of the ending in light of Partha Chatterjee's formulation that anti-colonial nationalism was imagining social space as separate gendered spheres of the 'home and world', with the elite woman bearing the onus of preserving the cultural 'essence' within a home 'unaffected by the profane activities of the material world'.[136] Likewise, the dance drama's closing seems to be drawing Chitrangada from her road of autonomy back into her essential feminine role of breeding the ideal heterosexual home and nation. Yet to reduce the work to this residual telos of gendered nationalism would mean foreclosing the more sahit-inducing narrative aspects in order to obtain a conventional linear plotline. The reductive linearity would foreclose the radical challenge *Chitrangada* is posing to all nationalist endeavours to resolve questions of women and heterosexual relations in the interest of a collective future.

Three imports of the work as a whole are salient in this regard. Upfront, the piece argues that heterosexual relationships ought to be forged in national society simultaneously at the corporeal (sexual/emotional) and at the active/intellectual level: woman must accrue *sanman* (dignity) from man as companion both at night and during the active day.[137] At a subtler level, the meaning of dignity itself takes on different nuances. Once we unravel the intratextual and the intertextual politics of the play's closing, as I have been attempting over the previous pages, we cannot but read the emphasis on a heterosexual alliance as a conditional one. Tagore's position overall seems to be that, in order for this gender-equitable relationship to be achieved, antagonistic gendered alignments of behaviour have to be dismantled and rethought. People have to exit sexualized structures in order to rethink how possessive and instrumental categories of knowledge devolve into human relations.

And then there is a third import of the closing, and indeed of the work as whole. Whereas *Chitrangada* enables the dignity of autonomous self-growth and companionship, as we have seen, it refuses to reduce personal autonomy to atomism. It seems to me that the point of the collective celebratory ending of the dance drama is to reject along the same lines companionate relationship between two atomistic individuals as found in the metropolitan Western romance of the period. What we see instead is that the new person is fulfilling her human dignity by taking a further step towards responsible collective relationality—towards engaging in the critical-affective endeavour to break-and-rebuild humanity for more egalitarian and mutual relations (as argued by Tagore also in *Narir Manusatya*). In totality, the dance drama is clarifying that these endeavours must transpire at once at the personal, the communal/national, and most crucially at the aesthetical-genealogical level (in social, aesthetic, mythic, religious communications of pleasing womanhood). That *Chitrangada* revivifies a better heterosexual family-to-be at the core of a national-society-to-come has a lot to do with the collective orientation of non-metropolitan feminist cultures. As African American feminist thinker bell hooks has argued in another context, feminists who want to imagine change from the grounds of racialized contexts must think of women and men as 'comrades in struggle' against multiple structures of domination; the drive, overall, should be for an undominated home and community.[138]

Yet such struggles as these launched by activist intellectuals to revise practice and perception invariably transpire both against and within institutional limits. We must find ways to read emancipatory conceptual strides and struggles such that we avoid the orthodoxy of placing an ontological faith in any one canonical activist thinker (be this a Tagore, a Gandhi, or another), while we sideline lingering complicities and compromises. This is my contention throughout the book. As argued in the Introduction, any activist's capacity for (self-) critique tends to be more compromised by some of his/her social investments than others.

Along these lines, Tagore's restorative critique of sociobiological imagination grows considerably more complex and conflicted once he begins exploring woman's desire in relation to caste and race hierarchy. To delineate this conflicted critique, I round out the chapter by looking at another portrayal of the ascetic man vis-à-vis the desiring woman, only this time she is a dalit village girl from the untouchable chandal community. The work *Chandalika* exists in a prose play and a dance drama version, written within a few years of each other (1933, 1937).

I look at the latter in order to retain my focus on the desiring woman as a dancer—the one poised to embody quotidian motions of feminine corporeality, according to the Tagore school of performance theory. On one side, *Chandalika* is even bolder than *Chitrangada* in taking in stride the 'disgrace'[139] perpetuated by current psycho-biological hierarchies. It condones that the chandal woman desires reciprocity from an elite ascetic man at the same time that it reinforces ascetic manhood's instrumental view of femininity. Put in another way, it shows this 'third' woman's road to autonomy forking into the deepest recesses of the modern Hindu familial order, namely, caste-racism and social clannishness. On another side, however, the work tilts towards developmental reform and, therewith, becomes embroiled in an imperialistic male order (upholding filiations of caste, race, and social position).

The dance drama opens upon a young chandal woman, Prakriti, who is rebelliously self-aware of her dehumanized status. Unlike her family and community members, she refuses to drown the *ghor anyay*[140] or severe injustice of her social status under the oblivion of daily routine. Prakriti's pessimistic lethargy gives way to hope for reconstructing her degraded life-condition when the Buddhist monk Ananda (literally bliss) breaks the taboo of bodily pollution by accepting water from her hand to quench his thirst. Moreover, Ananda accepts the life-sustaining water to the accompaniment of an ideal liberal (caste-blind) declaration of common humanity: 'You are a human same as I, my girl' (*je manaba ami sei manaba tumi kanya*).[141] The 1933 prose play by the same name elaborates the humanity in Ananda's gesture of dignifying Prakriti's care-work (that is, of doing the *seva*/care-work of offering water to the weary pedestrian) by contrasting it to the instrumental honour Prakriti had received from a princely suitor who craved possession of her for her looks.[142] In the dance drama, Prakriti turns with the thunder of Ananda's liberal rhetoric upon her routine-bound mother, asserting that it is a *pap* (wrong-doing) on their part to accept any ascription other than *manaber bangsha*[143] (a human ancestry) equal to all.

In the course of exchanges with her mother, the rhetorical tone of Prakriti's lyrics shifts and calls as well for an appropriate departure in bodily movement and spatial use. Prakriti begins to interpret the vocabulary of human equality not in accord with its original metaphysical usage (by Ananda, in this instance) but rather, viscerally in a corporeal way. She sings that as she the voiceless (*bachana hara ami*) begins to acquire new language (that of humanism), a snake of humiliation (*apaman nagini*) unfurls within.[144] This humiliation burns her body/

mind with *bicched dahan* (pangs of separation) from her desired man and it parches her eyes and her breast with thirst (*chokkhe amar trishna, ogo trishna amar bohsko jure*).[145] The implication is that it is not enough for an untouchable caste woman to be accorded in principle the dignity of commonality with a man who commands elite status. It is imperative that the principles of equality and autonomous worth be *embodied* in socio-sexual practice such that the crucial caste/race boundary between the pure and the polluted body is dismantled.[146] Hence when her more conventional mother warns Prikriti against the transgression immanent in desiring Ananda's return, Prakriti affirms that she remains fearless in her conviction that he will return to reciprocate her longing. What she fears is that, unless he does return to reciprocate, she will lose touch with her newfound self-dignity or 'forget her own worth' (*nijer ami mulya bhuli*).[147] Unmistakable in this critique of Prakriti's devalued feminine worth is Tagore's earlier commentary on the ascriptions of woman's mulya or worth customary to male discourses of his time, both native and foreign (see my discussion of *Narir Manusatya* above).

Building upon his larger critique of women's ascriptive mulya, here Tagore is engaging the ascription of feminine worth in contemporary ascetic-male nationalisms. He mobilizes the Hindu metaphysics of gender found in current bhakti nationalist language. He sets the ascetic *purush* or male principle, the one who repudiates worldliness, against *prakriti* or the fertile woman/earth who embodies *pravritti* or the cravings of this world.[148] Bengali nationalism was of course reviving and recasting the Hindu vocabulary so as to cope with colonial modernization and also rival dominant Victorian manhood, as noted in Chapter 1. Yet while Tagore invokes the vocabulary, he intercepts the self-oriented abstractions of male ascetic resistance with a concrete question. Through the mouth of yet another neglected woman, he once again raises the query he posed in *Chitrangada*. He asks what ought to constitute mutual responsibilities—intellectual, emotional, sexual—in heterosexual societies. Only now Tagore's critical query strides across the caste/race division of purity and pollution to shake the foundations of contemporary Hindu filiative order.

These explorations of humanness as embodied and as ideal grow far more complex and also contradictory when Prakriti prevails upon her mother to call back the monk by casting a magic spell. As a lower-caste woman, her mother is in command of magical machinations. Even though the immediate reference here is to Tantric Hindu and Buddhist sexual practices,[149] for the purposes of my discussion I will bracket the immediate reference and focus on what the dances of magic imply in regard to Tagore's larger concerns with the sexual politics of nation and empire. Reading intertextually, we must note at once that this low magic of seduction is the only kind under the control of our protagonists here because the godly seductive powers at Princess Chitrangada's command are unavailable to them both in social and in mythic imagination; an earlier lyric sung by Prakriti has established that she finds it pointless to supplicate the gods to right her wrongs.[150] The complexity posed here is that as Prakriti charts her own righteous path to redressing her neglected wants, she has no recourse other than to embrace the social image of lowly seductress. This image was of course constitutively vile under indigenous caste misogyny, and in Tagore's context even more so because it entwined Hindu caste biology with an imperialist Judeo-Christian division of primitive and advanced family-lines.

To spread her *mayajal* or seductive web of illusion, Prakriti's mother teaches her to do a predatory dance before the magic mirror and witness in it the *dasha* (resultant pitiful state) of uncontrollable lust to which the upright ascetic is reduced.[151] In dancing before this mirror of objectification Prakriti's body turns intertextual with the public woman's with the mirror, an image that became widespread in the urban folk art of nineteenth-century Bengal. As discussed at length in Chapter 1, such images as these of self-objectifying women spearheaded the shift of visual culture from the non-perspectival iconography of religious painting to voyeuristic directionality. A new masculine gaze had begun to proliferate through folk art itself and the overlapping technologies of still photography and illusionist proscenium stagecraft. Not unlike the mirror before which a seductive kamini such as Binodini Dasi had to practice self-transformation, the mirror before Prakriti as well is one of social chastisement. She is imaged as repeatedly cringing in lajja at her shamefully immodest craving for the man[152] at the same time that she turns back to pursue the seduction with a remorselessly devouring *khudharto prem*[153] (hunger of love). The image of her predatory lust undoubtedly carries the elite author's civilizing mission of rebuking the primitive and animal-like quality in any chandal's emotion.

And yet Prakriti's mirror scenes call for a textual rather than linear reading in that their bifurcation of subject and object tends to be convoluted, and lends itself to compelling variations in choreographic design (as we will see in Chapter 4 in discussing Manjusri Chaki-Sircar's feminist delineation). What the mirror trope focuses upon is not at all the woman Prakriti's image but that of Ananda, as this is enacted through shadow-play on stage. The image brought to life through Prakriti's performative lyrics about looking is the celibate ascetic's as he is cursing and flagellating himself with lightning. While the man's shadow act certainly chastises the lowly seductress, the mediating mirror metaphor in line with its popular cultural intertexts underscores as well the specular nature of his act. We confront a fracturing of the ideal of high-caste ascetic masculinism through a suggestive exposure. Beneath the overt calm of the ascetic is exposed a covert voyeur objectifying a lowly woman. In this provocative specular critique, we could perhaps detect a distant and non-Western pre-figuration of Jacques Lacan's notion of 'discordance' within the Ideal-I.[154] Through analogical extension, the specularity could be seen as implicating the male author as well.

At any rate, it is along this trajectory that Prakriti's sentiment of lajja takes a different rhetorical turn. We hear her averting her eyes not only through selfish guilt for her primitive craving, *also* because she is selflessly concerned about the agony Ananda faces. She registers the *bhayankar dukkher ghurnijhanjha* (terrifying whirlwind of grief) he feels as his *abhrabhedi guarab* (the towering glory/pride of ascetic manhood) comes crumbling down.[155] Note also that Prakriti's own desire for a human relationship with her desired man, a line of thought his own liberal vision had opened up for her, is quite at odds with Ananda's annihilating self-transformation from transcendent ascetic to objectifying voyeur. All that Prakriti seeks throughout is *mayabandhan* or a quotidian bonding of affection, as distinct from the mayajal or seductive net, which would bind the man she likes with her everyday laughter and tears (*amari hasi-krandan*).[156] Because various sociobiological structures of mediation and media come in the way of this very human aspiration of an underprivileged young girl, she is left with no recourse on hand other than that mayajal of mediation. Herein we see Tagore as also striving to look beyond his own caste-bourgeois eye in order to achieve a substantial 'mind-change', a more direct perception of what an untouchable young woman might need to be and to feel human; his narrative striving, as put by Gayatri Spivak, is for weaving an ethical responsiveness in with the 'compromised as teacher'.[157]

However, neither is Prakriti's human vision holistic nor is her autonomy as a humanist visionary unmediated by empire within the discursive compass of the work. For the 'web'[158] of Tagore's narrative shows her to be simultaneously embracing the chastisement of their ways by caste-racist society. She displays abject remorse for having pulled the lofty ascetic Ananda to the ground (*matite tenecchi tomare*) and ends with a supplication that she be uplifted out of her *pap* to his realm of *punya* (virtue).[159] Moreover, in this conclusive reaffirmation of socio-moral hierarchy, Prakriti's rhetoric derives from her mother's.

There is little doubt that the portrayal of Prakriti's mother (Ma) as well is 'multiaccentual'[160] and conflicted. On the one hand, Ma had all along apprehended that Ananda would return only to curse Prakriti for her wicked seduction. At the same time, with maternal affect, she was afraid that nothing of mulya would remain in her daughter's life were Prakriti to try fulfilling his demands.[161] Perhaps in these trepidations of the wise Ma, we find a necessary complement to and a reality check for the young chandal woman's visionary demand for an embodied equality with the socially/spiritually elevated Ananda; Ma's fears remind of the realities of their condition and that unless the social and perceptual hierarchies are dealt with, the liberal principle of (caste-blind) equality cannot be embodied.

On the other hand, however, the dance drama concludes upon the daughter demonizing Ma for the wicked seduction, whereas the prose play goes to the length of showing the mother's death. This telos of the narrative web underscores that Tagore is basically compromising with an institutionalized filiative order that combines caste-Hindu with Victorian-racial misogyny. The import of these plays' endings is unmistakably *developmental*, from a biological point of view. The point is that in order to attain the bliss of Ananda's sanitized humanity, the new chandal woman of the future must repudiate her polluted ancestry. Her individuality, in other words, has to be brought into or be possessed by his frame of understanding humanness. On this narrative line, Tagore's humanist aesthetic of knowledge becomes entirely embroiled in empire and self-reference. For we should not forget that the name of the monk coincides with the name Tagore gave to his ideal of aesthetic knowledge in *Vishwasahitya* (see above).

Even though I emphasize the issue of institutional mediations in Tagore's thought, however, by no means should this be taken as my conclusive word. To do so would be to damage my critical endeavour in this book from two directions. We would be reducing to our own teleological end the complexity in a monumental endeavour such as Rabindranath Tagore's to decolonize human agency by weeding out gendered imperial and national perceptions. As well, we would be reducing into a singular linear strand the apparatus for multi-accented textual reading, as I am elaborating the apparatus through my study. I have repeatedly noted that I find this realistic textual approach to modern thought crucial for distinguishing activist and restorative accents from compromised cognition. My extensive readings above of Tagore's gendered self-critique should have reiterated that, for one, I consider all critical analysis to be driven by lived affect (one's psychosocial investments and interests)—disagreeing with Dipesh Chakrabarty's position that one is able to separate analytical reasoning from lived reasoning in postimperial contexts.[162] For another, I want to parse all the ways that sexualized hierarchies have been engaged and still can be in the cause of autonomy in practice *and in concept*. My point of closely reading Tagore's *Chandalika* above is to amplify my general point that the dialectic of critical engagement is constitutively inconclusive. Activist thinkers' attempts to take disgrace in their stride ought not to be read in absolute terms as achievements or failures, rather, as conflicted yet cumulative endeavours; in complex hierarchical contexts some disgraces more than others are bound to be sidelined or misrecognized. To reinforce my position with attention to the context I study, I find it helpful to end this chapter on Tagore by turning back to Tagore's own perspicacious insight on cumulative humanism under gendered empire.

In the work *Red Oleanders* (1924), with which I began my readings, Tagore contraposes opposite forms of humanist knowledge. On one side, we encounter the king of a nation built for accumulating capital (as much in the form of gold as of knowledge); this governor wants to know and possess the other through a fiercely affective form of diagnosis— through probing her out 'back and forth ... part by part'.[163] We also meet a self-reflexive man of knowledge, a professor who thoroughly criticizes how manusatya or predatory humanness makes one 'kill' the other for self-survival[164] at the same time that he concedes to this self-serving rationality of objectification. Against this 'baroque allegory'[165] of ruinous humanity, Tagore pits the woman Nandini and her bliss-inducing autonomy (her name literally means, the 'giver of happiness'). Whereas there is much more to this rich text than fits the scope of my brief word here, I want to bring out two aspects I also raised in the Introduction. Despite the seeming gender binary we find in the allegory of knowledge sketched here, Nandini is not the idealistic symbol of a feminine alternative to male empire. By Tagore's testimony, her role explores the conflicts of attitude and practice he detected between a 'civilization of living through the tilling of land' (*karshanjibi sabhyata*) and another 'civilization of living by the means of attractions'(*akarshanjibi sabhyata*; while the literal translation of the prefixed word akarshanjibi in this context would be 'non-agrarian', I retain the Bengali pun).[166] As such, the form of 'attraction-less' or un-capitalized temporality conceived in bliss-begetting Nandini is not a denial of fetishistic mediation by imperialist capital and its masculinist humans. Instead, it constitutes a quintessentially non-teleological struggle for knowledge that can rip apart the mediating *jal*/net[167] of instrumental knowing. And it is a struggle that could very well end in the autonomous knower's death (the play closes with Nandini's assertion that her struggle will be unto death).

On that critical note, it is not irrelevant to finish up my own reading of Rabindrananth Tagore's gendered conflicts with empire by pointing out that in the last of the three depictions of the autonomous woman as dancer, *Shyama*—composed two years before his death (1939)—Tagore turned his lens of critique squarely upon an idealistic man.[168] Despite his reflexive acknowledgement of guilt, the male protagonist of *Shyama* fails to overcome the cognitive orthodoxy in his perspective upon a culpable yet vulnerable woman/other. He cannot perceive the ethical beauty in her self-committed desire. My view is that the lasting contribution Rabindranath Tagore has made to our gendered critique of empires, then and now, is to alert us both to the mediating role aesthetical moralities play and to how we might turn the gaze in another ethically pleasing way.

PART TWO

POSTCOLONIAL GLOBALITY

3

AUTONOMY AS
REPRODUCTIVE LABOUR

The Neoliberal Woman and
Visual Networks of Empire

A well-received telefilm titled *Amra* (We)—made in 1998 and to this day regularly re-aired—portrays multiple empowered women. Stringing together three shorts, the film presents, first, a high-profile call girl who refuses to be enslaved either to the father or to the son who both keep her; then, a Muslim village girl who resists seduction by her father's employer and instead migrates to the city and its opportunities for independent living; and finally, a disabled bourgeois homemaker, neglected and left in isolation by her upwardly mobile husband, who bonds with her servant woman and decides to adopt the latter's daughter. In the 'live interview' with which the film closes, telestar Aditi Choudhury claims that in each of the three roles she plays she finds a part of her 'I' (ami) since all such modern women as herself share in the same 'struggle to exist, to be' (*astwitter ladai*). Verifying the reality of the situation, the interview is interrupted by a phone call regarding Aditi's ailing son, followed by her anxious queries about how long her work day will last. When she returns to the interview, Aditi turns to her audience and states: 'I have a child at home: *this* is our real "existence/essence" (astwitya).'

Amra is symptomatic of imaginations of the *ekushe nari* (woman of the twenty-first) and the *aparajita* (the unvanquished feminine)—ideals of the millennial Bengali woman proliferating under India's new liberal economic order. We see here a nari embodying such core Enlightenment concepts of personhood as civil liberty, autonomy, and dignity as against subjection and instrumentality. The active individual agent is resurfacing at a new conjuncture of socio-moral change in Bengal. This new humanist aesthetic stems from financial policy changes that began in the mid-1990s as the Indian state moved out of 'over forty years of autarkically conceived planning and state-led development' into multinational capitalism.[1] Hand-in-hand with market growth, cultural imaginations started to drift away from the nation-based emphasis on collective identities prevailing in the autarkic eras and towards liberal individualism. Since cultural processes can hardly be periodized, we also must keep in mind that long before the recent economic liberalization such other routes of global capital as the growth of bourgeois Indian diasporas in Europe and America and accompanying transnational flows were altering social ideas and practices of Indian personhood. Earlier phases of transnational flow sometimes proved to be unsettling and alienating for the prevailing collectivism (as illustrated by the negative stereotype of the emigrant in Satyajit Ray's film *Agantuk*). The recent exchanges of self-images and lifestyles between 'non-resident' and 'resident' Indian populations, on the other hand, flourish with the support of the marketizing nation-state (as exemplified by the many diasporic peoples and places appearing in contemporary Indian visual media).

A first glance at the pleasures of *Amra* suggests that, at this new conjuncture of global capitalism with a decolonized nation-state, aesthetic individualism is substantially more activist than it was at the inception of subjectivist imagination in colonial Bengal. In fact, perceptions of the beautiful, the pleasing, and the good in women appear to be breaking down all patriarchal nationalist filiations and instead growing flexible and egalitarian. In striking contrast to the public women Binodini's and Monomohini's narrative struggles for rights under paternalistic bourgeois Hindu nationalism, for example, the shorts in question challenge all forms of sociobiological bias. Norms of sexual and ethnic purity, class status, as well as feminine ability are all brought into question. *Amra* represents in the same collective feminist struggle a sex worker, a rural Muslim, a bourgeois woman disabled for her typical roles (reproductive work at home as well as productive employment), and a public actress who appears in the provocative attire of an entertainment nayika. Moreover, the inclusive aesthetic of feminine agency we find here is not an anomaly at all, rather, a characteristic of contemporary Indian regional cinema and television as well as of Bollywood cinema. The immediate predecessors of this inclusive impulse are the various activist and state-sponsored movements for 'women's empowerment' or stree shakti[2] that have been underway in social and legal practice as well as in media aesthetics since India's freedom from colonization.[3] These include the women's movement, the Marxist-led peasant movements, and most recently, the sex workers' and disability movements. As illustrated by the popular feminist aesthetic of Amra, an expanding market fuels state-led empowerment. It produces images of how women and the underprivileged gain opportunities from the new liberalization—how they find new possibilities for independent income, geographic and social mobility, as well as consumer choice.

Nonetheless, something in the telefilm goes against the grain of nineteenth-century Bengali humanism rather than manifesting a teleological extension of the earlier trend in a more radical historical era. *Amra* is one among the large number of feminist stories in circulation today which finds no conflict between a woman's autonomy and her feminine roles as a self-sacrificing homemaker and a (son's) mother. The vocabulary of social change endorsing *individual choice*, dignity, and civil liberty *pleasingly agrees* with another terminology centring the essential sweetness (madhurya, to use a nineteenth-century term; see Chapter 1) of feminine self-sacrifice enshrined in the mother-figure of a *bourgeois Hindu filiative order*. The conflicts over femininity that had once raged in colonial Bengal between illiberal patriarchal-nationalism and indigenous-activist liberal voices are being reduced to cohesive imagery and storylines. Where imaginations and images had posed stark contradictions, they are now undergoing a (paradoxically) surreptitious yet decisive 'mortification'.[4] This surreptitious collapse and mortification of opposing cultures of social change illustrates the point made in the Introduction—that contemporary Indian liberal culture manifests a peculiarly economical trend. This trend wants to foreclose what Bakhtin describes as 'two-sided' frameworks of artistic reflection and social action—frames for thinking and seeing within the contemporary historical process yet outside and against it.[5] As such, our ideal individual woman of *Amra* self-reflexively identifies with the less-than-ideal and the socially discriminated, fighting for their equal rights through both aesthetic and social activism (as suggested by the 'interview'), at the same time that she manifests a feminine essence transcending all such devalued forms of womanhood.

This chapter examines the new cohesive imagination of the autonomous/maternal bourgeois woman, showing that it is symptomatic of a discontinuity in material conditions between the two relatively liberal eras of modern Indian thought. The altered character of capitalism in our multinational era is what requires this conformity between opposing liberal and illiberal approaches to women's agency. A post-Fordist American-style capitalism of networks is rapidly changing the face of urban India and much of the globe. As more social sectors and different people come to be drawn into the circuits of finance and communication, dominant imagery exposes and includes an increasingly varied cast of voices, bodies, and interests in its democratic public sweep.[6] The classificatory principles of virtue and pollution, or voyeurism and worship, which had characterized nineteenth-century representations of Bengali women, appear to have been replaced by principles of equal visibility and reflexive self-empowerment. Yet, this new humanist visuality also tends to semiotically crop[7] down the tensions and to resolve conflicts of agency and of communication that persist within its variegated filiative order. Instead, it reinforces biological stratifications of labour and reward across processes of sexuality, race, ethnicity, and class. In these visual-financial networks, we encounter a new flexible formation of empire coordinating across ostensibly decolonized contexts. Reducing the dialectical cultural heritage of liberal and indigenous selves, these coordinated processes of social change and social representation produce dichotomies of essence and difference. As such, the 'indigenous' also comes to be formulated in terms that are starkly illiberal and communalist yet eminently sustainable in our new liberal globe. To delineate this process of cultural reduction and mortification, I look below at how recent adaptations are altering Rabindranath Tagore's feminist works in contemporary Bengal and in selected bourgeois Indian diasporas in the US. I show that while these feminist works in particular find a fresh lease of visual life on the new liberal stages and screens of ostensibly democratic bourgeois communities, the alterations reduce internal conflicts in ways that cohere with larger national and transnational networks of governance.

Neoliberal Canons of Femininity:
Women's Autonomy and Reproductive Labour

The trends of reduction and coherence I sketch above characterize the canonization of cultural forms. Aesthetic canons invariably still and totalize dialectical activity, yielding what John Guillory has insightfully called 'dreams of consensus'.[8] The discourse of canonical value denies 'not so much the reality of conflict as the *constitutive* nature of conflict … that is to say, [aesthetic work] as an arena of social struggle' (emphasis in original).[9] Occurring in the course of the reception and reproduction of aesthetic imagination, canon-making reduces the multiple rational and affective evaluations within the work of imagination.[10] The work is recast in a way that accrues both 'knowledge capital'[11] and pleasure capital for the people in its circuit of reception. By valuing the given artistic work and its author for some perspectives while reworking or ignoring other perspectives, its new receivers enjoy the privileges of commanding coveted knowledge and/or feeling and making others happy. Therewith, they come to be entitled to tangible and intangible rewards and profits within their own social realm. Yet the promised rewards are never equal for all members of the valuing group in that deprivations come in the guise of rewards to the lesser in status amidst the group. In other words, the very ways works are recast as they come to be canonized reinforce existing inequalities both in social and in semiotic relations: women, for example, invariably come to be reimagined and reaffirmed as self-sacrificing in relation to men. All in all, canons reduce and stratify social knowledge insofar as they permit powerful voices and interest groups to rule over people's judgements and inclinations. Even as they persuade people to agree with and value their views, rather than enforce and brainwash through propaganda, they thoroughly hegemonize by extracting consent.[12]

It seems to me that dreams of hegemonic consensus have gained a *uniquely pleasurable* lease of life in our contemporary visually coordinated hegemonies. The technologies available for cropping away social anxieties and schematizing collective desires help to widely distribute canonical templates of aesthetic value. Since technological networks by and large intersect with global agendas, this canonizing of aesthetical evaluations (of human living) is easily governed by corporate interest. In this light, it is noteworthy that two contradictory canons of Indian womanhood—the woman with choice and the woman with familial obligations—are currently gathering aesthetical capital amidst Indians worldwide.

This contradictory requirement, as well as cohesive resolutions of the contradiction, in my view, stem from global imperialist processes of deregulating capital yet dividing labour.

Stuart Hall notes that, on the one hand, global capitalism today flexibly links the Third World sectors to the 'so-called advanced sections of the First World', reconstituting the once-backward sectors[13] in a way such that pre-existing divides between the 'Third' and the 'First' seem to be narrowing apace both across and within national borders. The specifically neoliberal character of today's transnational market is that it works 'through difference'.[14] utilizing and mobilizing a variety of productive labour forces that cuts across sexual, caste, class, and geographic boundaries. Along these lines, women from many social positions are being portrayed in Indian and in diasporic media as productive wage-earning workers and liberated individuals. They are shown to be making autonomous choices and freely pursuing their work and leisure[15] as well as criticizing patriarchy, racism, casteism, and the blind pursuit of male-dominant capitalism. Depicted as the 'natural' outcome of the benevolent capitalist socioeconomic forces',[16] the millennial Indian woman presents a 'responsive, active ... desiring subject'[17] rather than the sexually passive wife and mother recurring in nationalist representations of the autarkic post-Independence eras. This fresh cast of feminist individuals is well in tune with the future understood in both its senses, as increasing prosperity and greater liberation. It robustly blends Adam Smith's variety of hedonistic self-love with Utilitarian freedom as well as with Kantian reflexivity and the Romantic critique of capitalist progress. On the other hand, the portrayal is invariably double-edged. It inscribes the flexible form of imperialism immanent to neoliberal capital. For the gendered depictions of agency and empowerment invariably portray sexual divisions of labour entwined with other spatiotemporal divisions of caste, race, ethnicity, class, creed, and geographical location.

Paradoxically enough, these sexual divisions stem from privatization which, in principle, gives agency to the individual. Gayatri Spivak points out that as nation-states privatize under the 'New World Order'—and we witness an unprecedented systematic withdrawal of the distribution of goods and benefits based on principles of liberal civil society[18]—an irrevocably gendered form of inequity comes to prevail. In Spivak's view, 'it becomes increasingly correct to say that the only source of male dignity is employment just as the only source of genuine female dignity is unpaid domestic labour [because] across all class processes', the market manipulates the notion that it is ethical for women to be nurturing.[19] Feminine 'home work' should be understood at once as material and as notional. To begin with, it reproduces the relations of masculine production and maximizes accumulation through absorbing such costs as 'health care, day care, workplace safety, maintenance, management' at the same time that it remains characteristically subordinate and unpaid.[20] Furthermore, the emotional work of reproducing the imagined territory of a communal home—a unique non-temporized sanctum of national patriarchal tradition outside materialist progress— becomes crucial for counteracting experiences of global mobility. The work of emotional reproduction enables Indians to cope with new forms of social and affective dislocations. These include such fresh processes of historical mobility as transnational migration into the racialized global North, or the restructuring and globalizing of cityscapes in the Indian subcontinent. Note that 'mobility' in our global world has to be understood as adopting and adapting to changes of status which may or may not entail geographical movement.[21] As many scholars note, the hankering to step out of transience into an idealized belonging—once again to be completely at home in the locality and in the land—leads to a 'reprocessing of habits, objects, names, and histories that have been uprooted ...',[22] wherein the ideal Indian woman is imagined to be in charge.

The core contradiction between the liberal and the illiberal ideals of Indian femininity proliferating in the present, then, is that they stand at the opposite poles of the sexual division of labour under the neoliberal global market. Each remains equally marketable both in itself and in relation to the other. In both the locations I study in this chapter—the US-Indian bourgeois diaspora and the marketizing Indian nation-state— canons of femininity are evolving in ways that resolve the contradiction between the liberal and illiberal ideals respectively of women's dignity and render new images of consensus. Since remembrances of cultures past have everything to do with negotiating cultural pulls and pressures at present, these coherent pictures of social consensus determine what is or is not diachronically legible as community memory and where. Arjun Appadurai rightly notes that the planting of homes and localities in our global world is very much the work of 'mass-mediated' imagination comprising a 'palimpsest of highly local and highly translocal considerations'.[23] Yet how local imaginations intersect with the translocal has quite a lot to do with located histories of empire and of liberation. It is useful to begin with Indian diasporic imaginations born of post-1965 immigrant locations because they supply rather obvious instances of how canons of autonomous homemakers recast earlier Indian traditions of dissent and neutralize dialectic. Later I will show that, by contrast, feminine-canon-formation is relatively constrained in the contemporary volatile context of marketizing India, and therefore, also more complex and subtle.

Redomesticating Women and Homes: Canons of the Diaspora

At a fund-raising event held by Bengali Americans in southern California (2005), I watched the staging of an adaptation of Rabindranath Tagore's *Raktakarabi* (*Red Oleanders*, 1924). *Internet* (written and directed by Madangopal Mukhpadhyay) presciently reread within the present social context the Tagore play, challenge to male-dominant capital, yet it also altered the role of the female protagonist in a way that changed the import of the challenge for its Bengali diasporic audience. While I focus on the significance of the changes made to the semiotic schema of the Tagore work, my point is not to suggest that the adaptation somehow mistranslates or distorts the original Tagore text or that I, as an academic, command the knowledge capital to discern Tagore's correct meaning. To the contrary, I would maintain that, being a bourgeois immigrant Bengali woman myself, I am implicated in the socioeconomic processes from which these changes stem.

In this farcical adaptation, vignettes of *Raktakarabi* are performed together with other Tagore songs and dances within a plot set in contemporary Kolkata. The Tagore work is not only a play within the larger play—the characters are rehearsing *Raktakarabi* for an amateur production—it is thematically enmeshed. *Internet* portrays how two middle-class patriarchs (father and uncle) try to arrange an upwardly mobile NRI (non-resident-Indian) match for the daughter of the family through matrimonial advertisements on the internet. Deeply committed to her indigenous Bengali roots, which include her loyalty to her equally rooted boyfriend (Samir Chatterjee), the daughter Meera (Maitrayee Chakravorty) vigorously resists her father's (Sagar Rakhsit) plan, rejecting all the suitors he has lined up. These include caricatures of globe-trotting consumerist men and upstart Westernized women completely uprooted from indigenous moral values and social practices. The complications that ensue are amicably resolved when the line-up of suitors turns out to be nothing but a hoax staged by the uncle himself (Manab Datta) and the genial neighbourhood dada (big brother)

(Madangopal Mukhophadhyay) in order to safeguard Meera's emotional and intellectual rootedness and to disillusion her father about global upward mobility.

In more ways than one, *Internet* artfully reads and recontextualizes *Raktakarabi*'s approach to ethical autonomy. To begin with, Meera, who also plays the female protagonist Nandini in the inset performance of *Raktakarabi*, revivifies several key characteristics of Nandini's individuality (see the Introduction and Chapter 2). While Meera is a liberated woman in contemporary terms, seeking the economic freedom to choose her life-path, she is radically autonomous in electing a life of thrift (as a teacher) rather than falling in with the mainstream of upward mobility. As she declares, if she can get enough free time to relax amidst nature and whimsically snatch a tune, she 'wants nothing more from life (*jibone aar kicchu chai na*).'[24] As such, Meera reclaims in the life of a Kolkata college girl her textual predecessor's allegory of *phanka samay* (empty time). She recontextualizes the temporality of capital accumulation and instrumental reason which, as Tagore himself puts it, inscribe the mentalities to 'acquire' more and to (self) 'coerce' in the name of necessity.[25] In line with Nandini, then, the character of Meera is transcultural in scope. She combines vestiges of Romantic and Kantian critical individualisms with the Bengali Vaishnava conception of autonomous-self-knowledge as a sensually blissful state which effaces the proprietary self and worldly interests. In this respect, Meera's role overlaps with boyfriend Anandamoy's (literally, the blissful), in the role of the madman Bishu, the eccentric in Tagore's imagination of the kingdom of accumulation, the Yaksha Land. Together, yet with the woman in the lead, they reincarnate in the new context *Raktakarabi*'s notion of the radically itinerant, as inspired by the *sahajiya* poets who wandered through Tagore's rural Bengal and intermingled popular Hindu, Sufi mystic, and Tantric Buddhist elements in their devotional expressions. Intelligently recontextualizing these semiotics of autonomous movement, *Internet* implies through Meera's and Anandamoy's performances of dissent an autonomous contra-mobility to the capitalist routes of our times.

The portrayal of the routed, on the other hand, recalls Tagore's baroque allegory of ruined human beings bearing the 'imprint' of capitalist progress.[26] *Internet* depicts the organizing *techne*[27] of our new capitalism in the shape of successful or would-be consumers. The line-up includes, on the one hand, the mobile expatriates (a real estate developer, sexy women speaking for their male model brother, etc.) and, on the other, the mobility-desiring aged petty bureaucrat (Meera's father) who has stagnated within an otherwise globalizing nation-state. An even more subtle updating of Tagore's attack on capitalism is the way cyberspace is shown to have called upon these ruins of the human. This goes against the grain of the dominant view that the current 'cyber-libertarian development model'[28] enables a desegregated globalization that harmonizes corporate profits and equitable distribution of information and access amongst people. Instead, *Internet* showcases a world pervaded by progress-seekers who are simulacra of human beings, folding the real into the virtual in rapid succession. While humorously dramatizing our digitalized globe's way of overtaking 'mass' by the 'forces of speed', the work in effect laments the ruining of the individual and collective 'human body—with its capacity for consciousness, concentration, and voluntary memory'.[29]

Like her literary forbear, Meera works in antithesis to this landscape of decimation and amnesia in order to revivify the autonomously human mind and body. She leads the community in reclaiming self-consciousness about indigenous ways that interrupt the speed and the atomization brought on by a universal craving for metropolitan mobility. On stage, this performance of ethnic autonomy[30] became all the more evocatively persuasive in that it was replete with sights and smells associated with customs of orality and nieghbourliness in Kolkata. As friends collectively consumed street snacks (*jhalmuri* or spicy puffed rice) and bantered with each other while rehearsing *Raktakarabi,* the stage took on the nostalgic hue of neighbourhood literary *addas* (chat circles of friends). This evocation of a corporeal-intellectual comfort zone, which broke down the fourth wall and elicited responses from the audience, heightened the evaluating group's autonomy in belonging-together and being-at-home in a way at odds with the 'gravitational pull [of] the *telos* of productivity and development'.[31] Constituting an indigenous 'place-making practice'[32] for these diasporic people, this performance of neighbourly traditions led by the woman opened an interval of autonomous existence within their bourgeois American surroundings. In that South Asians are bound by the tensions of a 'racially indeterminate'[33] status in mainstream America, their easy ability for creating these autonomous times and places attests to American capitalism's flexibility and adaptation to difference.

In view of its prescient intertextual elaboration in an American diasporic context of *Raktakarabi*'s gendered vision of ethical autonomy, it is striking that *Internet* eventually settles for a bourgeois-male-dominant consensus about Indian global domesticity. It fails to come to grips with

Tagore's anti-imperialist notion that the ethical woman is perpetually autonomous—characteristically eccentric to male-dominant territories of home, land, and capital. Instead, the work resolves the conflict of desires in a way that gathers pleasure capital for the target professional audience in Southern California. It shows that Meera's boyfriend wins a prestigious academic scholarship (from Caltech, no less) and prepares to marry her and depart for California. Commanding the marketable knowledge to immigrate to the global North—to acquire the territorial male dignity of upwardly employment and allied proprietary rights—the boyfriend is readily persuaded to move with the promise of technocracy. On her part, Meera drops her resilience against the global track through the right balance of temporal reassurances. On the one hand, she is to move with the liberal cosmopolitan time and all that is new while on the other, she is to carry her authentic indigenous attributes into the California Bengali scene such that she may revivify *Raktakarabi* itself and authentic (canonical) Tagore wherever she goes.

The adaptation culminates, that is, by reducing Tagore's self-critical vision and resolving transcultural dialectics. Instead of the Tagore woman's eccentric individuality we end up with the cohesive image of an autonomous woman whose choices are compliant with the reproductive needs of globally-equipped possessive Indian men. Whereas initially Meera's employability had promised her independence from patriarchal agendas, ultimately it is troped into a potential only as she prepares to immigrate on a spousal visa as the homemaker of a technical professional. As such, Meera also emotionally nurtures male immigrant identity, quelling the anxieties of transience as well as of a racially contoured belonging in the Anglo North. In that capacity of culture-reproduction, Meera's role also complements boyfriend Anandamoy's. For Anandamoy collapses into one monolithic representation of bourgeois Bengali manhood—both the knowledgeable technocrat and the eccentric poet, Tagore's 'madman' Bishu.

Along these lines, Tagore's transcultural individuals come to be re-domesticated—female made to belong with dominant male—within a heterosexual Indian collectivity that at once embraces yet seeks to supersede Western possessive teleology at its non-temporized poetic (spiritual) core. Whereas the metaphorical characters born of Tagore's indigenous liberalism engage the masculine techne of an imperial capitalist state, then, their transfigurations in *Internet* come to be insulated from the teleology of imperialist capital rather than engage in a dialectic. In a new time and place, we once again encounter a collective effort to develop some Bengali national characteristics and to alienate others (as noted also in Chapter 1), only the processes of cultural idealism and differentiation are now far less conflicted than at their inception.

The syntheses of choice and obligation, self-love and selflessness, which build an apparent consensus amidst the male-dominant valuing group, also predictably stratify the rewards to group members. To women who are spousal immigrants, for example, hardships often come in the guise of reward. Perceived as second-wage earners, they often settle for part-time or piece work and inadequate compensation at the same time that they are putting in a second shift of labour at home to maintain an upscale family life. Masculine dignities also are stacked on an imperialist order of gendered knowledge. Upwardly mobile men who move with the times yet privately retain national ideals rank high above at least two other groups of men: those who mimic the West and those who are stagnant in time and space. A notable example of the latter is Meera's aged father, shown to depend both financially and attitudinally on mobile metropolitan men. In a binary of masculinities such as this, of the globally mobile enlightened man against the backward and aged, we find unmistakable residues of early nationalist imperialism such as in S.N. Banerjea's portrayal of an aging father in his *A Nation in the Making* (see Chapter 1). Whereas in earlier nationalism the binary remained stark and contradicted, however, in the present it pleasingly readjusts and combines the different patriarchal interests into one transnational familial resolution (albeit inherently stratified by knowledge capital and temporal capital). Gendered assignments such as these of power and of reward today are invariably adaptive to transnational networks of interest. In this instance, they interlink the two ends of the US-Indian diaspora—on one side, a right-wing-dominant superpower of the global North and on the other, a developing Hindu communalist nation.

Challenging the positivist fact/value split, Satya Mohanty reminds us that 'social and cultural identity' can be understood in terms of people's objective experiences of their 'social location'.[34] People's sense of identities are their 'ways of making sense of ... experiences',[35] that is, of processing available information[36] about their 'relationships' with the world and with themselves.[37] Furthermore, when identities are understood and negotiated in art, as I have noted before, 'extraverbal pragmatic'[38] frames of reference entwine with artistic choices, priorities, and deletions. The domesticated-woman-centred identity I discern in *Internet* refers to the experiences of the generation of elite professional Indians who came to set up home in the US after the 1965 Immigration Act lifted race restrictions and assigned uniform quotas for all countries based on the American market's need for highly specialized labour. Until recently, the technical immigrants from India have been predominantly men who benefited from the high-quality English-medium technical education of an industrialized nation-state and an ex-British-colony but failed to find satisfactory upwardly mobile employment in the autarkic economy of their home country. The peculiar contribution of women to the experiences of this professional bourgeoisie, as Anannya Bhattacharjee suggests in an important essay, is that they typically nurture the two obverse faces of the group's identity.[39]

On the one hand, the public face of right-bearing, employable 'model minority'[40] men, working with the agendas of state and multinational capital, is upheld by the large number of women who follow on spousal visas (which tie their rights to the men's sponsorship) to fulfil their appropriate individual dignity of nurturing male-privileged families. As captured in *Internet*, liberal practices of autonomy and gender equality are far from at odds with this track of women's immigration into upwardly 'Anglo-conformed'[41] Indian enclaves. In themselves, liberal values are accented by the 'autonomic impulse'[42] to immigrate and accumulate this immigrant generation as a whole receives from more than one quarter. The neoliberal American state extends the rights of economic participation and citizenship; from its end, marketizing India extends opportunities of individual entrepreneurship and ownership (the predominantly bourgeois immigrants to the US were the first in line for Overseas Indian Citizenship, for example); and the markets in-between visualize and sell ideals of overseas Indian production and consumption for the target groups. Moreover, what characterizes the transnational mobility of this bourgeoisie is that it is a movement away from inherited support structures into acquired property and privilege, accumulated through individual enterprise within a cycle of production and consumption. In the larger landscape of American progress (understood as both enhanced prosperity and liberty), double-income families and occasional equitable distribution of labour within homes, are not merely necessary but well could be desirable. Yet the complexity of such promises is demonstrated well by *Internet*: educated Indian women acquire (limited) autonomy in the public realm so long as they concede that their primary dignity lies in nurturing Indian immigrant masculinity through reproducing a heterosexual family and its authentic spiritual values.

Thus, on the other hand, value-carrying women also are poised to nourish the highly privatized face of the uniquely Indian ethnic identity produced of the idealist multiculturalism of post-Civil-Rights US. As Anannya Bhattacharjee puts it, the bourgeois Indian American woman's being at home means also belonging to the extended ethnic community and the nation of origin.[43] We see here a dual process of 'ethnification' (belonging as a distinct national group here) and 'diasporization' (belonging there in another homeland)[44] symptomatic of a general weakening of the nation-state structure under contemporary transnational capitalism. While in the US specifically, ethnification draws upon the earlier radical race-identity-centred movements of the 1960s and 1970s, the contemporary American 'Nation of nations' landscape of ethnic identities—sustained by a neoliberal multicultural market—also differs significantly in its social politics.[45] These politics are far from race-neutral for a people of colour such as the Indian, even when institutional racism officially recedes from the workplace and everyday transactions[46] under neoliberal multiculturalism. Not only do networks of American multicultural capital 'produce' and utilize Indians as a particular race-and-class category (selectively privileged or not),[47] American territorialism both at the state and at the local levels fluctuates for South Asians of all classes, revealing the treacherous flexibility of the American capitalist empire. This treachery has been well demonstrated through the violent racial profiling of South Asians under the processes of 'renationalizing' post-9/11-US.[48] Thus 'reinvigorations' of ethnic identity[49] through such gatherings and performances of national belonging as I describe above are political acts of self-reclamation, empowering Indian immigrants and sustaining their participation in public spaces. The remarkable privatization of the ethnic nationalisms born of the balkanized multicultural landscape[50] of neoliberal US, however, also promotes a politics of dominance. This level of privatization produces, as I suggested earlier, a form of non-temporized Romantic idealism in which autonomy means uniqueness. The self-possession of ethnic uniqueness enforces group unification, and thereby allows hegemonic interests and images to prevail over the consensus about group identity and indigenous tradition.

Among such upwardly mobile ethnic groups as the Bengali Indian the consensual challenge to capitalism on the basis of unique timeless values affirms not only patriarchal and heterosexual territories[51] but increasingly those of the majority, the upper-caste/class Hindus. This Western-educated immigrant bourgeoisie descends largely from the bilingual Hindu elite bhadralok (gentry) created by the British colony— and positioned above the Muslim in that context (see Chapters 1 and 2 for more discussion)—while its ethnic profile has also been reaffirmed by the US history of immigration. In the past, upper-caste Indian men were Aryanized and more recently, Hindu Indian identity has received a significant boost through US profiling of the 'new "evil empire" of Islam'.[52] Perhaps it is not unexpected, then, that *Internet*'s performance of a uniquely indigenized alternative to capitalist autonomy should surreptitiously creep into rivalrous Hindu nationalism. Whereas the Tagore play had been eclectic in its indigenous elements rather than solely Hindu, its adaptation domesticates the transcultural in the illiberal schema of an ethnic Hindu nation.

On stage, three images placed in parallel enframed the living room of Meera's home in Kolkata. A portrait of Tagore was juxtaposed with another of the saffron-clad monk Swami Vivekananda and a batik painting of the Hindu goddess Durga. This semiotic pattern entwined with others outside the performance. The event as a whole, which included devotional Odissi dance numbers, was a fundraiser for what is a common phenomenon in Indian American locations, the erection of a Hindu temple. In this instance, the temple was to be a centre for the Hindu missionary organization, Bharat Sevasram Sangha. Appropriately, the principal speaker was a saffron-clad missionary who conveyed a message characteristic of the 'communalistic ... spiritual movements' of our global times; he sought to replace the conditions of 'vagueness' and homogenization born of cultural globalization with an 'aura of [spiritual] authenticity' interlinked with development, thereby providing the target group with renewed 'vigour and autonomy in an otherwise thoroughly governed world'.[53] The monk waxed eloquent about how such community events and sites as the proposed temple educate the second-generation youth in their 'Indian heritage' at the same time that they are becoming models of achievement in American schools and workplaces. He was seeing no contradiction between encouraging the second-generation to imbibe competitive individualism of the American variety and to practice (his version of) Hindu religious values. He rounded out his speech by leading the audience in chants of '*Bande Mataram*'.

Conjoining with these other semiotic elements of the programme, the stage décor framing *Internet* in effect persuaded the audience to accept the two key signifiers of the contemporary Hindu nationalist (Hindutva or 'Hinduness') movement: the saffron-clad holy leader and the cardinal Indian hymn of erotic nationalism, '*Bande Mataram*' (hail to the motherland). For holding the centre stage, was the foremost among saffron-clad ascetics—especially from the viewpoint of the international arm of the Hindutva movement, the Vishwa Hindu Parishad—the celebrated exponent of Hinduism, Swami Vivekananda. At the Chicago World Parliament of Religions in 1893, Vivekananda had expounded Hinduism in imperialist terms as a monolithic 'rational and masculine' faith whose superiority lay in its liberal 'tolerance'.[54] Vivekananda had successfully won over the first raft of Western Hindu devotees from an America already influenced by European Orientalism and its Indo-Aryan myth. A not dissimilar message of muscular-individualist Hinduism was being reiterated at the programme itself by the new-generation Hindu leader from the Bharat Sevasram Sangha. A fitting accompaniment of this message was Bankim Chatterjee's hymn *Bande Mataram*, which currently maps the 'magical wholeness' of the Hindu motherland in right-wing narratives both in India and in the diasporas. In passing we should note that the spreading influence of Bankim's parochial nationalist hymn has nearly displaced the centrality of the official national anthem by Rabindranath Tagore, the ecumenical *Jana gana mana*.[55]

The visual and rhetorical resonances between the staging of *Internet* and the rest of the programme suggest that in this location Tagore and his indigenous-liberal imagination were being folded into illiberal Hindu heritage. This heritage reclaimed Bengal and India into a modern Hindu homeland centring the ideal woman. She spoke for autonomy both in the liberal sense of individual opportunity and in the nationalist sense of unique identity. Moreover, this event's visualization of Tagore's rightful place amidst the canon of Indian-nation-thinkers stands not alone but within an iconic pattern in the larger Indian diasporic imagination. One such iconic composition recently published for the Indian Independence Day celebrations by the UFICA (United Federation of Indo-Americans of California) included both Tagore and Dr Keshav Hedgewar, founder of the foremost militant Hindutva organization (the RSS). Without a doubt, all such maps of nationalist belonging are drawn against an imagined 'thousand-year-old struggle of Hindus and Muslims'.[56] Still, the Hindu communalist profile of India's other has considerably hardened in the US since 9/11. Now Hindu Indians themselves face racial profiling and strive, with heightened anxiety, to conform to the anti-Islamic sentiments fuelling America's imperialist renationalization. This was well revealed by a recent controversy over the representation of Hinduism in California textbooks,[57] or, on a lighter vein, by the strident call in a letter to the editor in *India West* for a new line of T-shirts declaring 'Proud to be a Hindu from India' or 'Not a Muslim, not from Pakistan'.[58] It is hardly surprising, then, that the inimical Muslim also should hover as the other of the canon of bourgeois Indian individualism I consider here.

Incarnating global cyberspace's 'homogenization of knowledge',[59] which *Internet* tried to challenge, cyber networks of the Bengali bourgeoisie of Southern California join voice with the American Christian Right in pitting the barbaric Muslim opposite a supposedly secular and enlightened Hindu Indian intellectual. Projecting ethnic empires back into South Asia, these 'mass'-less and faceless browsers from the diaspora recast indigenous humanist critiques of orthodoxy. Bearing witness to the easy way Jurgen Habermas's vision of the public sphere of rational exchange turns vertical through desensory digital networking, for example, editorials and reports from the critical liberal Pakistani newspaper, *Dawn,* often are re-articulated with leading subject-lines in these cyber networks. One such ethnic-imperialist caption presented a *Dawn* review of Amartya Sen's book, *The Argumentative Indian,* in the light of extremist Pakistani politics with the subject line, 'The Argumentative Indian and His Non-Argumentative Brother'; another *Dawn* report of atrocities on Christians in Pakistan was sarcastically pitched as 'Left Without a Prayer!!' Such cyber-narratives as these of Pakistani Muslims as an anachronistic species of irrational and fierce people are complemented in these diasporic circles by the reinvention of a Bengali intellectual telos. For example, such Nobel-laureate celebrities as Amartya Sen and Tagore himself are cast in the forefront of a triumphal Hindu history of tolerance and reason, whereas such other Muslim Bengali writers as the anarchist intellectual and poet Kazi Nazrul Islam are described as being relatively 'crude' and primitive in aesthetic practice. It is arguable that the tension between the peripheral social position of merchant- and working-class Bangladeshi immigrants and the professional status of the Bengali Indian majority is displaced on to this negative profile of an eminent voice of modern Bengali literature such as Nazrul.

By now it is widely accepted by scholars that Indian diasporas show strong trends of right-wing nationalism (separatist movements like Hindutva and Khalistan). My point in the reading above is to emphasize one key factor contributing to this communal imperialism. Self-critical approaches to indigenous and liberal humanist concepts to be found in earlier decolonizing imaginations of modern India are being synthesized into paradoxically illiberal-liberal canons that aid the agendas of majority groups. Then what, if anything, alters when contemporary people self-consciously attempt to be critical of majority agendas and to mobilize for minority rights? What shape do activist intentions commonly take in the ethnic Indian enclaves of post-Civil-Rights US?

Comaroff and Comaroff maintain that the 'autonomic impulse' of 'millennial' capitalism decontextualizes and distantiates people from place and its 'sociomoral pressures'.[60] For post-1965 Indian immigrants the capitalist autonomic impulse, as I describe above, is Janus-faced. It drives at once towards public hyper-individualist autonomy, albeit unequally gendered, and towards private and unitary group autonomy. I would extend the insight of Comaroff and Comaroff to suggest that, for this generation, it also becomes difficult to re-enter place and critique social morality. This may be one reason why, as Jenny Sharpe has noted, the radical multicultural conception of individual rights which emerged from earlier race-identity-centred movements in the US (which also challenged the racialization of class privilege) has tended to devolve into canons of immigrant ethnic identity. I think my point is illustrated by the circuitous linkage forged by a contemporary reproduction of another woman-centred play by Rabindranath Tagore, the dance drama *Chandalika*.

Atlanta-based Kuchipudi Dance Academy's *Chandalika* was first rendered into Telugu verse and the Kuchipudi dance form by the eminent exponent Vempati Chinna Satyam (1975). Vempati's foremost disciple and director of the academy, Sasikala Penumarthi, has brought the work to US audiences. Vempati's politicized choreography and dramaturgy—while encompassing traditional elements of attire, music, and voice—adeptly humanize the depersonalized rasa-based[61] gesture language of Kuchipudi dance in order to revivify Tagore's message against caste-discrimination. Working through antithesis, this version sets the fluid 'rhythmic patterns'[62] of Kuchipudi dance numbers, sensually accented by lighting and song, against interruptive dramatic episodes that portray how hatred for the chandal (outcaste) girl's polluted body erupts within the affective bonding of women in an Indian village. Vempati's *Chandalika* captures a relatively secular moment in post-Independence Indian aesthetics in that it was conceived just before the 'Hindu culture' rhetoric started to proliferate in the Indian public spaces dominated by government-controlled media.[63] On one level, it develops and makes more legible Tagore's use of Buddhism's humanitarian embrace (as inflected by Enlightenment values in Tagore's view) to challenge the caste orthodoxy of Hinduism. It closes with an evocative multi-media tableau (combining slides, lighting, and body groupings) which depicts the chandal woman being inducted into Buddhism and its mission of egalitarian community.

In 2005, Sasikala Penumarthi's dance drama found a most appropriate home at a fundraiser of a very different hue than the Hindu missionary event I described earlier. It was the centrepiece of a fundraiser for setting up a Gandhi Foundation at Atlanta, US, in association with the Martin Luther King historic site. Introductory speeches and cyber newscasts—by such activist voices as Gandhian Giriraj Rao (who was himself a part of Mahatma Gandhi's non-violence movement before Independence) and journalist H.V. Shivdas (who hails from an eclectic multiracial background)—celebrated that the *Chandalika* production brilliantly encapsulates the 'overriding mission' of the Gandhi Foundation and its Civil Rights affiliates. The consensus was that the work shares in the mission pursued alike by Gandhi and by Martin Luther King of challenging the production of 'outcastes' in all societies and advancing the cause of individual rights 'regardless of race, gender, creed, class, or financial status'.[64] A videotape of the event suggests that, in this context, the performance was crossing multiple borders of activist imagination. It was linking Tagore's and Gandhi's challenges to social hierarchy in decolonizing India with the secular critique of religious orthodoxy in post-Independence India as well as with US traditions of minority-identity-centred movements (based on race, gender, and labour-centred identities).

The complexity of the cross-racial activism invoked by this performance of *Chandalika*, however, is that its paths have been contradictory. It has sought affiliation and visibility in starkly opposing sites of ethnic Indian mobilization. The same production featured in another fundraiser held by the Hindu Student Council of Atlanta (1996), an organization sponsored by the openly communalist Vishwa Hindu Parishad. In entering this other venue, Sasikala's performance was networking with the other face of humanism, that of the imperialist who translates and reduces difference to dominant interests. This assertion of majoritarian self-interest is to be found on the Hindunet web report of the programme. The report reduces the 'exposition of terrorism' by keynote speaker Wajaht Habibullah (former commissioner of Kashmir) to a plea for the victimized 'Kashmiri Hindu community'.[65] While the site does note in passing that, as a Muslim, Habibullah himself has faced kidnapping and assassination threats, it makes the speaker voice the imaginary consensus that the rights alike of visible victimhood and of reparation for victimage belong to the authentically Indian Hindu citizens of Kashmir. Both the rhetorical and factual frameworks of the Hindu Student Council event, as revealed by actual practices of Hindutva followers, reiterate a definition of human-rights-bearing community that is typical of anti-Western global spiritual movements.[66] It binds libertarian agendas of community progress with a timeless ideal of indigenous values (seva or community service, for example), justifying erasures of difference and stratifications of reward both within local communities and across their global outreaches. This begs a question: what in the Kuchipudi *Chandalika* could have fitted and been legible in this context, making it an appropriate central spectacle for ethnic imperialist mobilization?

To answer this we must first note that such activist liberal causes behind the Tagore work as the equality of Hindu women and of outcastes apparently may not clash with Hindutva nationalist ideals. Not only do foremost women exponents of the movement advocate the woman's economic autonomy and leadership (especially where Hindu male leadership is perceived to flounder and to emasculate), caste distinction is also formally negated in the everyday practices of some communalist groups.[67] Nonetheless, Hindu-communalist equality is drastically at odds with the dialectical approach to liberalism taken by such activist intellectuals as Tagore in that neither caste nor class hierarchy is actually challenged.[68] Moreover, bourgeois women's rights are selectively endorsed only if they refrain from obstructing women's 'collective identification'[69] with the times and spaces of the dominant Hindu male. It seems to me that the Kuchipudi *Chandalika* forged intertextual ties with the conceptual agenda of the communalist Hindu Student Council in question because it contains an already appropriately developed sexual politics overwriting Tagore's own conflicted critique.

Vempati Chinna Satyam's *Chandalika* diachronically resolves the conflicts in Tagore's depiction of the male ascetic in relation to the autonomous desire of an untouchable-caste woman. As I detail in Chapter 2, Tagore's portrayals of the desiring woman challenge what he sees as a separatist and irresponsible strand in the anti-colonial sexual politics of his time—that of casting the Hindu ascetic ideal of male celibacy against the hyper-virility of the Western colonizer. Debating this position from a transcultural/European feminist perspective, Tagore's feminist dance dramas assert through their lyrics and their choreography the woman's needs at once for intellectual, emotional, and sexual companionship. Arguably, these aesthetical-political rebuttals were levelled at such key proponents of male celibate politics as Vivekananda and perhaps also M.K. Gandhi, even though Tagore's performative self-critiques in these works were always limited by his bourgeois Brahminical biases. Imagined within a nationalist history that has sanitized pre-colonial South Indian dance forms to produce modern traditions of Kuchipudi and Bharat Natyam,[70] Vempati's choreography reproduces the sexual binary in a hardened form. In this instance, the choreographer functions as a 'bestilling' historian of the conflicted strands of lyrical desire and accompanying bodily movement to be found in Tagore's versions of *Chandalika* (as discussed in Chapter 2); he is practising from a disembodied distance what we could describe in the words of Susan Leigh Foster as a choreography of 'stillness that spreads across time and space [and] ... masquerades as omniscience'.[71]

The upshot of the stilling and mortifying choreography is a piece that pits the glorious 'moral authority [of the] celibate male'[72] against the blatant pollution of untouchable women's desires. It recasts Tagore's uneven challenge to sexual and caste hierarchies into a linear narrative of motion and conclusion. On the one hand, it emphatically depicts how the ascetic temporarily loses his celibate sexual *virija* or strength[73] through the polluting magical machinations of the mother and her Tantric priestesses (*yoginis*). That he gives in to the 'infirmity' of desire and drops his semen is choreographed through a performance of his limp and malleable (feminized) body. On the other, it celebrates how the ascetic reclaims his male celibate psycho-spiritual poise. He is shown to paternally guide the chandal girl into a similar state of sexual-self-sublimation such that she can be inducted into Buddhist humanitarian community work. Thus, Vempati's *Chandalika* reduces verbal and corporeal tensions. Contrarily, Tagore had envisioned the chandal girl's desires and struggles, showing how she strives for reciprocity and accountability from the ascetic

On stage, a spectacular performance of lithe bodies and flowing hair represented the misogynist Hindu notion that the bodies of the outcaste yogini priestesses, shown to be inducting the chandal girl into desire through forbidden magic, are sexually 'open'[74] and polluting (Figure 1). Permitting abandoned movement beyond the disciplined patterns of Kuchipudi, this dance number did momentarily subvert the vilification of women's desires. Soon enough, the self-abandonment had come to be controlled by a recentring of the ascetic celibate as a pedagogue able to restructure the virija of his celibate sexuality. Moreover, there is little doubt that in this Hindu-centric context the saffron-robed image

Figure 1 Choreographing Pollution—The Faceless Priestesses
Courtesy: Sasikala Penumarthi, Kuchipudi Academy, Atlanta

of the celibate would have been persuasive for the target spectatorship only by way of another cannibalistic feat of visual mortification—that of deadening Tagore's Buddhist monk and devouring him into the vibrant figure of Hindu ascetics of the new millennium. This visual feat would be cropping away the Buddhist man's antithetical role vis-à-vis misogynist Hindu nationalism in Tagore's dialectical text, and instead solidifying the majority consensus regarding who the ideal Indian male leader of indigenous community work could be (none other than an ascetic Hindu man). Note also that this diasporic Hindu consensus coheres well with the nationalist canon of Kuchipudi dance upon which Vempati based his *Chandalika*. For Vempati Chinna Satyam is one among the several eminent dance gurus in Chennai who have attacked the acclaimed feminist dance innovator, Chandralekha. Vempati has inveighed against Chandralekha's call to mobilize against Hindu (right wing) patriarchy by eliminating 'Hindu gods and goddesses' from the dance forms of 'Kuchipudi/Bharat Natyam'.[75]

A question still remains: what do we make of the way that an explicitly activist performance such as this *Chandalika* has roved interchangeably through divergent sites of ethnic Indian mobilization? At the least, the blurring of distinction between critical and misogynist-communal aesthetics is symptomatic of the way orthodox views bleed into the 'respectable niche' of minority group identity which Hindu Indians claim in post-Civil-Rights and anti-Islamic public spaces, especially in the wake of Martin Luther King's endorsement of M.K. Gandhi's philosophy of non-violence.[76] This specific instance of interchangeable activist routes, in my view, also reveals why it may be difficult to uphold distinctions. The autonomic impulse that sustains the mobility of this immigrant generation in the transnational track makes it uncomfortable for people to internalize the sociomoral pressures of challenging hierarchy (sexual, racial, and economic) within ethnic Indian locations. For this can upset the delicate balance of public-individualist and private-majoritarian autonomy upholding group identity. On their part, bourgeois women affectively/rationally performing Indian ethnicity on or off stage tend to move into and outside ideals of individual autonomy and of group autonomy understood in diametrically opposite ways. Overall, they tend to be visualized as complying with their primary dignity in this immigrant location—that of nurturing the dual faces of the patriarchal ethnic home and its extended ethnic-imperialist national group.

Mobilizing Women and Homes: Flexible Canonicity in the Nation-state

At first glance, it appears that in contemporary liberalizing India, canons of reproductive femininity are less noticeable and sustainable in comparison with North American diasporic spaces. If dominant imaginations born of bourgeois diasporas tend to make autonomous women isomorphic with the patriarchal home and the Hindu nation, those born of the contemporary nation-state conversely appear to *mobilize* women as independent challengers. This contrast stems, in my view, from the differing ways that the bourgeois Indian patriarchal family and community alter in the respective locations of globalization. There are two significant differences—one pertaining to changes in social conditions and communicative media, the other to aesthetic traditions.

To begin with, sexual hierarchies are less stable in contemporary urban Indian locations than in the US-Indian bourgeois diasporas. Whereas the American diasporas grant autonomy and independent mobility primarily to elite professional men—by virtue of their status as model minority immigrants and principal wage-earners/property owners—marketizing India distributes opportunities for upward mobility and impulses for self-creativity more equitably across genders and social ranks. As such, bourgeois patriarchal domesticity comes to be in tension with women's escalating independence in matters of financial and social choice. Mary E. John observes, in reference to contemporary Indian visual media (Bollywood and allied films, advertisements), that even though 'class-caste endogamy remains the overall norm, ensuring the very reproduction of the middle class, there is ample evidence that an increasing number of women, especially from professional groups, are not getting married, are prepared to leave their husbands, or have other relationships outside marriage'.[77] These familial upheavals, moreover, are relatively widespread across the social spectrum since the very contours of the 'middle class' are changing faster than ever under the deregulated market. Thus, in urban India today, innovative images of professional femininity—of women claiming the privileged 'male dignity' of specialized employment—also cut across socioeconomic divisions of status and space (homes, neighbourhoods).

Seen in another way, popular representations of autonomy (individual and/as group) in the diaspora tend to fulfil the conditions of Roland Barthes's well-known characterization of the 'ex-nominating operation' of bourgeois imagination—that is, the operation of obfuscating the 'particular historical' conditions of class formation.[78] By contrast, similar representations of bourgeois women in Indian popular media instead seem to disprove Barthes: rather than obfuscate, they expose the historical particulars of inequality at the same time that they promise an unprecedented democratic distribution of embourgeoisment. A visual media that now spreads beyond the metropolitan centres (especially via television) and across national boundaries forges communication links between the spaces respectively of the traditional haute bourgeoisie (descending from British colonial education), the petty and the nouveau bourgeoisie, and upwardly aspiring working-class and rural people. Further, it interlinks more closely than ever before regional trajectories of expression such as the Bengali with Bollywood, Hollywood, and Hong Kong. Communication being the primary way to be intimate and in community[79]—to exchange ideas, feelings, choices (in practice and in taste)—new liberal ideals of bourgeois womanhood and belonging are negotiated in and mediated by these virtual communities. We saw in Chapter 1 that nineteenth-century Bengal had produced a traditional 'intellectual'[80] madhyabitta bhadralok (middle-class gentry) whose haute 'middling' social codes germinated from a unique combination of European liberal education, second-tier wage labour, and anti-colonial nationalism.[81] In transnational Bengal today, on the other hand, mediatized democracy is destabilizing those codes to an unprecedented degree.

What also differs between the bourgeois Indian diasporas of the US and the Indian nation-state is that in the latter location literary and visual productions are relatively less distanced from the socio-moral tensions and activist solidarities of their postcolonial place.[82] Whereas upwardly mobile US diasporic imaginations find it difficult to engage with local/global 'workings of power'[83] in any way that impedes the autonomy of the modular ethnic group, popular Indian imaginations conversely link up with radical aesthetic legacies.

Since the recent spate of economic liberalism in West Bengal is allowing diverse women to gain financial opportunities for independence,[84] it is not surprising that indigenous liberal imaginations of women's independence and gender equality—vis-à-vis the patriarchal structures of an earlier era[85]—find a new legibility and social salience. Tagore's feminist works are widening in appeal in popular-commercial Bengali media hand-in-hand with similar feminist depictions of women's autonomy (such as the television-film *Amra* I described at the start of this chapter). This new visibility of an earlier progressive trend overlaps with the reworking of other local legacies of progressive aesthetics.

Of these, two secular traditions are noteworthy. The Marxist People's Theatre (IPTA) movement of late-colonial and early-independent Bengal/India was inspired, on the one hand, by such transnational aesthetical movements as the European Anti-Fascist Progressive Writers' Union, German agit-prop, Workers' Theatres in Britain and the US, Soviet Shock Troupes (1920s and 1930s)[86] and, on the other, by the anti-imperialist drama of Bengali writers like Tagore and Michael Madhusudhan Dutt as well as by religious folk traditions. Driven by a radical self-conscious pragmatism, IPTA-allied multi-genre dramaturges, performers (Bijan Bhattacharya, Utpal Dutt, Shobha Sen), and filmmakers (Mrinal Sen, Nemai Ghosh, Ritwik Ghatak)[87] sought to 'excavate' the past and the present from the 'viewpoint of the subaltern populace'.[88] No doubt, the ties between the intellectual and the populace were at times less than integral (the latter being reduced, once in a while, to a homogenous category in the bourgeois imagination). While overlapping with this Marxist aesthetic centring collective autonomy and subaltern rights, another Bengali aesthetic charts a somewhat distinct path. This is the critical humanist tradition centring individual autonomy. Its path winds circuitously through tentative explorations of the bourgeois individual and the autonomous woman vis-à-vis orthodoxies in popular Bengali cinema of the 1920s through 1950s[89] into more obviously critical routes. They include feminist theatre and dance drama, such as the work of IPTA performers Tripti Mitra and daughter Saoli as well as of the mother-daughter dance team Manjusri Chaki-Sircar and Ranjabati Sircar. They also encompass art cinema's reflexive explorations of the ethical individual. Works by such filmmakers as Satyajit Ray, Aparna Sen, Rituparno Ghosh, and Mrinal Sen himself[90] are noteworthy.

In the next chapter, I look at a few of the latter. For the moment, I consider how dreams of consensus about gender and class do arise in popular-commercial Bengali media notwithstanding these seemingly progressive trends in society and aesthetics. New illiberal/liberal canons of feminine autonomy position the woman within the primary female dignity/labour of nurturing patriarchal domesticity, and in ways that also atomize and stratify women. Therein, the marginal remain so or become even more marginal[91] as systems of 'economic dependence [become] a non-negotiable or even non-debatable topic'.[92] Ideas about autonomous development—women's, men's, the family's, and society's—are played out and played off against each other in a way that yields a new coherent group identity. This identity inflects to social conflict at the same time that it 'manages' and suppresses[93] the anxieties of conflict by overwriting critique in pleasurable ways.

The satellite channel ETV Bangla recently aired a telefilm dramatizing and intertextually updating Rabindranath Tagore's well-known feminist poem *Sadharan Meye* (1928; see my discussion of the poem in Chapter 2). Presented on Tagore's death anniversary (August 2006), and advertising Tagore himself as the 'storywriter', the film was described on the channel's website as yet another tale of a 'dark-complexioned' Bengali girl 'with no hidden talents' losing 'the battle with fate' in the 'marriage market'. The blurb added that Bengali society had not 'changed much' since Tagore's time.[94] The film itself revolves around one evening when the protagonist Deepa, dolled up in finery, is being shown to yet another prospective groom and family and encountering one more rejection. The typical Indian filmic device of the flashback, used to convey inexorable life patterns, is here employed to link this evening's experience to a lifetime of humiliation heaped upon the unattractive and under-achieving girl. We see that Deepa has failed to meet the standards enabling bourgeois Indian women's upward mobility in all such salient respects as fashionable looks, academic achievements, and extra-curricular activities. Unlike her literary forbear, Deepa however does not concede to underprivilege. Instead she strikes out on an autonomous life path with an independent income. Directed by popular feminist telefilmmaker Anindita Sarbadhikari, whose claim to fame includes films on sex work and workers' rights, *Sadharan Meye* was cast as a part of the anti-domestic-violence movement and co-sponsored by the feminist radio station, *Amar* (Mine).

The film itself is made in the common commercial Indian cinema genre of the humanist family melodrama. It pits the individual against coercive social systems, interiorizes and personalizes social conflicts (of gender and class),[95] and 'displaces' emotions and psychic tensions onto expressive codes[96] like sound and music (Tagore songs and recitation), lighting and space use, and mythic spectacles of good and bad. As a melodrama, the work is poised between social subversion and escapism,[97] showing on the one hand how a woman without capital 'confronts' and critically corrects an over-capitalized male dominant world and, on the other, how she accepts status-based femaleness.[98] However, the latter supersedes in the overall meaning. The film demonstrates how easily televised communication turns into canonical signification[99] serving global urban interests. Note however, that here I am viewing the telefilm vis-à-vis its medium and its techniques of networking. Robust studies, such as Purnima Mankekar's, analyse the complex ways in which television programmes are received and understood within everyday Indian social conditions.[100] The discussion of reception lies outside the scope of my study.

To return to the issue at hand, the telefilm *Sadharan Meye* develops the Tagore poem's utilitarian critique of the privileged (high-caste) Bengali woman's confinement in the physical conditions of patriarchal domesticity, as well as in its norms. It reads into a new historical context and genre of John Stuart Mill's well-known formulations that each individual human being has the right to fulfil volition, desire, and impulse in making his/her life plan and that social systems which divide spheres of space and opportunity in ways crushing individuality are despotic.[101] On screen, the notion that division and confinement are despotic towards autonomy is adapted to the melodramatic expression of claustrophobic trauma.

On the one hand, protagonist Deepa's body and the spaces it/ she occupies are shown to be closing in upon her. This useless and unprofitable body comes to constitute a standpoint for critically exposing the sadomasochism of a patriarchal capitalist world in which only commodification matters in satisfying an individual's desires and needs. Medium and long shots of Deepa in company have the effect of shocking spectators out of their complacent expectations about human community and instead evoking self-critical sympathy. These shots portray either that the 'ugly' girl's presence is being insulted, ignored (by peers), or lamented (by family members), or that she internalizes this dehumanization by abjecting herself to the point of becoming suicidal. The film connects the commodification of 'whitened' feminine beauty in present-day Bengal with earlier genealogies such as misogyny among Brahmin and Aryan bias in the Hindu elite under European rule. Drawing more intertextual links with Tagore's social criticism, for example, a quite memorable portrayal of traumatized corporeality shows young Deepa watching her classmates rehearse Tagore's dance drama *Chandalika* for a school performance. As she views violent caste-racism being hurled at the outcaste/untouchable chandal girl—performed through Tagore's well-known song 'Do not, do not touch her'—a visceral loathing affectively contours Deepa's own body, delineating it as yet another outcaste's in a new Indian time and space and therewith connecting native sociobiology with a new global racism. That the trauma of being confined in an unsaleable body and mind is crushing Deepa's human core of wants and impulses is effectively emphasized, on the other hand, through the *melos* of Tagore songs. Especially powerful is the use in this context of another song from *Chandalika* expressing the individual's inseparable corporeal and intellectual trishna (thirsts) and inclinations (see Chapter 2 for a discussion of the song).

The film places its portrayal of social despotism within an unevenly restructured neighbourhood of the rapidly globalizing city of Kolkata. Along the lines of Marxist and critical humanist cinema's habitual emphasis on the 'charged environment'[102] of the postcolonial metropolis, *Sadharan Meye* exposes the particularities of bourgeois inequality in the global urban landscape. It depicts how lower-end and nouvelle bourgeoisie jostle in the same locations (neighbourhood, schools, colleges), rupturing neighbourliness and peer bonding. Deepa's best role model and worst insulter is no longer the self-seeking foreign woman of Tagore's *Sadharan Meye* (see my discussion of the poem in Chapter 2). She is the Indian girl in step with global progress, the supermodel-like and overachieving Ananya (played by tele-screen sex idol June Malia) living in an upscale ownership-flat-complex next door to Deepa's run-down and primitive rental apartment. Ananya's privileged status—in looks, intellect, and location—is what snatches away Deepa's only promising marriage prospect, a multinational executive whose traditional father had wanted family-oriented Deepa as his daughter-in-law. In this way, the film plays out the pathos of gender disparities brought about by urban development. The point is that polarities of masculine and feminine ability erupt within urban homes and neighbourhoods as super-achiever young men and women (Ananya and her executive spouse, for example) keep in step with global progress and leave behind them the backwardly under-achievers and elders (Deepa and executive Sandip's elderly father, in this instance). As such the film interestingly recontextualizes and gives new meaning to Tagore's critique of capitalism in *Sadharan Meye*, emphasizing that in the tracks of capital an individual's worth is determined solely by her resources for material advancement. Indeed, it gives a more democratic turn to Tagore's high-caste bhadralok politics by exposing the conditions of inequality amidst the bhadralok elite of today.

Beyond using the standpoint of the victim for social critique, the film revivifies in the cinematic medium Tagore's transcultural explorations, in the poem and elsewhere, of material and philosophical individuality. For one, the camera cuts back and forth between Deepa's shamed body and her face framed in close-ups as she writes or sings, showing how the protagonist reflexively reclaims the agency to self-create and self-position herself in relations. She is portrayed to be writing in seclusion (exactly like the protagonist of Tagore's poem) in order to vent to an imaginary lover her trauma as well as her hopes. In the vein of parallel feminist cinema, such as Aparna Sen's *Parama* (see Chapter 4), the film invokes the classic Romantic-feminist motifs of privacy and being in touch with one's inmost inclinations and desires. It depicts a space of Deepa's own and the 'un-violated' pen with which she 'give[s] birth to [her] suppressed or repressed thoughts' on a 'virginal ... empty page'.[103] At these moments, an erotic feminist camera frames and caresses the woman's eyes, lips, and breast-line—teaching the spectator to be intimate with the voluptuousness of the woman's desiring body. The film closes with Deepa once again privately reciting Tagore's poem *Sadharan Meye,* and effectively reworking its hopeless ending. The telefilm closes upon a Deepa resolved to market her one talent by applying for a professional cooking job at a 'home-delivery' kitchen.

Furthermore, and importantly for the purposes of this study, a 'sonorous envelope'[104] marks Deepa's mystical inwardness as well as its transcultural scope. The one song to which she gives herself fully recalls into the contemporary consumerist context Tagore's Vaishnava-mysticism-inflected critique of what he had once attacked as the capitalist civilization's '[visual] attractions'. On screen, Deepa's song-performance is pitted against the attractive sounds and images of patriarchal domesticity that include a voice-over from the widely popular E-tele-magazine *Prothoma* (the first) targeting success-oriented bourgeois Bengali women (it features makeovers, high-end home décor, as well as tips for advancing in the professional world). Presenting a counterpoint, the song-lyric Deepa lipsynchs asserts the radical autonomy of the one who effaces the instrumental reasoning of her worldly eye/I and finds inmost sight at that moment when there is no light around to illuminate her gaze ('*Chokher aloye dekhecchilem chokher bahire/Antare tai dekhbo jakhan alo nahire*').

The complexity of this film is that while it stakes a subversive and transcultural feminist perspective in its portrayal of globalizing urban India, at the same time, it escapes from the onus of subversion by *flexibly adapting* transcultural critique to the pleasures of a multiculturalism serving the neoliberal consensus about development. In the imperialist-libertarian way, it segregates opportunities by type and status. It promises autonomy to multiple subjects at the same time that it stacks women and men within a patriarchal cityscape which stratifies the dignities of work and mobility according to gender as well as social rank. Indeed the film's rejection of the Tagore poem's gloomy affirmation of the woman's hopelessness in favour of a democratic optimism—that a free country and an expanding meritocratic market offer unprecedented opportunities to hitherto marginalized women[105]—proves to be little other than a flexible adaptation to the needs of an *un*democratic meritocracy. For exactly in portraying the protagonist's entrance into the workforce in the capacity of a cook in a *home*-delivery kitchen (distinct from a public restaurant), the adaptation erases the gender dialectic in the Tagore work. Instead, it reinforces a peculiarly *flexible yet filiative hierarchy of choices* speaking to urban redevelopment and market expansion in Kolkata.

First, the narrative confirms a temporal division of labour by implying that under-achieving lower-middle-class women can earn a livelihood only through commodifying women's care work. In depicting such positions as these—characteristically underpaid, labour-intensive, and unpromotable—as 'opportunities' for underprivileged women, this telefilm and similar media portrayals perpetuate the perception that women's (physical) care work is devalued in a world system wherein efficient mental/knowledge-work gathers capital. This market fetishism of feminine reproductive labour reappears in other tele-feminist images as well. For example, another film by Anindita Sarbadhikari—aired on ETV soon after *Sadharan Meye* in the same 'soft-art' Sunday afternoon telefilm series—portrays (and bemoans in voyeuristic pity) how attractive lower-middle-class women are selling sexual labour by becoming call girls in prospering Kolkata. Second, the telefilm makes the woman's seemingly autonomous and merit-based choice of a profession signify with father figures' choices and assumptions. Deepa comes to realize her only saleable talent because her father applauds her labour-intensive traditional preparation of *mochar ghanto* (banana-flower-curry), a dish that has grown rare and exotic in nuclear middle-class households as more women run against the double-day clock whereas the men still largely refrain from assisting in the daily grind. In fact, the 'home-delivery' professional kitchen where Deepa seeks employment is a type of professional service sprouting all over the metropolis. This new service sector fills the gap in traditional homemaking practices opened by middle-class women's entry into the workforce alongside the breakdown of extended family structures under the pressures of lucrative transregional and transnational mobility. In this regard, it is noteworthy that the one other man who is impressed with Deepa's Bengali culinary repertoire is the favourably-inclined prospective father-in-law.

An episode such as this manages and represses the prevalent social anxiety regarding the breakdown of the patriarchal/patrilineal family together with its ideas and practices of elder-care based on the seva work of family women. Hence the professionalization of elder-seva-work—by such authentic/surrogate daughters-in-law from underprivileged strata as Deepa—performs the crucial symbolic task of reaffirming Hindu patriarchal hierarchy. The implication here is that the woman's seeming autonomy depends on male support both financially (through the sale of cooking skills) and affectively (through the nurturance of patriarchs and providers). This striking canonical move, and one which diachronically reduces Tagore's work to the terms of neolibertarian patriarchy, is that the telefilm overwrites the poem's dialectical self-critique of masculine authorship (as discussed in Chapter 2). What out of Tagore's poem is aesthetically affirmed, on the other hand, is the familiar patriarchal nationalist binary of virtuous and profligate femininities. Whereas such configurations of domestic and public female sexualities had opposed and clashed with each other at their inception in the colonial era (as seen in Chapter 1), now their conflicts are resolved into a pleasing telos of stratification.

Heightening the melodramatic contrast between the good native woman and the bad foreign woman, which in the poem itself had been complicated by ironic male-self-critique, the televisual adaptation pits the globally equipped Ananya against the virtuous sari-clad and authentically Bengali girl Deepa. This contrast suggests that even though the neoliberal order of universal self-development enables both to be productively employed and potentially fulfilled in desires, it sexually divides the two women's forms of work and self-desire (or self-denial as the case may be). Whereas Deepa's seemingly autonomous choice upholds both the 'timeless' reproductive and self-giving obligations of national-patriarchal domesticity as well as the timely virtue of reproductive wage labour supporting market and (high-end) workforce expansion in Kolkata, Ananya's choices of competitive mobility and free consumption place her at the masculine end of the division of labour. In that the super-achiever and consumer Ananya models the appropriately autonomous wives and daughters of multinational executives in this fast-growing metropolis, however, her *reproductive* function melds with Deepa's and resolves the conflict. Moreover, that women are becoming divided in this way—as bonds between neighbours, friends, mothers and daughters begin to crumble in the tracks of global mobility—is both consumed as a spectacle of patriarchal pity and at the same time blamed upon the women.

In a recent work on globalization in South Asia, Achin Vanaik contemplates the conflicted nature of televisualization. He notes that in a country of low literacy such as India, television definitely 'personalizes' and democratizes politics to an unprecedented extent by sending out information to myriad people in their homes and in principle reneging control over their 'reception of the images'. At the same time, it dangerously weakens public debate.[106] Working along these lines, Bengali popular-commercial television is adjusting to the anxieties and pleasures of a context which not only registers major social change but has a political-aesthetical tradition of fervid debate about social hierarchies. It is attempting to play out current debates around gender and class in a way that promotes information which 'sell[s]commodities or generate[s] profits' while sidelining other information and viewpoints that could hinder profitable trends (such as challenges to patriarchy and class divisions).[107] The film in question falls in the train of the innumerable femininity-centred Bengali television programmes which role-model women as at once 'consumer, product, and promoter'.[108]

The two womanly images in *Sadharan Meye*—apparently polarized yet reducible—are sutured to the two currently profitable visual canons of bourgeois Bengali womanhood: the modern mobile woman appears as either the global-fashion-clad supermodel (consuming sexy tops and designer jeans) or the stylishly groomed and efficient working homemaker (promoting makeovers, seasonal fashions, exorbitant home décor); the nativist homemaker/mother, on the other hand, appears in traditional sari-clad and bejewelled splendour (promoting the growing market for traditional garments and embroidery, ornamental work, culinary art, children's clothes). Like in the film itself, these idealizations of femininity are polarized yet reducible. Together, they propagate a consensus about how the dignity of middle-class women's economic development (as productive workers and as consumers) can reconcile with the dignity women command as nurturers of the patriarchal home and community.

Moreover, there is a consistency in mass-feminist Bengali visual culture today about how the 'ekushe nari' or new women of the millennium are able to resolve the contradictory demands globalizing Indian society places upon them. The consensus that seemingly pleases all is that they are able to do so only if they command the heroic versatility of (Aryan) Hindu woman as the aparajita homemaker and mother-goddess. Across televised imaginations—whether in telefilms, drama serials, self-help shows, game shows, or advertisements (notably of religious as well as secular national events such as the Durga Puja and the Indian Independence Day)—this mystique of the heroic millennial nari comes to be mortified into the Hindu.

The aesthetic cult of the Hindu mother and wife as a goddess figure is of course a trope at least as old as the inception of heterosexist nationalism in nineteenth-century India (as I discussed in Chapter 2). Throughout the early decades of nation-state politics as well, it was revived and reinflected in many ways by popular media. In Bengal the mother-goddess Durga as the domestic woman who at the same time is the 'furious'[109] unvanquished slayer of demoniacal adversity, has held centre stage as the national ideal of femininity. She has come to symbolize the dual force of motherhood—on one hand, the matriarch who fights against evil to restore order in the world, on the other, the 'tender and familial'[110] mother-figure of quotidian Bengal who periodically visits her natal home with her four children (during the annual Durga Puja celebrations).

Still, something is new about the mediatized neoliberal present. We saw in Chapter 2 that during the Independence struggle, the communalist Hindu image of femininity characteristically reaffirmed *illiberal* patriarchal idealism. On the other hand, it now sutures with and hegemonizes liberal and subaltern humanist imagery. These include women's social and sexual autonomy within and outside marriage; single and divorced motherhood; and the self-development of hitherto underprivileged people from the dalit (untouchable), tribal, and non-Hindu communities. The overriding characteristic of this multicultural imagery, however, is that it is consistently Hinduized. Note, for example, how the widely-consumed daily game show *Rojgere Ginni* (The Earning Housewife), also aired by ETV Bangla, surreptitiously enfolds its female viewing public in this communalist homogeneity. The show claims to be going into every corner of the region of West Bengal in order to embrace diverse women and families (urban and peri-urban, inter-caste, inter-creed, dual career, child-free, and so on). To these multiply-located women and families—including Bengali Christian families—it carries games that celebrate Hindu marital and fertility rituals hand-in-hand with women's reproductive home work and care work. No doubt radical Bengali aesthetic traditions (such as the critical humanist and the Leftist that I mentioned earlier) as well as official Indian secular agendas add an egalitarian colour to televisual media; ETV Bangla's newscasts about Hindu-Muslim amity resonating with the officially secular government channel Doordarshan, vindicate this trend. Nonetheless, consumptions of pleasure reclaim all such progressive traditions into the imagination of an India modelled on the patriarchal and heterosexual Hindu family. In a typically neoliberal configuration of communal empire, this family/nation is shown to be morally distinct from the temporalities of other racial and ethnic families—whether the global Western or the backward Muslim. The distinctive national temporality at the same time is eminently flexible in that it allows its model families to seize the commercial tide of opportunities and satisfactions.

It is not surprising, then, that Hindu imagery similarly should work its way into the contemporary Tagore canon of feminism. A telling case in point is a well-marketed video production by Atlantis Music, Kolkata, of Tagore's celebrated feminist dance drama, *Chitrangada* (2005; director and principal performer: Piyali Basu). Once again, at first glance, Piyali Basu's video adaptation appears to build upon ideas of feminist autonomy and masculine self-critique to be found in the Tagore work (see Chapter 2). Yet in the characteristic mass-feminist way, it reduces these ideas and pleasingly mortifies the woman's choice. She is morally obliged to choose according to the dictates of the patriarchal Hindu family, obliterating elements of gender debate that had surrounded the publication and revision of the work in its day.

This video version robustly develops such feminist strands of the play as the visionary strength of the woman leader and the intellectual and sexual self-development of women within the erotically charged circle of same-sex companions. Notable is the colourful choreography by Piyali Basu of the protagonist's self-realization of sexual/emotional desire within her same-sex support group of *sakhi*s and at a distance from her austere patriarchal upbringing. Spectacularizing 'the erotic component' involved in the coloured image,[111] the choreography of body movement and costuming depicts the *matrika* ('mothering') composition of women's dancing bodies. Signifying the collective gestation of a woman's sexually creative self, this composition has been made famous in the Indian dance scene by Manjusri Chaki-Sircar for one. Of the latter I will have more to say in Chapter 4. For the moment I wish to emphasize that Piyali Basu's feminine gestative formation evolves along a historiographic line strikingly at odds not only with Chaki-Sircar's, and with the performative implications of the Tagore text. As choreographed by Piyali Basu, the protagonist Chitrangada's sexuality is aroused only to be 'bestilled'[112] and channelled into a Hindu patriarchal marriage leading to the basic reproductive labour of biological motherhood (made sacred).

A clear demonstration of this Hindu canonical interpretation of the Tagore text appears at the close. Chitrangada's sakhis regroup, decked in the auspicious yellow of Hindu marriage rites, while the protagonist herself appears in their midst decked in the fertility-enhancing vermilion-red of weddings. Furthermore, this communalist Chitrangada drastically undercuts her (accurate) performance of the Tagore song about gender equality wherein the woman calls upon the man to see her as an equal companion rather than as a goddess on a pedestal or/and a servant. Directly after the song-performance she bows at the feet of her groom-to-be. This pose not only resonates with the Bengali Hindu wedding rite in which the bride stoops at the groom's feet to acknowledge the sacred role being taken on by him and his *bamsa* (patriline) of providing sustenance (*bhat*/rice) to her and her progeny-to-be. In being presented directly after her performative demand for equality, the pose implies a canonical reduction of the independent and desiring woman Chitrangada into a chaste and submissive patibrata as codified by the authoritative text on Hindu social hierarchy, the *Manusmriti*.[113] The conflict between these two views of womanhood is erased in a new coherent configuration of a feminist Hindu wife. The image entwines home-grown Hindu patriarchy with orthodox Victorian ideas absorbed through colonization.

Tellingly, this unequal alliance is blessed with the sacred promises of a prosperous home and an upper-caste virtuous progeny. The final full-screen image is of the three icons of Bengali Hindu femininity: Lakshmi, the Goddess of Hearth and Wealth; Saraswati, the Goddess of Virtuous Learning; and at the centre of all, Durga, the Mother Goddess. Overlapping with popular Hindu mythological imagery, pervading festival and calendar art as well as epical telefilms, this video in effect redomesticates Tagore's imagination of a woman leader within contemporary illiberal Hindutva nationalism and its fetish of the mother goddess. Written over is Tagore's effort in the dance drama itself and elsewhere to humanize myth and to reclaim the metaphysical in a way that challenges social hierarchies underlying religious mystique (see Chapter 2). As such, this video is one of the numerous mass-produced portrayals today which tellingly illustrate Rajeswari Sunder Rajan's prescient observation about the 'expansionist and adaptable' character of Hindu communalist politics—that it incorporates 'various "progressive" elements in the political interests of enlarging its appeal' to women and minorities at the same time that it reasserts 'the authority of majoritarian religious discourse'.[114]

Yet, do oppositional strands of communication and community surface today and what forms do they take? Might media activists approach ethics or conceptualize democracy at odds with global spectacles?

4

AGENCY UNDER NETWORKS

Belonging and Privacy in Feminist Visual Culture

The popular South Asian works presented in Chapter 3 demonstrate that even though today's liberal economies distribute promises of choice and opportunity more widely than ever before, a person's range of choices is curiously homogenized. Hand-in-hand with the transnational market and its empires of labour, communication networks persuade various people about what it means for each of them—as a person of a specific gender, race, creed, and social status—to succeed or to fail in life, to work with dignity or not, to remain static or become mobile, to belong to the national community, or be alienated. If possession and consumption rank high in people's conception of choice and reward, hardships also wear the disguise of choice for less privileged persons (notably underprivileged women). Since people's identities develop from their ways of processing cultural information about their relations with the world,[1] the information about choice provided today by *available* texts invites self-objectification and restrain transcultural critique. Pleasing visual images of opportune choice and appropriate self-development, in particular, erase alternative approaches.

Does this network of neohumanist mediations mean that the indigenous activist-intellectual cannot but refuse the humanist ethic of choice in favour, say, of a non-subjective ethic of self-surrender drawn from the indigenous past? Not necessarily. Thinkers who take on the responsibility to correct social inequalities cannot afford to settle only for embracing non-humanist values. Not only have non-subjective cultures systemically upheld sociobiological boundaries (of sexuality, property ownership, caste, skin colour), non-subjective frames of reference are inextricable today from orthodox modern revivals. Selected pre-modern values go hand-in-hand with instrumental and filiative self-images. In other words, the comparatively fluid non-subjective selves of precapitalist Indian society are unavailable today in their pure form[2]—that is, unmediated by some variety or another of modern self-reflexivity. The deployment of 'Hindu' values by communal and misogynist nationalists from the early twentieth century onward is our case in point. We have also seen in previous chapters that the sacrifice of women's bodies and needs for the collective good forms the core of such illiberal national moralities as these both in anti-colonial Indian nationalisms and elsewhere. Hence, feminist intellectuals on anti-colonial grounds find it particularly difficult to reject out of hand the Enlightenment ethics of personal choice and egalitarian belonging. This chapter will reveal that, under the practical conditions of contemporary capitalism, feminist activists face a twofold struggle. First, they must conceive how women could choose life-paths in a way unmediated by neoliberal patriarchal canons of feminine choice. And then, through their re-visions, they must break apart available beguiling yet mortified imagery of women's self-development such that the gendered contradictions beneath are exposed.

Feminists under Networks: The Indian Visual Perspective

To claim that today's financial and communication networks by and large are detrimental to underprivileged lives, however, would be to take a one-sided and politically regressive stance. Raymond Williams reminds us that social arrangements comprise not only 'power, property, and production', they encompass modes of communicating information (persuasion, learning, and exchange).[3] As the material arrangements of production and distribution shift, new communication technologies emerge to meet the practical demands of the altering political economic conditions.[4] At present, communication channels (such as interactive television, mobile phones, the internet, as well as the traditional newspaper or magazine) are proliferating in India together with the access to opportunities of a widening spectrum of previously underprivileged people. This increasingly democratic distribution of communicative and financial resources has indeed enabled the emergence of 'organic'[5] intellectuals from different social locations in independent India and also in diasporas.

Notions of women's autonomy born of the male-dominant anti-colonial struggle were determined by patriarchal reformist agendas or, at the least, tied to male self-critique (as in Tagore's instance). By contrast today's feminists envision women's agency organically, that is, with reference to the 'practical' activities[6] of various women's lives.[7] Such feminist artists as Manjusri Chaki-Sircar and Aparna Sen try to think critically in reference to the demands of the core social framework in and through which Indian femininities have been defined since the inception of anti-colonial modernity—the bourgeois home and authentic-Indian domestic work. Both thinkers depict feminist protagonists as challenging key assumptions of patriarchal capitalist femininities through reconfiguring the woman's home in relation to the world, women's nurturing labour in relation to wage labour, and the personal female body in relation to the social body. Availing of linkages across social and geographic borders, bourgeois intellectuals such as Chaki-Sircar also attempt to learn in solidarity with marginalized women activists about how to think themselves 'out of colonization'[8] by ideas and rewards.

Despite the fact that transnational linkages have brought about many such democratic changes, lives within these networks are bound to present their own organic difficulties to those who are struggling to become activist-intellectuals, that is, to learn from the practical situations on hand of ways to conceptualize their world and also to modify and improve it. The particular problem facing feminist activists today is that notions of agency that are at odds with prevalent liberal capitalist terms of self-help and free choice appear to command no resources for intervening in and changing historical trends, whether pragmatic or textual. In a world where the dominant notions of freedom are beguilingly visualized as ideal self-images, which encourage narcissistic subject positions, some of the toughest struggles are to be found in the work of visually expressive feminist thinkers. And so are some of the more prescient possibilities for alternative autonomy. The struggle for visual autonomy, in my view, centres around the sutured gaze.

I briefly suggested in Chapter 3 that in our visually dominated economy, agreements are brought about between contradictory images and ideas through a suturing process. In this discussion the 'suture' or 'tutor-code' (as Daniel Dayan calls it)[9] should be understood both as a visual practice and also as a metaphor for an economy of meanings. The economical logic wants to resolve 'multiaccentual'[10] conflicts both in the texts and between texts and contexts. Within the scope of conventional narrative cinematography and continuity editing, sutures comprise a succession of shots in which the first makes spectators conscious that they are watching framed images, while the 'reverse' shot sutures or meaningfully closes and unifies the 'hole opened in the spectator's imaginary relationship with the filmic field....'[11] The suture is a technique for inculcating in the viewer a sense of 'unity and continuity' of self-conception.[12] The previous chapter discussed how Indian popular global/local media links are suturing spectators' desires to dominant ideals. These media include cinema, television, commercial print, as well as corporeal performances including fashion modelling. We are incessantly exposed to images of idea and value that drive us to gaze back and reread ourselves in relation to and mediate our judgements through dominant conceptions (and accompanying rewards).

This chapter explores different ways that feminist visual/performative texts are attempting to break out from this specular gaze upon women's autonomy, and from the supporting organization of sutures. Instead, they try to open the spectation to contradictory and competing images of gendered belonging and agency. I demonstrate that while this struggle occurs in different eras of woman-centred feminist art in Bengal, it grows comparatively complex in works that are organically bound to the new liberal feminist practices under contemporary marketization. To this end, I juxtapose below the performance art of Manjusri Chaki-Sircar and Ranjabati Sircar with the cinema of Aparna Sen. The latter has been entrenched in the structure of popular Bengali visuality and attuned to its altering trends.

An Un-sutured Feminism: Corporeal belonging and the Nurturance of Autonomy

Manjusri Chaki-Sircar's acclaimed dance drama *Tomari Matir Kanya* (Daughter of your Soil) was first presented in the East-West Dance

Encounter in 1985, casting her daughter and collaborator Ranjabati Sircar in the title role. This year also saw the return of another acclaimed feminist dancer, the Bharat Natyam innovator Chandralekha, to an Indian stage that appeared ready for critical choreography. In contrast to Chandralekha's early training in the regimen of the Bharat Natyam, as this dance form had been reconfigured through the nationalist movements of revivalism and anti-nautch reform,[13] Manjusri Chaki's background embraced an eclectic variety of dance forms as well as choreographic thought. Having dwelled not only in India but in Nigeria and the US, she had trained rigorously in the Bharat Natyam form and also in Manipuri folk dance, as well as in African and Sri Lankan folk dances. The two core concepts of her *Navanritya* or New Dance choreography—that is, of her thoughtful process of composing bodily movement in physical space[14]—are a 'chemical synthesis' of differing performance artistry and continual 'innovation'. Each composition is to process into a new synthesis of corporeal movement and meaning such bodily practices as classical and semi-classical dance forms, folk dance forms, and martial arts, as well as daily gestures.[15]

By her own testimony, Manjusri Chaki-Sircar had been inspired in her innovative combination of cosmopolitanism and quotidian practice within bodily thinking by Rabindranath Tagore's dance drama legacy. Along Tagore's lines she was embracing, on the one hand, myriad folk arts that were intimately related to the 'functions of daily life' as well as adaptable to alterations in 'physio-geographical ... and social environment' through new experimentation in form.[16] On the other, she was developing Tagore's challenge to the objectification of the female dancing body in the male eye. She wanted to build on the way these dramas depict women in their 'full individuality'[17]—as 'self-respecting, self-reliant, and sensuous human beings'—rather than in the roles of nayikas[18] whose sexuality is made available for male pleasure in classical Indian dance and Vaishnava poetry. Since at the same time Manjusri and Ranjabati were working outside both the nationalist canon of the *Rabindrik* or Tagorean dance (and its sanitized presentations in the post-Tagore eras) and the neo-Orientalist canon of the Uday Shankar school of choreography, also entrenched in Kolkata,[19] this enabled their radical innovations.

Tomari Matir Kanya combines Tagore's male-ascetic-centered dance drama (1936) with his earlier prose play (1933) which, as we saw earlier, emphasizes woman-to-woman and mother-daughter dialogues. The Sircars develop with remarkable prescience one critical aspect of the Tagore works—the (imperfect) challenge they level at the mind/body split in liberal thought, that is, at the separatist mentality that has propelled the control of supposedly irrational peoples and bodies since the inception of imperialist modernity. Manjusri and Ranjabati perform the inalienable corporeal dignity of disenfranchised women's desires and labours. Manjusri's choreography elaborates the untouchable chandal woman's sensual desire while also emphasizing how one individual's psycho-sexual urges flower within her same-sex support group. This embedding of the individual in women's collective process of self-actualization is framed by the chandal community's history of struggle against the exploitations of their bodies and their work. Manjusri dialectically interweaves this humanist relationship of an autonomous self with community into the pre-modern Hindu conception of 'dividual' personhood,[20] which assumes that the person is both psychologically and biologically open to nature and the cosmos. Her transcultural choreography seeks to respond to social change with the kind of immediacy Kapila Vatsyayan detects in everyday forms of folk arts.[21] Bodily practices of openness and fluidity indigenous to village art displace the self-interest-driven individual of liberal capitalism at the time when these practices adapt the Enlightenment ethic of social justice. Choreography and narrative come together to challenge the biological bias ingrained in the pre-modern Hindu assumption of psychosexual openness (the bias that women's and low-caste people's personhoods are more open and sexually available than the high-caste males). Overall, the transcultural feminist performance of autonomy gestures at a caste-and-class-less Indian future.

In the video production of *Tomari Matir Kanya* I watched,[22] Ranjabati performs this transcultural critique of caste and class patriarchies through an aesthetic of movements mingling bodily self-creativity with 'responsiveness' to other bodies and 'alongside' them.[23] Her realization of desire, following her encounter with the Buddhist ascetic, is choreographed to vigorously express the synergy of sexual with intellectual. This is implied by Tagore's song on the chandal girl's *notun janma* (new birth) into a humanity replete with physical wants and trishna (thirsts) (see Chapter 2 for my discussion of the original Tagore works). While Ranjabati creates the fluidity of her sexual self through what Luce Irigaray would describe as a plural expression of sexuality[24]— replete with deep back arches and combined hand-breast-movements— she also reflexively interjects her anticipation of intellectual intimacy with the monk through joyful enactments of imagined companionate conversations. Pushing further against the potentially imperial liberal notion that the mind is an internally coherent rational entity, sovereign over matter and body, Manjusri's composition reorganizes corporeal and dramaturgic semiotics to portray interiority as a social process. In a memorable performance of community-facing inwardness, Ranjabati as the chandal girl moves as both an autonomous body and a desiring entity. She performs alongside and amidst companionate and compassionate bodies, opening herself to nurturance and protection. While she vents her inner agonies and inclinations through her performance in the illuminated front of the stage—literally and metaphorically spotlighted as a private psychological space—three of her sakhis or companion-women co-perform her psychological condition in silhouette at the back. The composite performance underscores not only that inwardness is an embodied process, which can be fluidly partaken by a supportive (same-sex) community, but that the individual woman's subjective suffering is grounded in the oppressed collective's history of struggle.

The scene is one of a sequence extending and recontextualizing the socioeconomic implications of Tagore's portrayal of the struggles of low-caste peasant women in his two versions of *Chandalika*. The sequence powerfully elaborates Tagore's critique of how outcaste peasant women's bodies and labours are dehumanized and put to instrumental use in the service of the leisured upper castes. And not only does it draw out the anti-capitalist vision of modernization found in this dance drama as well as several other Tagore works, including the allegorical play *Red Oleanders* (*Raktakarabi,* see Chapter 2), it also implies an extension of the critical vision into present conditions, specifically the sexual division of labour in post-Independent India's economy. For Manjusri's choreography and dramaturgy, as strongly embodied in performance, affirm that not only is women's agrarian work an essential component of a productive economy, the nurturing activities entwined in the everyday practices and rituals of village women are equally important for socioeconomic sustenance. Performances of the chandal women working together and struggling for survival are complemented by portrayals of leisurely companionate nurturing which can in no way be exchanged with clocked work and wage labour. Through accented responsive gestures of the dancers, we view the bodily rhythm of peasant women's quotidian practices of sustainable belonging—of how they play and laugh together, or sit around supporting and helping relax one another's fatigued bodies. By according non-instrumental dignity to both wage work and to the respite necessary for re-energizing workers, this choreography of self-sustenance reclaims both employment and nurturing as *productive* forms of socioeconomic activity. As such, the work rebuts the sexual division of productive-reproductive labour which not only is central to capitalist patriarchies but, as Chapter 3 has shown, especially informs the new canons of feminine autonomy in neoliberal India today.

Investing an inalienable dignity—as Kant puts it, an 'inner worth' which has no equivalent and cannot be exchanged[25]—in the feminine work of nurturing bodies and minds is integral to Manjusri's larger feminist project of reconceiving the home and domestic work against the grain of filiative capitalist categories. In fact, she powerfully rebuts the imperialist filiative order, as entwined in modern Indian caste prejudices. For she reimagines the family as a woman-centred site in which to practice and through which to universalize egalitarian relationships. *Tomari Matir Kanya* depicts the growth of a remarkably comradely mother-daughter relationship as it presents real-life mother and daughter Manjusri and Ranjabati 'following and framing each other'.[26] As a performer of motherliness she moves in affective synergy with the daughter's body, presenting fluidity of emotions and reasoning (Figure 1): the non-objectified compassion in a mother witnessing her daughter's agony of unrequited love blends into the non-psychological Sanskritic ethic of karuna as a self-reneging desire to bond with another.[27] This performance of mother-daughter synergy is at odds not only with Hindu mythological and everyday imaginations of family relationships[28]—which customarily present daughters as dowry burdens or at the least as pieces of property to be alienated through marriage into another patriline—but also with some Western feminist views. For example, Julia Kristeva's notion of motherly bonds as invariably compromised by 'the *consecrated* (religious or secular) representation of femininity'[29] conflicts with the Sircars' assertive performance of the uniqueness each of the mother and the daughter as well as the mutual nurturing of sexually and intellectually self-reliant individuals. This mutuality culminates in the staging of a collective birthing which comprises a dialectical *bricolage* of indigenous and liberal European notions of the self.

Low-caste priestesses (*bhairavi*), who include the biological mother, are depicted as performing two birthing rituals drawn from Hindu and Tantric iconography. The first is the matrika or birthing canal passage which turns the chandal girl into a sexually mature individual holding in her hand the *yoni* (vulva) symbol of the erotic Hindu goddess Kali (see Figure 2).[30] The second is the *sarpa-bandhan* or 'snake coil ... of [the]

Figure 1 Performing Family—A Mother-Daughter Bond
Courtesy: Avinash Pasricha, New Delhi

never-ending itinerary of life'[31] which, in turn, implies that this women's group is breeding and nurturing in the girl her potential for making her way with self-reliance through heterosexual social relations. This choreography of birthing, while it draws on the Brahminical Hindu anthropology of open and outflowing selves, retorts against the high-caste-male bias that corporeal openness is tantamount to sexual looseness. Humanizing the sexual openness of the ritual dancers by fully exposing their faces and lending dignity to each individual, *Tomari Matir Kanya* emphasizes their respective rational capacities to concentrate on the sexual ritual. As Figure 2 shows, both the priestesses themselves and their collectively birthed new chandal woman wear their hair neatly tied up so as to represent that their sexualities are self-developed and mature rather than out of control. In the final reckoning, the protagonist both autonomously leads her collective mothering by the priestesses,

Figure 2 Choreographing Desire—Matrika, the Birthing Canal
Courtesy: Avinash Pasricha, New Delhi

and she fluidly partakes of this collective energy of the fully individual women she has mobilized. Now, she is poised to work for an egalitarian heterosexual society precisely from the grounds of this low-status and non-filiative feminine family.

Note that this affirmation of the sexually open self poses a striking contrast to the dehumanized performance of the sexually open snake-women in the *Chandalika* choreographed by Vempati Chinna Satyam, a contemporary of Manjusri Chaki-Sircar's in the Indian dance scene. There the priestesses appear animal-like, their faces covered with the traditional Hindu sexual emblem of flowing hair (see Chapter 3, Figure 1). By contrast Manjusri's choreography as well as the full-bodied per-formance express the inalienable dignity of the women's sexual desires, going against the grain of masculine orders of pleasure. These orders include not only the nayika dance tradition, which Manjusri explicitly critiques, but also reproductions of the sexually available nayika in modern Indian scopophilic[32] cultures of performance and visuality (exemplified in Bollywood dance, for one). And even though Manjusri herself considered her vocabulary of *Navanritya* (modern dance) to be an outgrowth of the woman-empowering 'chemical synthesis' of Tagore's *Rabindrik* school of choreography, as noted above, her own aesthetic undoubtedly discards the nationalist anxiety we encounter in *Rabindrik* dance about sanitizing the exposed rhythmic bodies of dancing Indian women.[33] All in all, Manjusri Chaki-Sircar's *Tomari Matir Kanya* substantiates that cross-border encounters made possible especially in our time by translocal networks matter in this development of ethical autonomy.

This visionary interpretation of Tagore's *Chandalika* emerged at once from Manjusri Chaki-Sircar's varied life experiences and education as well as from her encounters with women activists in diverse historical locations. Raised in a liberal bourgeois Bengali family, Manjusri completed a doctorate in anthropology at Columbia University during the second wave of the women's movement in the US. As an ethnographer inspired by Western feminist ideas as well as by a groundswell of dalit mobilization in India, Manjusri also encountered Meitei rural women in Manipur and low-caste bhairavi priestesses in a Kali temple in Assam. Volosinov reminds us that an artist's choices—in matters of form, content, and their mutual interaction—are inflected by her/his 'living interrelations ... with the world'.[34] Manjusri's eclectic artistic choices stemmed, in my view, from her varied worldly interrelations. These encompassed, on the one hand, her experiences with organic female intellectuals in diverse local and translocal, rural and urban places and, on the other, her personal endeavour to build a liberal Hindu home of conjugal companionship and comradely mother-daughter relations.[35] Yet a question remains: in what way does a feminist vision as cohesive as the Sircars' position itself vis-à-vis the dominant visual economy? In my exploration of empires old and new, I am compelled to consider to what extent the choreographic aesthetic in question is adaptable to ongoing postcolonial engagement with a world constantly being *reordered* by empire.[36] As Argentinian postcolonial dance scholar Marta Savigliano puts it, a continual performative engagement is necessary with gendered 'objects of collective desire'.[37] We have seen that *Tomari Matir Kanya* is well poised to engage with the sexual divisions of labour under racialized masculine capital; my question regards visual structures of objectification and distribution. Under the spate of financial reforms, mainstream visual culture of the 1980s was promoting middle-class consumerism in India, at the same time that it identified the prospering modern middle-classes as elite Hindu.[38] While government-sponsored television incorporated women's advancement into its portrayals of national development, the roles played therein by Hindu women and men in leading and unifying the community remained paramount; no doubt the various secessionist movements in Punjab, Kashmir, and the Northeast were fuelling a defensive communalism at this historical moment.[39] One choreographic choice exemplifies the position the Sircars' expressive philosophy takes with regard to the visual economy of its time. In diametric contrast to such canonical *Chandalika* productions as Vempati's which tend, in a Hindu communalist vein, to glorify the saffron-robed ascetic of the Tagore drama, the original stage production of *Tomari Matir Kanya* altogether refrains from embodying the ascetic man. Instead, his role is visually choreographed with flickering lights.[40] It is arguable that Manjusri's refusal to visualize the saffron-clad celibate man constitutes an aesthetic choice referring to its context. In choosing not to personify the ascetic on stage, Manjusri effectively arrests any inclination her spectators might have of linking her work with the Hindu imagery of saffron-clad virile celibacy that had begun to populate commercial media and government-sponsored television by the mid-1980s.[41] This choice, in other words, blocks the possible suture, and seeming agreement, of her liberal indigenous Hindu imagery (the saffron robes, the Tantric rituals) with the Hindutva nationalism and misogyny germinating in the popular gaze. This blockage of the sutured gaze—the refusal to cross the popular media boundary and engage with its way of seeing—creates a feminist spectatorship at odds with the prevailing scopic drive. Yet we cannot but question the longevity of this ideal spectatorship as we note that the video production of *Tomari Matir Kanya*—precisely by the government television channel Doordarshan (1991), in line with its agenda of uplifting women's conditions—reinserted the male ascetic as in more conventional interpretations of the dance drama. It is also indisputable that this televisual version was distributing the work and its feminist message to a far wider viewing public than ever before.

Following the logic of Manjusri Chaki-Sircar's visual politics of blockage, current Director of Dancers' Guild, Jonaki Sarkar, noted to me in a personal conversation that their project is to produce *chintasheel nritya* (thought-provoking dance) rather than *binodon nritya* (dance-for-pleasing-another). Yet it seems to me that a refusal such as this to engage with the pleasing logic of objectification—which pervades our visual times—limits our ability to challenge an issue organic to neoliberalism. We fail to engage with the issue that our best efforts to think and to act autonomously have a way of re-entering dominant networks of imagery and resource. By reinserting the ascetic into its video, Doordarshan television's multiculturalism capitalizes on unifying the spectator's gaze with the misogynist Hindu nationalist's fetish for the saffron-clothed male. Yet the Sircars' approach partially idealizes visual autonomy by failing to address this problem of the financial hold popular visual capital exerts over the means of all artistic productions. Therewith, it curtails the interventionist potential of an otherwise prescient feminist aesthetic.

For our purposes, it is useful to juxtapose the Sircars' anti-mediated feminism with another which is more organically invested in the visual networks of our new liberal present. Our case in point is the intellectual trajectory of Aparna Sen, a foremost nayika/matinée idol of the Bengali screen and also the founding editor of the widest circulating popular Bengali women's magazine, *Sananda*. In the line of Manjusri Chaki-Sircar's humanist imagination, Aparna Sen also conceives Indian women's autonomy as a transcultural process. At the same time, her films wrestle with a more basic question. Aparna Sen had once said that her work is about the 'private spaces of individuals'.[42] It seems to me that in her recent works privacy and belonging work together as concept-metaphor in the imagining world. As proposed by John Stuart Mill's philosophy of individual liberty, privacy constitutes a person's freedom to self-develop intellectually and morally without interference from authoritative structures. However, this private self-growth is achievable not in isolation but rather through participatory association and understanding—a free 'discussion' of one's experiences within the larger social context is what allows for rectifying 'mistakes',[43] one's own and others'. Aparna Sen's cinema explores the notion of privacy in tandem with ideas of nurturing and of understanding. She is struggling to visualize a space wherein people self-develop such that they avoid interference by dominant images of the pleasing, the good, and the safe life. In one sense, Aparna Sen's approach to liberal media politics converges with poststructuralist feminism. Her work interrogates 'gendered' power, questioning the 'subordination' of women and the feminized 'in all of [their] mani-festations'.[44] In another sense, Aparna Sen is a critical feminist indigenous to Bengal and India. Her films attempt to correct dominant sight and knowledge by drawing upon bourgeois Bengali women's daily habits and their philosophical bases.

Autonomy in the Eye of the Camera: Networks and Private Belonging

Hailed in commercial Indian media as 'an icon for the spirited, intelligent Bengali Eve'—at '50 plus [still the] strikingly beautiful [and] … somewhat regal' director and mother[45]—the public figure of Aparna Sen is fetishized today as a popular ideal of the Indian feminist. She is visible both as the liberal nayika who flaunts and utilizes her modern body and mind, and as the tacitly conformist mother who publicly exemplifies her filiative brata of breeding her own bourgeois feminist progeny and that of the liberal patriarchal nation. It is not that Sen herself is averse to this form of self-utilization for advancement, as her characteristically neoliberal self-help advice to women demonstrates in print and on screen.[46] As noted in the Introduction, Aparna Sen's life as a visual media figure straddles divergent genres and philosophies of aesthetic production.

Aparna Sen began her career as a child star in Satyajit Ray's *Teen Kanya* (*Three Daughters*, 1961), her father the film critic and filmmaker Chidananda Dasgupta's co-founder of the Calcutta Film Society. Then she was recruited by commercial Bengali cinema and moulded into a star persona in box office hits (in the 1960s through early 1990s).[47] While involved with the divergent parallel and popular cinematic traditions, Aparna Sen chose to learn the art of performance from a foremost dramaturge of the Marxist People's Theatre/IPTA movement, Utpal Dutt. It is arguable that these various visual and performative approaches have been intertextual with the feminist experimentation in Aparna Sen's own films. As briefly noted in the Introduction, we find in her works three strands of indigenous visual tradition, in addition to influences of Hollywood melodrama that percolate through popular Bengali cinema as well as auteur films (such as the works of Satyajit Ray, Mrinal Sen, and Tapan Sinha).

In my view, one strand clearly intertextual with Aparna Sen's works is the urban cinema of Satyajit Ray. This is his series of productions exploring women's and marginal men's autonomous inclinations and merits, against and despite narcissistic[48] complicities with the masculine and racialized discourses of Bengali urban associative life (in the bourgeois family, at work, in leisure and on vacation, and so forth). Noteworthy in this regard are Ray's *Mahanagar, Aranyer Din Ratri, Pratidwandi, Shakha Proshakha* among others. A less obvious inter-text is the postrevolutionary/postmodern Marxist critique of bourgeois relations in the late works of IPTA filmmakers. One case in point is a family melodrama by Mrinal Sen such as *Ek Din Protidin* (released in 1979, a few years prior to Sen's first bourgeois family melodrama, *Parama)*, which parses how 'economic, social, and political conditions infiltrate and reconstitute familial relationships' and trigger '*individual* psychic traumas'.[49] Another remoter resonance is to be noted with Ritwik Ghatak's subversive specular critique of the bourgeois agent and the radical intellectual. Ghatak was criticizing how these 'colonised individual[s]' are caught within the grand myths of history[50] while being 'seduced' by the commodification of activist meaning (in such works as *Jukti Takko ar Gappo* and *Meghe Dhaka Tara,* for example).[51] Whereas Ghatak genders his visual subversion by portraying in *Meghe Dhaka Tara* how the woman as an individual is produced as a gendered object for the division of labour alike by 'social forces' and by the 'primordial images [presented by] ... mass arts',[52] Aparna Sen refuses to entirely let go of mass aesthetical femininities. Indeed, the third inter-text I detect in Aparna Sen's work comprises precisely the liberal representations of autonomous women in early post-Independence Bengali cinema,[53] as well as in visual productions of the contemporary transnationalizing economy (such as ETV's films *Amra* or *Sadharan Meye,* discussed in the previous chapter).

All in all, it seems that Aparna Sen's feminist critique of gendered filiations ought to be seen as working organically within a *post* postrevolutionary liberalizing Bengal and world. As amply discussed earlier, rapid transnationalization grants more and more people across social sectors democratic mobility and visibility and at the same time it masks or displaces oppressions and violations. Sen's portrayals take with pragmatic seriousness the social and economic rewards bourgeois Indian women gather from conforming to institutional images of self-development under the prevalent climate of opportunities. What her works also attempt is to push beyond. They seek to organically engage with the contradictions of masculine transnational imperialism by juxtaposing these pleasures women gather from conformity with their unpleasurable difficulties and oppressions *and also* with the general objectification of feminine homework and nurturing practices in the global economy. Aparna Sen has been cumulatively trying to develop what I see as a combination of illusionist cinema with meta-cinematic techniques that make spectators conscious of the camera's framing of objects and pleasures. Her technique of re-orientating the spectator's eye is well described by Gayatri Spivak's term 'counterfocalization'.[54] Building on Mieke Bal's notion of 'focalization' as 'the relation between the vision and that which is 'seen', Spivak suggests that a reader is 'provoked' to actively 'counterfocalize' and transact alternative ways to read when a narrative (self-consciously) 'fails' to produce a cohesive focalized reading.[55] This metaphor helps us to think about the moments when Sen's camerawork and imagery fail to cohere with (suture and make sense in terms of) available mortified images of women's autonomy and belonging. At these moments, spectators are provoked to 'enliven' alternative sensuous registers for the social activities they view in Sen's filmic text.

Aparna Sen's *Parama* (1986; in both a Bengali and a Hindi version) is the first of the series of films in which she has been attempting to conceive a notion of the autonomous Indian woman in relation to her home, to the larger community (nation, the world), and to her labours therein. It is a controversial tale of a repressed Bengali bourgeois housewife who has an extramarital affair with an NRI photographer, is exposed, and subsequently ostracized within her patriarchal home, and is driven by temporary insanity to attempt suicide. Cast in the genre of the woman-centred bourgeois family melodrama, the film mobilizes the malleable textuality of this cinematic form. On the one hand, melodrama has a binary proclivity to balance spectacles of 'female transgression' with 'capitulation' to patriarchal order[56] (accented in conservative productions such as the ETV film *Sadharan Meye* discussed in Chapter 3). On the other, melodrama's excessive elements of spectacle and narrative have the ironic potential to act 'subversively'[57] against the socio-moral order, giving rein to 'female desire'[58] as well as exposing the 'contradictions' of personal and familial living under capitalism.[59] Along these lines, *Parama* presents spectacular binary contrasts between social oppression and psychosexual transgression, suggesting that the bourgeois woman is able to free her body and mind by breaking out of her reproductive roles in patriarchal domesticity and seeking an independent life and income. Produced in a Kolkata beginning to creep into a new and more transnational phase of capitalism (in the late 1980s),[60] transgression is understood as the free rein of individual desires. In the filmmaker's utilitarian vocabulary, the work explores 'the physical and emotional wants of the Indian middle-class married woman and her quest to find her identity as an individual'.[61]

The film exhibits the backward abuse by patriarchs of the patibrata or virtuous and sexually submissive wife. Combining filiative values of the extended high-caste Hindu family with 'self-love' of the Adam Smith variety,[62] the high-level executive (Dipankar Dey) does not hesitate to effectively rape wife Parama when he himself is aroused (by no less than the prospect of a promotion in the multinational corporation at which he works). Moreover, domestic patriarchy is complemented by the public practices of the benevolent medical patriarch (Anil Chatterjee) treating Parama's mental illness. While this physician extends a ministering 'solidarity'[63] with Parama's supposed guilt and madness, he coaches her about retrieving her proper social '*jayega*' (place). That patriarchal Hindu rituals are interwoven in the physician's communalist science is spectacularly highlighted through the way Parama is tonsured (prior to a brain procedure)[64] and made to look like the conventional desexualized high-caste Hindu widow.[65] Against the images of patriarchal domination, the film pits Parama as the sexually heated and self-propelling modern nayika (appropriately casting the Bollywood superstar Rakhee) going on trysts with her lover out to the streets and into his bedroom.

All in all, the binary spectacles of Aparna Sen's *Parama* combine the scopophilia and exoticism of the popular Indian film and television melodramas—wherein 'subversion' is inextricable from 'escapism' into pleasures of objectification[66]—with the classic temporal binary of the imperial civilizing mission and its Western feminist counterparts. Confinement in the circuits—private and public—of the backward Hindu familial order is this Indian woman's 'problem that has no name'.[67] Out of this order, she steps into her desired autonomous status, yet with the pedagogic aid of a liberated and divorced working woman (tellingly spectacularized by the filmmaker herself). While Parama's autonomy subverts patriarchy, that is, it reinforces the Western progress myth in a way that classifies homemakers and family traditions as devalued categories. It should hardly be surprising that this work cohesively sutures with the popular feminist tele-dramas I discussed in Chapter 3, being the most frequently telecast of Sen's films today (especially on the sexually 'liberated' satellite television Bangla channels).

Nonetheless the film, in my view, is integral to Aparna Sen's cumulative effort to conceptualize an ethically indigenous feminist present, for, at the same time, *Parama* works through spectacles such that underlying contradictions are revealed and challenged. Spectators are made to approach spectacles reflexively, to become conscious that the camera (or visual art) has conflicted roles vis-à-vis women—it can be at once a mediator for scopophilia and a medium of woman's autonomous agency. The larger implication is that women must struggle for ethically un-interfered spaces of self-development from underneath multiple mediating structures of gaze and resources. They cannot easily avoid or forego these practical arrangements. Aparna Sen's experiments with the camera and femininities are grappling with the conundrums of self-spectacle another Bengali visual artist faced in the very early days of technological modernity, none other than Binodini Dasi (see Chapter 1).

The photographer in this film is the first in a line of professional men with cameras who appear in Aparna Sen's films, reminding spectators that subjects are invariably mediated and commodified by the medium of view. Revealing how local and neocolonial global 'structures of representation compete to produce the Indian woman',[68] the photographer from the *Life* magazine, Rahul (Mukul Sharma), acts like something of the imperial anthropologist. With detached expertise, he uses his camera to document the 'reality' and assign the meanings to a variety of alien bodies[69] that include at once the 'gorgeous' exposed breasts of aboriginal women and the 'traditional' exotic beauty of the Indian housewife Parama (as he himself names them). Implying the ubiquity of this professional's instrumental gaze, his camera also roves into Parama's erotic growth of desire for him, and violates the privacy of her body. Rahul splashes a sexually explicit close-up of Parama's nude bust and wet hair in *Life*, indiscriminately juxtaposing it to Parama as the patibrata performing fertility rituals, and unwittingly exposes their illicit affair to her husband (causing her abject humiliation). At the same time, spectators are alerted not to homogenize masculinity. For after all, this man with a camera is *other* than the husband representing the filiative order. Precisely this subversive element of contradictory manhoods is reinforced through subsequent images of camera-holding men—Srivastava in *Paromitar Ek Din* (*House of Memories*) and Raja Choudhury in *Mr. and Mrs. Iyer*. To these examples I return below. For the moment, we should note that in *Parama* the contradictions of maleness extend to Rahul's ethnographic camera. For it also presents to the woman a resource for self-reflexivity—for seeing her own actions and oppressions. For the resource to be put to use, however, the camera has to be loosened from the man's decisively instrumental grasp.

A telling representation of the camera, in my view, impels spectators to rethink its roles and find ways to read afresh. A medium shot shows a camera sitting upon a tripod facing Parama who lies satiated in bed with Rahul and happily hums a tune. While the camera's presence undoubtedly reminds us of voyeuristic intrusion, which sutures with similar pleasures in dominant Indian visual networks, at the same time it disturbs the focalized eye by the way it is displaced from the hand of an obvious voyeur at the significant moment when Parama shows a self-fulfilment of wants, and that with a momentarily *companionate* male partner.

This disjoining of the depiction of the individual woman's agency from imperial masculine visuality proves to be a central rather than tangential theme of this narrative, and indeed, of other films to come. The process extends to the various other ways in which the dignity of representation—of politically 'speaking for'/making visible[70]—is given by the ethnographic camera to Parama's daily life. It enables her growth of self-consciousness about the unique importance of her lived experience: of her personal taste (how she enjoys chewing on a morsel of food), of her body (that rituals such as wearing the fertility mark of *alta* on her feet can be an independent erotic act of self-adornment), of her talents and passions (how she cherishes playing the sitar and wandering about her natal home and its memories), and of the daily details that used to be part of the routine of her reproductive/nurturing feminine work (such as sewing and tallying everyday expenses). Further, at one significant moment of the narrative, we find Parama herself holding the camera and also deviating from Rahul's tutelage about how to see. While Rahul is trying to educate her in looking with an omniscient bird's-eye view at what he calls, with an Orientalist flair, the 'interesting' (exotic) city of Kolkata, Parama introspectively breaks into a snatch of her favourite poetry about 'my city' (*amar shahar*) to capture what she is viewing through the lens. This romantic outpouring about the 'her-ness' of city life—daily corporeal habitations, mobilities, trading—reveals just how differently from her anthropological male guide the woman is seeing the city and what living there freely could mean.

In a similar vein, we see the feminist camera offscreen disconnecting from sadomasochistic spectacles of patriarchal oppression and instead creating spaces wherein the woman can privately rethink herself in relation to the world and human bonds. How Parama claims her space of self-knowledge, disengaging from the physician's scientific sanity, is spectacularly captured by a full-screen close-up of the 'Big-Brother'-like physician's soundless moving lips cutting to Parama lovingly gazing at the plant on her window sill and finally remembering what it is called. Her reclamation of memory is also a healing of her splintered (mental/corporeal) autonomy because this plant is the kind that grew by the window-side as she was learning to play the sitar in her childhood, and whose name she had repressed, along with her other personal desires, beneath her filiative roles as daughter, wife, and mother. Thus, it is also around and through this plant (in practice and in metaphor) that Parama forges *non-filiative* same-sex family ties. Her teenage daughter finally understands in what ways Parama is claiming the dignity of individual worth, rather than conceding to a 'relative' sense of self-worth that is conditional to the roles she plays in her husband's family.[71]

Almost fourteen years later (1999), Aparna Sen revisits several tropes of autonomy and family presented in *Parama*. Under the influx of the new liberal capitalism in Bengal and India, her cinema significantly rethinks and retorts against the temporal binary of free versus tradition-confined women that had limited the transcultural feminist scope of the earlier film. While *Paromitar Ek Din* explores more radical possibilities of woman-centred personal and associative choice, against the grain of filiative dictates, at the same time it approaches autonomous choice with a more nuanced grasp on mediating structures. If the film follows *Parama* in thematizing the classic modernist dialectic between custom and the individual made famous by John Stuart Mill, it is subjecting 'custom' to heightened scrutiny. For it sees instrumental rationalities to flexibly encompass all patterns of behaviour that enforce public 'sanity' upon personal judgement: men's *and* women's domestic and worldly labour, traditionalism and progressive adaptability. Hence, this is also the first Sen film to press upon us the question of just *how private* the feminist's sanity can remain despite mediating structures of social comfort and visual pleasure.

Like several of Sen's films, *Paromitar Ek Din* begins self-reflexively from a life experience of the filmmaker. Aparna Sen had wanted to evaluate an apparently minor factual detail of contemporary bourgeois Bengali life—a divorced woman's experience of kin rituals:

The idea [of *Paromitar Ek Din*] first came to me when I went to a *shraddha* ceremony [that is, last rites] some six–seven years back. The former wife of the deceased was sitting in a corner; she looked completely bereft, she was crying. In the central area, the children of the dead person sat around the widow—the new wife. Because of the laws, the earlier wife had no right in the rituals. But she was no less a widow than the other. So I started wondering what happens to a relationship, one which is socially determined by marriage, after a divorce. What happens to the feelings when the relationship does not exist any more? That is where it began.

(Shoma Chatterji, *Parama and Other Outsiders*, 2002, p. 218)

At the time, Sen pinned on the woman's courageously private approach to family 'feelings', against the grain of 'public' ceremonies of kin sentiment. Satya Mohanty's formulation of a 'postpositivist picture of knowledge'[72] suggests that germs of oppositional awareness such as Sen's uncomfortable 'wonder[ing]' about non-customary family emotions comprise 'confused feelings' and 'vaguely felt ethical judgements'[73] that might be linked to 'more developed normative theories of right and wrong'[74] but are not articulated as such. Clearly, Sen's empathetic evaluation of the cruel customary 'laws' underlying the divorced 'widow's' marginalization grows at the intersection of her own social location (as both a divorced woman and an activist female intellectual in a still largely male-dominant society) and the ethical norms of the different local and translocal cultures in which she partakes as a modern-educated elite Indian.

On the cognitive basis of a lived experience, the film develops a visual narrative of how autonomous women could lead the way to transcultural conceptions of non-filiative familial and human belonging within our atomizing and terrorized world. This exploration revolves around the 'day' in the life of the title character, Paromita (Rituparna Sengupta), on which she attends the last rites of her former mother-in-law, Sanaka (Aparna Sen), and sits in tears in a largely abandoned corner while becoming the butt of whispered ridicule by some married women. Paromita's life-story unfolds through flashbacks that depict how this modern-educated liberated woman (holding a postgraduate degree in comparative literature) comes as a new bride to an orthodox extended family home, divorces her sexist and alcoholic husband Biresh (Rajatabha Dutta) after giving birth to a child with cerebral palsy and losing the child, and how she returns to tend to her dying (former) mother-in-law with whom she had forged an unexpected bond.

Since much of the film explores in what way the customary desires and warmth of the bourgeois Bengali family life could be reprised within a feminist visual framework, the imagery sutures with prevailing pleasurable melodramatic conventions of visualizing femininity and kinship (pervading Bengali film and television, Hindi television, Bollywood cinema, and advertisements). In line with the Indian family melodrama in particular, the film displaces character interiority and contradiction, born of capitalized personal life, on to habitually indigenous expressive codes of colour, lighting, space use, and song. However, Sen's deployment of the conventional expressive habits are transculturally individuated and dialectical, for her camera redirects the focalized eye such that the spectator emphasizes some layers of expression and dialogue while sidelining others.

Two mise-en-scène are exemplary of the transcultural approach. One is a flashback to the moment when Paromita, as an exquisitely decked bride, crossed the threshold of her marital home and was ushered by Sanaka in the customary manner through the Hindu ritual of *badhu-baran*: the ritual welcome of a young *grihalakshmi* (woman/goddess of the hearth) by the aging lakshmi-like mother-in-law. Deliberately saturating the screen with the fertility-coded colours of vermilion and yellow, while it also combines key and fill lighting to lend a fiery brightness to the bride's face, this mise-en-scène easily unifies with dominant Bengali visual conventions of eroticizing the bride and mother in patriarchal wedding representations as, for example, in Piyali Basu's *Chitrangada* (Chapter 3). Yet the mise-en-scène is also disturbing conventional wedding portrayals in the way it displaces the characteristic male focus and casts Paromita's husband in the background. Through close-ups, our eyes are led to focus instead on the two women and their interaction. Mother-in-law Sanaka's triumphant remark about the beautiful daughter-in-law she has chosen, while still conventional, is personalized by a look of affectionate pleasure. Greatly heightening this personalization of a kin relationship sealed through ritual, daughter-in-law Paromita returns the look with intent happiness. This reciprocity between the women encodes the start of an intimacy that is to enable non-filiative imaginations of the extended patriarchal home itself and also its links with the world.

Similarly, another series of mise-en-scène sutures with the seductive ideal of Hindu domestic femininity yet radically reorients the focal assumption. The opening shot of the dining room of a conventional bourgeois patriarchal family seductively promises domestic peace through preserving a gender hierarchy of time, space, and resource. The men are shown to be eating first, sitting comfortably, and getting the choicest food. The two daughters-in-law (Paromita for one) serve them according to *grihalakshmi*'s tradition of *seva* or care-giving, holding in their own appetites for leftover tidbits. Then, at a stroke, the feminist camera upsets this tableau-like synchronicity of movements, retorting against its assumption of patriarchal stability. It cuts to a Sanaka sitting with her back to her husband and sons, watching her favourite film on television. Angles and cuts heighten the contrast between Sanaka's comfortable perch and her daughters-in-law's tense scuttles around the dining table, further provoking spectators to consider how domestic routine exploits women's health and labour in the name of auspicious family seva. Sanaka's radically private control over her own domestic habitation grows clearer still as a sonorous code begins to 'envelope'[75] the men's chatter and its vestiges of family equilibrium, the sound being of a walking stick that announces the arrival of Sanaka's childhood sweetheart Monimoy (Soumitra Chatterjee). We soon learn that this impoverished poet is a frequent visitor; naming him a cousin from her village, Sanaka has chosen to share with him some of her own inheritance. Whereas this choice on Sanaka's part of an extramarital kinship turns her into a stridently self-willed *Alakshmi*, in terms of patriarchal custom, it does not however override all her custom-bound choices. Rather, we see it as constituting one of a bricolage of self-propelling decisions.

At the moment in question, Sanaka is committed to responding to a call from her husband and sons for her expert hand of seva, even though she appears to resent this customary demand from the male members. She commits time and energy to the domestic care-work called for before proceeding to her un-domesticated attention to Monimoy. She voluntarily completes the task of frying *luchi* (puffy bread) for her hungry family members before she departs. In the final reckoning, neither Sanaka's obviously rule-defying choice of relationship with another man nor her seemingly rule-bound choice of care-giving can be seen within patriarchal codes.

The grihalakshmi or Hindu Bengali icon of domesticity is best described in the words of Dipesh Chakrabarty as the 'housewife imagined in the divine model of Lakshmi, the goddess of domestic well-being'.[76] Drawing on David Kinsley, Chakrabarty elaborates that while the Hindu goddess Lakshmi had been venerated in popular Bengali practice for her 'auspicious nature and her reputation for granting fertility, luck, wealth and well-being', she took on a particular significance in the aesthetic of nationalist modernity in nineteenth-century Bengal. This aesthetic combined the codes of bourgeois Victorian domesticity with a very different culture, drawn from the authoritative Hindu text on social laws, *Manusmriti*, by emphasizing the 'connection between the pleasant and the auspicious in the desirable aspects of the feminine'.[77] On this anti-colonial nationalist view, such key elements of conventional Bengali feminine pleasantness as lajja (modesty) and obedience were pitted against a shrewish Alakshmi who destroyed the peace cementing domestic ties.[78] In this veiled parlance on chastity (see my detailed discussion in Chapter 1), the Alakshmi was unsurprisingly associated with the selfish defiance of authority born of Western education.[79] While acknowledging the patriarchal and fraternal nature of this nationalist aesthetic of homemaking, Chakrabarty goes on to underscore that this aesthetic reveals the inherently multiple position of the modern Bengali subject, and that this multiplicity presents 'significant points of ... intractability' when read through the lens of the 'subject of European modernity'.[80] In particular about the aesthetical representation of family and kinship, Chakrabarty remarks that kinship sentiments are not required to be the 'expression of the personality of the individual', as in the expressive individualism underlying the European family romance, but rather of the 'demand' placed on 'any member of the kin group without reference to the differences between their individual personalities'.[81] The nationalist politics representing authentic family relations, then, traditionally endorses a non-intimate and un-private form of domesticity resting on the presupposition that obligatory kinship is the preeminent morality. This nationalist aesthetic of kinship, replete with its filiative polarity of Lakshmi and Alakshmi femininities, also has been appropriated by the popular cinema of post-Independence Bengal. As we saw in Chapter 3, the aesthetic is now readjusting to our neoliberal visual culture by imaginarily domesticating the personalities of educated and independent feminist women, potentially the Alakshmis resisting patriarchal authority, through folding their images into dominant kin structures.

Aparna Sen boldly challenges this misogynist polarity of femininities in popular visual cultures through the aesthetical appeals of such defiant female characters as Sanaka and Paromita. Her point, it seems to me, is neither to simply dismantle such dichotomies as Chakrabarty's between personality and kin obligation, and to settle for the underlying postmodern affirmation of cultural difference despite the negative implication of this affirmation for Indian women; nor is it instead to endorse a competitive individualism (celebrating Alakshmis who defy custom) in the vein of some Western liberal or radical feminisms. The point here, in my view, is to radically aestheticize the messy transcultural interweaves being forged through the material processes of modern Bengali family life, that is, the dialectical weavings wherein personality routinely works through custom. Therein kin relations are forged both in accordance with customary interpretations of family 'demands' and also against them.

Aparna Sen's depictions of personalized kinships—such as the marriage and domestic rituals described above—reveal that private interpretations of family demands are those that endure under adversity whereas filiative obligations by demand wane, or they reduce into self-interest. Precisely, an Alakshmi-like defiance of the authority of biological kin structures could enable private kin relations characterized by voluntary self-sacrifice. Along these lines, *Paromitar Ek Din* expressively codifies women's ethical privacy as spaces and intervals for mutual self-development. It portrays the forging of an unconventional interpretive bond between modern-educated Paromita and tradition-circled Sanaka, across the borders of their respective cultures of being and doing. And this intimate support also culminates in what is perhaps the most unconventional exploration of interpersonal association in the film.

A divorced Paromita voluntary returns to care for Sanaka on her deathbed, tending the dying woman with untiring and intent sensitivity until her very last breath. Through this last episode, the film decisively dismantles the customary patriarchal Hindu assumption regarding the grihalakshmi. The assumption is that the chaste and monogamous married woman is the one naturally committed to doing self-sacrificing seva to parents-in-law and kin whereas an unchaste and self-driven Alakshmi in no way could command this auspicious feminine virtue. Pointedly disconnecting the virtue of voluntary self-sacrifice from the obligatory filial virtue of kin-seva, the film instead shows a flagrant Alakshmi (no less than the divorced woman Paromita) giving utmost care. The depth of Paromita's personal bond permits her, at one point, to save the aged Sanaka's life by creating a secluded space (make-shift toilet by the bed) where Sanaka can urinate in private and maintain dignity while performing her bodily functions.

Nonetheless, the film is pragmatically anti-teleological in its treatment of the political economy of feminist choices in contemporary urban India. Not simply does it undo the Orientalist dichotomy between the modern autonomous woman and oppressive patriarchal demands (found in *Parama* and many other popular-commercial feminist works), it also takes the further step to evaluate in what ways the sanity of seeing itself inhibits ethical self-development and human ties. And also in critiques such as these of historical sanity and sight I see an overlap of Aparna Sen's aesthetic with Ritwik Ghatak's postmodern exploration of the colonized individual. At the same time, Sen's own aesthetic 'discussions' of historical sanity remain tied to a feminist challenge of contemporary transnational empires of labour, pleasure, and violence.

Reclaiming the Private: Sane Individuals and the Freedom to See

We see a bitterly tearful Paromita retreating from the ceremonial public space of the *shraddha* rituals of her one-time mother-in-law. She claims the privacy of a bathroom to vent her anguish at losing her companion, Sanaka. In a desperate bid for comfort, she then turns to phone her new husband Rajiv Srivastava (Rajesh Sharma), brokenly crying out for support and solace. Her trust in this new partner is not misplaced since, to date, Srivastava has proven to be the perfectly committed companion. He had begun by assisting her to procure an intellectually fulfilling and also gainful job, and therewith enabling her release from the daily grind of an oppressive marriage to Sanaka's son. Subsequently, their camaraderie and shared emancipatory goals (of helping disabled children and raising awareness through filmmaking) blossomed into an ideal companionate marriage. At least so it had seemed until this narrative moment.

The storyline builds up to the moment of the phone call through a camera cutting between three temporal layouts whose priorities radically disconnect: the first portrays an efficient Srivastava engrossed in filming the star Indrani Haldar's performance of emotion and in utilizing every expensive moment; the second shows the (slightly comical) inefficiency of Paromita's colleagues in meeting an important deadline because she has chosen to attend the funeral ceremony instead; and the third depicts a Paromita steadfastly devoting time and concentration to Sanaka's last rites and being only irked by disruptive phone calls from work. Paromita's call to Srivastava potentially bridges the disconnect between their disparate allocations of time and value. It seems to me that her implicit expectation behind the call is that he will take the time out to lend her some badly needed emotional support. In other words, he will be reciprocating her autonomous way of assigning value to time and defying work routine through a voluntary exit from his own profit-making task; instead, he will be prepared to enter into un-clocked moments of familial bonding and care.

But Srivastava's response disappoints her, and it temporarily widens the disconnect between them. He quite simply fails to understand why she is so distressed because he is prepared to devote only a passing moment from his cost-efficient filming schedule to even listen to her. The self-love this little episode uncovers in the man is of a more complex order than Rahul's in *Parama*. For this narrative, unlike *Parama*, is not faulting a male photographer for commodifying women and the feminine for his own profit (although this is exactly what Srivastava is doing in shooting the melodramatic self-display of the film star). Aparna Sen appears to have settled for deeming this pursuit of commodification necessary for any and all filmmakers wanting to survive under the visual commodity structure. Much more subtly, however, this episode is faulting the fundamental logic Srivastava pursues in failing to give attention to his anguished partner at this moment—the logic of measuring time itself as a commodity, invariably in terms of monetary exchange and not in terms of human investment. By failing to exert this specifically ethical choice to selectively break away from the codes of capitalist growth, Srivastava upholds the more basic stratifications of time, work, and dignity enforced by the dominant political economy (as discussed in Chapter 3). Yet, even though this episode makes us aware of his ethical limitation in comparison to Paromita, it also leaves us to wonder whose form of social agency is after all more viable under the new liberal structures of opportunity.

For, due to this failure of cognitive intimacy between the two, Paromita's emotional retreat comes to encapsulate her completely self-isolating privacy. Figure 3 shows Aparna Sen's semiotic metaphor for the anguish immanent in the woman's isolated independence from public rationales of time, space, and purpose. Paromita is holding in her hand the commonest tool today for maintaining interpersonal communication and for compressing the divides of space and time brought on by capitalist mobility: the mobile phone. Only here, it is the *technology which failed to maintain network*—as spectators, we are left to make sense of this failure by connecting it to social situations of the same order. By implication, this powerful semiotic metaphor for communication failure constitutes an ironic commentary on the celebration of technological networks to be found today in popular Bengali media (as noted also in Chapter 3).

That this degree of privacy encrypts one away from a conceptual system wherein only visible and customary moods and meanings matter

Figure 3 Failure of Communication and Community
Courtesy: Rajesh Agarwal, Suravi Films, Kolkata

becomes apparent when this ethically private moment proves to be only a passing phase in Paromita's existence. Even though a momentary gulf yawns between the private woman and her commercially-oriented male companion when he finally finds time for her—a telling mise-en-scène reveals the still tearful Paromita failing to communicate and maintaining her distance from Srivastava—it soon disappears. Paromita resumes customary companionate gestures, marking a relationship partly limited by self-love, as they enjoy a bite together and then share in the joy of feeling the movements of their unborn child within the expectant mother. Vindicating maternity, and to that extent suturing with hegemonic glorifications of Hindu-mother-centred bourgeois family ties in popular Indian media, the closing shots of the film are enveloped by the melos of a song by Rabindranath Tagore celebrating the *bipul taranga* (majestic flow) of blissful life through the 'dance' of everyday domestic realities (*nache sansar*). Yet something is also left over from this narrative, a strand that radically misfits the enclosed web.

Shoma Chatterji rightly notes that the schizophrenia of Sanaka's daughter Khuku is simultaneously psychological and metaphorical. It questions 'conventional notions that define the dividing line between "normal" and abnormal, between sanity and the lack of it'.[82] Khuku's un/canny intuitions and decisions, on the one hand, cut to the core of nurturant homemaking, against the grain of the normal taranga of self-interested lives, individual and filiative. Defying all psychobiological rationality, this bumbling and confused offspring is the one who is shown to be tending to her mother in her own peculiar way when all others have abandoned the aging woman and her decrepit home (Figure 4). She is also the one who summons Paromita to Sanaka's deathbed, realizing that the seva of Paromita alone can give succour at this moment. On the other hand, Khuku's intuitive judgements imply a connection between the disturbances born of the local taranga of self-and-family interests and the violence born of territorial strife across the globe. As the filmmaker herself points out, elucidating the tragicomic implications of the metaphor of Khuku's schizophrenia, 'While news of widespread violence and terrorism is being broadcast on the radio, the schizophrenic Khuku keeps on asking whether she is the only one who has a diseased brain'.[83] Blending a disturbed inwardness with an autonomous ethicopolitical awareness as well as a mystical prescience, Khuku presents a provocative transculturation of the liberal notion of privacy. Her portrayal draws on classic European formulations of private identity such as the inward self,[84] interpersonal intimacy,[85] and the liberty to pursue the good in

Figure 4 An 'Insane' Care-giver
Courtesy: Rajesh Agarwal, Suravi Films, Kolkata

one's own unencumbered way.[86] It also invokes the indigenous (Hindu and Buddhist) ontology of the 'surplus' or incompleteness of the *atman* (innermost human soul) that exceeds existential meanings and craves deliverance from the sufferings of everyday *sansar* (domestic existence).[87] Khuku's irreducible privacy is spatialized in the recesses she chooses for herself that are *unmediated* by everyday flows. These include the rooftop where she sits unperturbed feeding the birds while the family mourns her mother's death in the customary ritual way, as well as the window sill to which Khuku retreats with her *tanpura* after throwing a tantrum, and where she reclaims her inward calm through the strains of a Vaishnava-inflected Tagore song. Forging an inter-text with Tagore's anti-capitalist critique, the song performs a profoundly mystical inwardness seeking the *prakash* (exposure) and the wedding of *hriday* (an inmost human soul) to the cosmic *ananta akash* (infinity of the sky).

All in all, Khuku's germinal insights into racialized terror, non-filiative domesticity, and human nurturance constitute, on one level, a deconstructive site of cognitive excess which subverts the normal coherence of people's existential understandings, including of those (such as Sanaka and Paromita) who are the most radical in their approaches. In other words, Khuku's irreducibly private cognition presents a postmodern historical critique underscoring that all normal reasoning and emotions will eventually reduce into individualist interests or anxieties about property and propriety (*qua*-normality). Yet far from only deconstructing history in this vein, Khuku's private sanity is poised for intervening in imperial history by spawning witnesses to the prevailing insanities. At the least, thoughtful 'normal' people—standing in for the thought-provoked off screen—stop to reflect upon what is different here (as portrayed by Paromita's and Sanaka's rapture in Khuku's performance of the mystical song). At the most, responsible thinkers begin to connect Khuku's dis-ease to global imperialism in our era of violence. The poet Monimoy reiterates Khuku's key question—which of us is diseased and who is sane in our so-called normal world? Khuku carries elements of a shamanic leader prophesying a possible future of private persons and nurturing relationships irreducible to conciliation with empire. Precisely this role has been intertextually developed by Aparna Sen in her recent English-language film, *15 Park Avenue*. I arrive there via a look at the previous film which eschews these dialectics of schizophrenic privacy and instead endorses a human agency radically at odds with dominant history.

The critically acclaimed Anglophone film *Mr. and Mrs. Iyer* (2002), following on the heels both of the massacre of Muslim minorities in eastern India and of the 9/11 attack in the US, is an optimistic delineation of the woman as an independent thinker about the family and national belonging. Enveloped again and again by the thematic song 'Don't look away', the film implicitly asserts that the camera ought to be reclaimed from dominant agendas in the cause of emancipatory social change.

Drawing once again on lived experience, Sen conceived the work after hearing about how a busload of people had been caught in a communal uprising in the eastern Indian region of Bihar.[88] The film portrays Meenakshi Iyer (Konkona Sen Sharma), a young Brahmin woman from the southern Indian state of Tamil Nadu, travelling with her infant son to her marital home in Kolkata. Raja Chowdhury (Rahul Bose) is a Bengali wildlife photographer who has been requested by Meenakshi's father to help her on the way. When the bus they are riding is stranded in a remote hilly region and attacked by Hindu terrorists, Meenakshi learns that her travel companion is also a Muslim. Despite the fact that initially she recoils with ethnic prejudice, she intuitively turns to protect him from the rioters by naming him as her Hindu Brahmin husband, Mr Iyer. Their bond grows into intimacy in the forest bungalow where they find shelter as husband and wife and share moments of disagreement, fear, and (implicit) conjugal joy. However, they eventually go their separate ways, cherishing only a memory of their privacy as recorded on a roll of film which none but the two know of.

Three aspects of the film are salient for the present discussion. First, the work elaborates the kind of self-love we encounter in *House of Memories*—grouping some together while turning others into instruments or alien objects, or at the least making people drift along with accepted ideas about satisfaction and security. *Mr. and Mrs. Iyer* further parses this self-love by suggesting that it can yield imperialist identities which outright minoritize and destroy the 'others'. In the Indian subcontinent, these complex biopolitics of minority violation descend from colonial methods of 'essentializing and enumerating human communities' in tandem with allocating 'space, time, resources, and relations',[89] and they escalate under the partisan resource allocations of a caste-Hindu-dominant nation-state. Constituting a microcosm of a multiethnic and multilingual India travelling along with imperial history, the people on the bus demonstrate how a homogeneous minority is constructed and vilified not merely under imminent threat but far more systematically through individuals' craving for the prosperity and security that come to majoritarian identities. Despite the fact that they learn that the rioters in this instance are Hindu terrorists, a good cross-section of the passengers drift into blaming the Muslim minority for inciting this kind of terror both in India and worldwide. The cross-section includes such people as Sikhs and Jews who have also suffered for their minority status. That in Sen's imagination majoritarian imperialism has a masculine profile is already evident in the way *Paromitar Ek Din* portrays that men most consistently uphold patriarchal capitalist customs because they enjoy the privileges. Here we are reminded of the binary biopolitics of majority manhood, that it has a fundamental racial and ethnic cast against which alien bodies are profiled. Further, the film opens with a collage of worldwide hatred and victimage—a rapid succession of stills flashing newspaper headlines and photos of conflicts in Palestine and Lebanon, Osama bin Laden, and Hindu terrorists mobbing Muslim village children. The collage implies that local ethnic fundamentalism is embedded in convergent processes of global power which produce diverse aliens at the same time that they homogenize majority racial interests. Along these lines, the most troubled of episodes portrays that when Hindu terrorists begin unclothing men to identify the alien (circumcised) Muslim body, a Jewish man reveals to them the presence of an elderly Muslim man in the panic of protecting his own ethnicity, lest his circumcised body be lumped in the fundamentalist gaze as the alien.

Even though the film emphasizes that this malaise of group allegiance is customary in contemporary communal India—Kwame Anthony Appiah rightly notes that this form of allegiance is 'conjured up' through a 'dynamic of antagonism, lumping as it splits'[90]—against the grain it pits an intuitive human desire to associate in peace and mutually preserve. This intuitive humanity surfaces in the passengers' horrified protest against the violence being inflicted on the elderly Muslim man and his wife, and it enables a new all-embracing community that includes the Jewish man (as signified by the way he breaks down into an un-defensive, self-reneging shame). Precisely this intuition to preserve and nurture life also catalyzes the central relationship—a most radical manifestation of a non-filiative family-like tie between the conservative Hindu Brahmin woman and the Muslim man. Even though intuition sows the seed of their intimacy by impelling the woman to overlook her Hindu filiative bias against the polluted body of the alien (*mleccha*) Muslim, however, a blending of desire with self-critical reasoning is what is shown to inculcate in her a loving solidarity with the man.

The second key aspect of the film for the purposes of my study, then, is that the biological boundary between the ideal/pure Hindu patriline of the nation and the alien/polluted Muslim intruder is bridged through a singularly private relationship (enabling 'beauty, love, and gender emotions', as the filmmaker puts it)[91] forged by the woman outside these boundaries. The growth of this relationship is portrayed through a transcultural range of narrative and expressive codes. These intermingle the psychobiological emotions invoked by such rasas as *vatsalya* (tenderness towards children), *sringara* (erotic love), and karuna (compassion);[92] a Rousseauvian spontaneity in adoring and protecting innocent childhood against destructive culture; companionate eroticism between two desiring individuals; and the call to bear witness to human suffering and sympathize as critical historical subjects, which entwines the human 'sentiment' theories of such thinkers as Adam Smith and David Hume with Kant's ethical 'imperative'.[93] This interweave of affects and historical reasoning precludes a disembodied subject position on screen and off.

The most notable instance of the embodied historical witness, in my view, emerges from an episode which follows the growth of in/dividual intimacy between the two. Watching terrorists slaughter a man, Raja and Meenakshi viscerally experience a horror that thickens their relationship and makes them cling to each other through the rest of the night. In the clear light of the new day Meenakshi stands before a mirror reviewing what is, in my opinion, her self-in-relation. This self-mirroring is quite at odds with the specular fragmented subjectivity associated with the mirror image in the postmodern Lacanian tradition. Her reflexive position implies a realization that she can belong with and desire for others only if she chooses to take victimage 'in her stride'[94]—whether this victimage stems from her own custom of defiling the other, or from the way her particular habits come to be generalized in imperial history's alienation and carnage. Subsequently, Meenakshi enacts her new way to build an intimate (heterosexual) home by exerting the ethical choice to demolish Hindu nationalism's fundamental ethnobiological barrier, that between the pure and the polluted/alien body. Confirming their corporeal intimacy she elects to sip water from Raja's bottle, whereas precisely this act had initially signalled to her Raja's alien descent and made her recoil (since Hindus view sipping water directly from containers as the alien's typical way of polluting the body).

Thus, *Mr. and Mrs. Iyer* outright reclaims and un-filiates the orthodox nationalist trope of the woman as the homemaker and mother (of future communalist citizens). At the same time, and this brings me to the third salient aspect of this work for my purposes, the film implicitly urges us to ponder if the woman's autonomous choice should be made visible to the biased public eye, or if publicity will reduce it to misreadings. Encoding a need to protect the privacy of the relationship, to prevent commodification, Raja is portrayed to be taking a step that is the exact opposite of *Parama*'s Rahul. At the moment of parting, he hands Meenakshi the roll of film which memorializes the intimate 'family' moments they spent in the seclusion of the woods by the forest bungalow (playing with the baby as they came to realize their mutual desire). Meenakshi reciprocates their private belonging by re-endowing him with the family name 'Mr Iyer'. However, this ideal ending also leaves us to puzzle over the status, in visual history, of Raja's intimate camera and its relational process of viewing people and the world.

Earlier, we learned that Raja's habitual lucrative modes of using the camera encompass not only commercial photography, which commodifies tropical wildlife for the nostalgic eyes of the world's urban elite, but also activist documentation of political violence. That something is interchangeable between these two visual modalities has been revealed through Raja wielding his lens the morning after the terrorist attack, zooming in on the glasses and dentures of the Muslim man who has been butchered and then telescoping toward the distant hills. What is shown as interchanging between these two foci, it seems to me, is the quest for 'distantiated'[95] objects appropriate for commercial photography. As such, the exotic appeal of landscape photography in the eye of the metropolitan buyer becomes interchangeable with the sympathy-appeal of terrorism photography in the eye of the social activist. Thus we have been reminded of being in a world where knowledge is most easily transmitted and peddled via publicly agreeable channels of information. As the film closes upon Raja walking away from their alternative, relational practice of photo technology—as the two had intimately conceived this practice in their hideout from customs— and back into his profession of dispassionate photography, we are left with questions. Can this private camera intervene in visual history and alter the informed and dominant ways to see? In the light of the meta-cinematic technique recurring throughout Aparna Sen's oeuvre—that of making the viewer camera-conscious and interrogative—we wonder if this assertion of perfect privacy idealizes and protects the alternative lens. In my view, Aparna Sen returns to this issue in her recent production, *15 Park Avenue* (2005). She further explores and self-revises precisely the interventionist possibilities of the private camera and the private photo-allured eye. She returns to the motif of the schizophrenic's ethical privacy through portraying her as a photo-journalist and a television buff.

Journalist Mithali (Mithi to family and friends; Konkona Sen Sharma) is seen on an assignment to report the post-poll terrorism being inflicted on Muslim minorities in an eastern Indian village. We note that her camera and tape recorder are aids in forging cross-border community with the terrorized, not merely technology useful for commodifying victimage. For Mithi uses these aids to capture emotionally charged face-to-face encounters, shooting at very close range and amidst talk that flows with tears and smiles of bonding (see Figure 5). Whereas the many men with cameras in Aparna Sen's films invariably stand apart and focus their lenses on distant objects, this woman with a camera breaks down the subject-object split. In this respect, she is a *decolonized* transcultural visual agent who combines nurturing camera work— entwining expressive individualism with an overflowing karuna or compassionate desire for the oppressed—with the promise of publicly transmitting image and information about the terrorized and asserting their human rights.

Later, when Mithi's schizophrenia is at its height, we see her looking precisely for the space to nurture life privately, in a way unthreatened by objectification and its violent consequences. She perpetually seeks the home she has lost and hears in the distance the voices of her small children calling out to her. Her peculiarly politicized schizophrenic look is encapsulated in a full-screen close-up of her eye intent upon telecasts both of George Bush's justifications of the war on Iraq and of Saddam Hussein's resistance. Interacting with the global power narrative in a way that is also radically private, un-interfered by the mediatized 'relation' between on-screen images and that which is publicly 'seen',[96] Mithi allies with Saddam while perceiving many people around her to be 'in league with Bush'. Whereas she avers that Saddam alone can point her way back to the home she had made at 15 Park Avenue with her sweetheart/husband Joydeep Roy (Rahul Bose) and their five children, she equally insists that the Bush people around her only misunderstand and misdirect her quest.

These 'Bush people' are several. Her nursemaid Charu (Yama Shroff) not merely keeps chiding Mithi for misbehaviour, with the consent of Mithi's mother Mrs Mathur (Waheeda Rahman), Charu summons a saffron-robed exorcist to rid the girl of her supposed demon-possession. We also have Mithi's dispassionate analytical psychiatrist Kunal (Dhritiman Chatterji) whom she perceives as being under her sister's influence (Kunal is attracted to Anjali). And finally, there is a primary 'Bush' person in Mithi's more intimate circuit, her divorced older sister

Figure 5 Autonomous Camerawoman, Cross-border Vision
Courtesy: Bipin Vohra, SPS Arts and Entertainment, Kolkata

and guardian figure Anjali (Shabana Azmi). Even though she wants to protect and care for Mithi, Anjali always feels burdened that family obligations encroach upon the time and space of her successful career as a physics professor with deadlines and milestones of achievement. Anjali draws to the fore the elements of narcissism in Aparna Sen's repeated portrayals of independent bourgeois Indian women (Parama's liberated friend; Paromita) as well as the self-pitiful angst with regards to burdensome and backwardly family obligations that riddle these portrayals.

Mithi's perspective effectively interrogates the pervasive self-orientation by deciphering a connection between everyday people's proclivities to objectify or alienate/demonize with global imperial power. Mithi's looking alerts us to how the major, able, and secure identities rise above the minor, the dis-abled, and the perpetually vulnerable (in racial, sexual, and corporeal terms). Her involvements with the visual economy—whether through composing and shooting or viewing and reading images—present what could be described in Immanuel Kant's terms as an autonomous 'synthetic' vision. It operates 'beyond the [practical] cognition of objects' and instrumental relations.[97] Along this line, Mithi also envisions how nurturing practices and non-instrumental relationships of a true home can heal stratifications in a way that rejuvenates human belonging both at home and in the world. That in her transnational reading of power the Muslim (villagers in eastern India; Saddam Hussein) is revealed, in fact and in metaphor, to be the most vulnerable and un-nurtured of all minorities seems to have a lot to do with Aparna Sen's own self-critique as a woman of the Hindu majority. By her own testimony, Sen has been most concerned with the 'pogroms against Muslims' in India and abroad.[98] These days she is deliberately using the English language to make activist films against the pogroms to appeal to wide audiences in India and the diasporas. Indeed, her challenge to Muslim minoritization in the two recent Anglophone films, in my view, implies an attack both on Hindu nationalism in India and on the Hindutva networks with racial majorities in such global contexts as George Bush's US (see Chapter 3 for examples). The films present a fine instantiation of global activism in the visual field.

Yet, what in Aparna Sen's view is the ethicopolitical future of a healing vision as private and ethically original Mithi's? At first glance, none. For no normal person around Mithi—who stand in for the norm-conforming viewers off screen—appears to understand or embrace her visionary quest in the way they claim social agency. In contrast to the schizophrenic Khuku's private ways of knowing home and nurturing bonds in a disintegrating world, which are at least partially legible to thoughtful normal people around her, Mithi's in *15 Park Avenue* by and large are inscrutable to the mainstream. On one level, her tale of hallucinations and epileptic fits represents an aberration of the healthy human mind and body that is to be pitied rather than conceptually engaged. The film most directly refers to Aparna Sen's own experiences with a close relative who is mentally ill. In this light, Mithi's original camerawork fails to make a mark on public practices, just as the camera she holds is literally destroyed as she is being gang-raped. The film presents a particularly bleak 'baroque allegory'[99] of how nurturing values and sentiments (associated with birthing, self-effacing motherly care, karuna) are coerced and 'ruined'[100] within a social fabric comprising aggressive self-loving individuals and groups. We learn that Mithi has forced her gentle temperament, inclined to homemaking and child-rearing, into the daring venture of covering post-poll communal violence in order to prove her competitive worth in the instrumental eyes alike of her employers and her aggressive upwardly mobile boyfriend Joydeep. Moreover, Mithi has to venture alone on the dangerous assignment because her sister Anjali, another self-interest-driven individual, refuses Mithi's request that she accompany her. Anjali cannot spare the time from her academic pursuits (she has an 'important seminar' to attend in Delhi in this instance).

Nonetheless, in a number of ways, *15 Park Avenue's* Mithi is a more sophisticated version of the shamanic schizophrenic we first encounter in Khuku of *Paromitar Ek Din*. Once again, Aparna Sen revises and complexly develops a motif she had earlier conceived. For Mithi not only makes people see differently at decisive moments of the narrative, she actually *dislodges* some from their 'normal' tracks and habitations. For example, she repeatedly pulls her self-driven sister Anjali away from the time and space of an over-achieving academic life back into her self-reneging commitments of seva to the family; therewith Mithi rekindles in Anjali a dormant transcultural loving nature (as Anjali's mother Mrs Mathur remembers it). Anjali not only takes numerous phone calls from home about Mithi's difficulties, despite the fact that they disturb her work schedule, she chooses against opportunities that would bring her emotional fulfilment and material mobility (such as taking a sabbatical to accompany her boyfriend to Princeton University; gaining a lecturership; and travelling in the Americas). Beyond this, Anjali questions the kinds of logic customarily understood as progressive such as the psychiatrist's objectifying prognosis and treatment of the mentally ill. Similarly, Mithi impels her ex-boyfriend Joydeep to stray from customary routes. While vacationing with his wife and two small children in Bhutan (in the attempt to repair a dysfunctional family life), Joydeep suddenly sees Mithi eleven years after he has broken off their engagement following the virulent turn her mental illness took after the rape. Certainly, as he himself tells his wife, Joydeep's guilt drives him back to be with Mithi (even though she seems not to recognize him) and then to agree to help her strike out of the circle of 'Bush people' and find her home at 15 Park Avenue. Joydeep shares this guilt-ridden specular subjectivity with Anjali, who also claims to have been driven to her decision to tend to Mithi through guilt.

However, the thematic point of their strayings, in my view, has to do with something more than just self-oriented specularity. These are among the normal people who are portrayed as being led into the schizophrenic's private quest for that autonomous nurturing home—a home which could protect humanity against interference by the world's violent ways to group and to split, to love the self, and to profile the unhuman other. The point is most clearly made by Joydeep's wife Lakshmi (Shefali Shetty). Upon hearing Mithi's perpetual quest for home—an information she wrests from Joydeep while agonizing over her own emotionless sexual intimacy with her spouse—Lakshmi meditates: are they not all looking for the home (of nurturance) they have lost?

Mithi herself directs this collective quest at least at two crucial points of the narrative. In a fleeting shot that captures the one moment of *unmediated* visual clarity the normal people share with Mithi's radical eye, we see Anjali, Joydeep, and Mrs Mathur stare in horrified distress with Mithi as she bursts into hysterical tears over the telecast of Saddam Hussein's arrest (Figure 6). Mithi cries out that now that Saddam has been captured by the Bush contingent, turned 'fragile' and 'weak', and poised for the gallows (a prescient forecast in view of Saddam's recent hanging), never again will she find the way to her home. Through Mithi's schizophrenic eyes, the three around her also momentarily witness the metaphorical face of the minor/dis-abled victim of majority-enabling imperial history: This is the face of the quintessentially homeless one which encompasses Saddam, the terrorized Islamic collectives, the violated Muslim villagers in India, and Mithi herself as objectified by both social and psychiatric sanity. At the film's close, Mithi emerges with an even more prophetic eye to lead people out of the threat of homelessness. The closing sequence of mise-en-scène shows Mithi

Figure 6 Facing the Minor—A Moment of Sight
Courtesy: Bipin Vohra, SPS Arts and Entertainment, Kolkata

striking out on the road to 15 Park Avenue with Joydeep, Anjali, and the psychiatrist Kunal behind her.

This portrayal of the road, in my view, is an apotheosis of the motif of the radical road to conceptual autonomy that recurs in Aparna Sen's earlier films. These metaphorical roads to freedom have been taken by Parama, Paromita and Sanaka, and Meenakshi Iyer. And they powerfully resonate as well with the metaphor of the autonomous road we found to be central in Rabindranath Tagore's works, as discussed in Chapter 2. Down this path, Mithi on her own terms seems to see her destination. She 'arrives' through a surreal mise-en-scène in which a house at '15 Ballygunge Park Road' metamorphoses into *her lost home* at 15 Park Avenue, with her long-lost sweetheart Jojo (the intimate name she had given to boyfriend Joydeep) and their five small children running out to embrace Mithi. We could read in her arrival to safety the closure of a visionary struggle on the part of one minoritized by the transnational empire of sane violence; on this trajectory, Mithi's surreal haven brings an optimistic closure to the pursuits of all those others across her world who are being terrorized out of home and hearth (the Muslim villagers, Saddam). Moreover, Mithi's shamanic stride into deliverance is vindicated by the three behind her who also launch a quest for the home into which Mithi seems to have disappeared. One last shot audibly encodes Anjali's voice-over saying 'perhaps there is a 15 Park Avenue ahead'.

The residual conundrum here is that her three followers really have nowhere to go. Even though Mithi has dislodged them from habitual assumptions about what is normal, as much topologically as socio-morally by urging them to seek the home at 15 Park Avenue on Ballygunge Park Road, ultimately these individuals wander aimlessly around the upscale neighbourhood; a resonance with the Absurd Drama is unmistakable in their aimlessness. Moreover, in a presciently final long take, Aparna Sen's camera stays with the topography of this upscale Kolkata neighbourhood as it is emptying of people, showing up only a plush but lifeless house with a closed door and a young man strolling along with a nonchalant whistle on his lips. On the Absurdist note as well, spectators are strongly reminded by this that all Mithi's destination amounts to is an *insane* hallucination. In the end all roads metaphoric and real cannot but converge toward the planned and safe neighbourhoods wherein the world's 'major' groups dwell. That route of convergence upon which *15 Park Avenue* ends is, of course, tellingly transnational in scope: Its 'major' locations include not only the supposed wealthy neighborhood of Ballygunge Park Road in Kolkata but also Park Avenue in New York, where all the logical people around her place Mithi's hallucinatory home.

The Autonomous Self and Ethical Journeys:
A Retrospective on the Eras of Empire

To round out this study of the eras of global empire, I find it helpful to take a relational look at another aesthetical journey for autonomy. Born of an earlier era of global empire is an anti-war poem which Rabindranath Tagore wrote amidst the First World War in 1915. Such scholars as Abu Sayeed Ayyub and Promothonath Bishi point to the poem itself and the collection *Balaka* where it appeared as constituting the turn in Tagore's thought toward global conflict; as discussed in the Introduction and Chapter 2, from hereon Tagore acquired a new consciousness of time, space, and activist ethics. Presenting some compelling parallels with Aparna Sen's recent films on war, the poem reminds us that Sen's imagination of autonomy is intertextual with Tagore's in that it partakes from different global eras the same indigenous tradition of ethical liberalism. At the same time, the intertextuality is broken at significant points. By attending to where these breaks occur, we are able to obtain a vivid sense of ways in which possibilities for conceptual autonomy have altered between the two eras in response to alterations in 'extraverbal' pragmatic frameworks[101] of aesthetical communication. Most revealing in this regard are the space-time metaphors of everyday lives and ethical journeys interlinking the poem to Sen's films. The point of my remarks to follow is not to present two exemplary activist thinkers from different eras, rather to consider in what ways and why communicative aesthetics alter in reference to differing material conditions.

Just as Aparna Sen's films interconnect the everyday biases of a Meenakshi Iyer or the 'Bush people' of Mithi's life with communal and racial violence, Tagore's poem interrelates the coercive mentalities 'clouding' people's everyday habitations with violence across the globe. The respective conclusions they draw with regard to these interrelations are, however, notably different. The poem in question is one among Rabindranath Tagore's multi-accented poetic critiques of contemporary world politics published in the periodical *Sabujpatra*.[102] These poems together with the lectures he was presenting simultaneously in a literature class at his Viswabharati University were soon published as an anthology titled *Balaka* (collective flight of geese).[103] In an introductory note, Tagore explains that the poems had arisen from *byaksha* (annotations) that were running through his mind at the same time that *bhangachora* (destructions) were being planned worldwide; like the journeys of geese, these poetic notes flew out of his *manaslok* (mind-world) on a *byakul* (anxious/perplexed) quest.[104] Tagore's language of Romantic inwardness does presuppose a teleology that comes across most clearly in some of the prose lectures (collected and collated not by Tagore himself but by Pradyotkumar Sen). In my view the telos of quest-and-destination, however, is repeatedly re-opened and *re-annotated* through the condensed poetic logic of intonations and imagery. I agree with Sukumar Sen's assessment[105] that in the *Balaka* poems Tagore was self-consciously trying to entwine poetic elements with prosaic face-to-face reasoning.

Poem 37 of *Balaka* presents an impassioned analytical exhortation in an irregular verse form intermingling alliterative couplets with prosaic face-to-face dialogue. It makes every individual accountable for such shared divisive mentalities as arrogant self-love, racial pride, and defensive self-pity born of deprivations. Moreover, this core individual is both gendered masculine and not, a point to which I will return:

Hear you not from afar the roars of death,
O you who are wretched, O you who are callous?
Those tumultuous cries,
The gushing of blood from a million breasts—
…
O my brother/O my companion, whom do you slander?
Hang your head [in shame].
These crimes are mine, and they are yours—
The cowardliness of the coward,
The arrogant wrongs of the mighty,
The cruel greed of the greedy,
The daily-agitated spirits of the deprived,
The conceit of race ….

[*Dur hote ki shunis mrityur garjan, Ore deen
Ore udaseen—
Oi krandaner kalarol,
Lakshya bakshya hote mukto rakter kallol …*

*Ore bhai, kar ninda karo tumi?
Matha karo nato.
E amar e tomar pap …
Bhirur bhiruta punjya, prabaler uddhata anyaya,
Lobheer nisthur lobh,
Banchiter nitya chityakhobh,
Jati abhiman …*][106]

The poem goes on to argue that these little 'deaths' of the human spirit
now burgeon into a worldwide deluge of hatred and destruction:

Deaths play hide-and-seek the whole world across
They float away, they go away, for moments they mock life along the way
Witness today their stupendous stature piercing through the clouds

[*Mrityu kare lukachuri, smasta prithibi juri
Bhese jay tara chale jay, jibanere kare jay khanik bidrup
Aj dekho tahader abhrabhedi biratswarup*][107]

At the same time people at large are portrayed as being called to
account for their complicities with the accepted norms underlying this
violence against humanity:

No longer will it do to peddle around your age-old stocks,
Deceptions grow apace, accumulated truths fast deplete ….

[*Purano sanchay niye shudhu bechakena*
Ar chalibe Na.
Bannchana bariya othe, phuraye satyer jato punji ....][108]

Responding to a call from beyond the 'harbours' of secure lives and habitual identities, they collectively plunge into a voyage on the quest for a fresh normative direction:

The commandment has come, at this time the ties of the harbor must end.
...
From all corners, people leave home and rush forth with oars in hand
...
Even then must we row on against the grimmest obstacles,
With the world's heart-rending moans ringing in our ears,
Bearing upon our heads wild stormy days,
Clinging in our hearts to hope without end.

[*Esecche adesh, bandare badhankaal ebarer mato holo sesh.*
...
Taratari tai ghar cchari charidik hote danr hate cchute ase danri
...
Tobu beye tari sab thele hote habe par, kane niye nikhiler hahakar,
Shire laye duranta durdin, bakshe laye asha antaheen.][109]

On this epochal voyage launched by responsible individuals each also is vested with a peculiarly transcultural historical agency. Each agent, according to Tagore, must strive for ethical autonomy through *tapasya*, that is, through a soul-searching practice of austerity in the pursuit of deliverance from indulging in the deathly attitudes in his/her everyday practices. This notion of the individual's austere pursuit once again appropriates a pre-secular Hindu norm to intervene in history and pose a retort to possessive individualisms. It complements such other appropriations of bhakti poetry imagery as the crossing of the sea of worldly tribulations and the divine helmsman. The particular this-worldly bent of the collective tapasya and journey is revealed in Tagore's recurrent questioning of human deliverance, and that these questions reveal a self-doubt referring to the specific material structures and social attitudes which obfuscate (benight) the path to a transparent and absolute truth. As such the poem is intertextual with the vocabulary of *dharmabodh* or religious-self-realization constituting *gamay* (the journey to transcendent bliss), elucidated by Tagore as a spiritual teleology in one of his appended lectures on the Upanishads.[110] At the same time the closing stanza reinforces Tagore's emphasis on the gamay through material history while it defers the destination:

Will not the tapasya of night bring about the day?
In the deepest despair of night,
Under the massive blows of death,
When humankind has crushed to bits all the limits of earthly existence—
Might not we then perceive the godly grandeur of the eternal?

[*Ratrir tapasya seki anibe na din.*
Nidarun dukharate,
Mrityughate
Manush churnilo jabe nijo martyaseema
Takhan dibe na dekha debotar amar mahima?][111]

Notwithstanding the reiterative self-doubt and historical critique, Tagore's vision of the ethical human journey out of possessiveness, not unlike Aparna Sen's, is imperfect and partially specular. In part, it refers to his elitist and gendered interests and anxieties. One subtext of the secular spiritual journey portrayed here—as clarified by a prosaic annotation on *swarga* (heaven) in sansar (quotidian life) appearing in the Appendix—is that fellow Indians must be awakened into a world-critiquing human agency out of the *nishphal achar-bichar* (fruitless rituals) in which Hindu conventions of world renunciation have accustomed them.[112] No doubt this binary of ritual/soporific-versus-enlightened/human agency resonates with the poem's assertion that the 'age-old stocks' of truth must now be cast away for a new purposeful understanding. At the same time, however, the poem's imagistic logic re-annotates and supersedes the binary in at least two ways: it depicts that the torpor of dwelling in age-old truths is a condition shared by people in all corners of the world; and moreover, that across contemporary historical contexts, the most obdurate of these soporific norms stem from material structures of power and disparity (of race, class, and so on) rather than from religious or social habits per se. Along these lines, the imagery also plays with yet collapses the self-anxiety-driven gender binary we repeatedly encounter in the works of both Rabindranath Tagore and fellow writers of his time. We momentarily glimpse the familiar male-nationalist dichotomy of the nurturing and haven-making woman against the world-driven combative man in a portrayal of tearful mothers and lovers/wives standing at the doorways of emptied homes.[113] As we see above, however, the images of voyaging forth that follow allow neither woman nor man any 'harbour' of transcendent truth or secure identity. Tellingly, this call to universal self-critique is couched in a gender-equivocal form of address: Even though in the colloquial prosaic appeal, '*Ore bhai kar ninda karo tumi* (Whom do you slander)' *bhai* literally means brother, in everyday Bangali the word is widely used by women to address female companions.

In the final reckoning, then, the transcultural voyage towards emancipation undertaken by Tagore's autonomous self is unconcluded and non-teleological at the same time that it is persistently and collectively cumulative. I have amply discussed in Chapter 2 that Tagore's autonomous self, on the one hand, is 'unfinished'[114] in his/her struggle to be free of the (domesticated) security of normative habit; on the other, s/he strives on autonomously and also together with a collectivity supporting mutual emancipatory change. In the parallel I find in such visions as Aparna Sen's of responsible persons' collective journey against global violence, by contrast, the claims to autonomous agency are both relatively limited *and* puzzlingly teleological. In other words, there is a relative despondence in critical humanist visions of the present. In my view, the clue to this despondence lies in the difference between Tagore's and Sen's handling of the dual motifs of journey and domestication vis-à-vis their material frames of reference. As discussed at length in this chapter, the referential framework for Aparna Sen's aesthetic motifs is the new flexible empire of our transnational times. This is an empire being surreptitiously 'reordered'[115] by a pleasurable deception being perpetuated by neoliberal capital—the deception is that all and each can secure majoritarian destinations in this world. Pleasurable communications regarding that universally accessible telos is what stymies today the activist self's potential for freedom from imperial thought. This pleasure is vitalized through the pleasing socioeconomic destination upon which we are left to gaze at the close of *15 Park Avenue*. While this film reflects, exactly like Tagore's poem, upon how people could ethically mobilize against the global terror of our times, that is, it also *mediates* the import of mobilization. This is the metaphoric point I glean from the contrast I see between the portrayals respectively of an energetic human landscape such as Tagore's of individuals concentrating on a common journey, and of a landscape such as the one at the film's close which is emptying the journey of human agents. The prescient import of this closing seems to be that all ethical journeys today could scatter because the norms of competitive and possessive individualism pleasingly mediate and colonize other potential choices. Herein is the crucial discontinuity between the ethical liberal visions born under the heterogeneous spaces of a decolonizing struggle and those emerging under the relatively homogeneous framework of a free and liberalizing postcolonial country.

A close attention such as this to how the political economies of critical liberal Indian imaginations differ between the colonial and our neocolonial global eras, thus, also reveals the one-sidedness of analyses of Indian modernity that emphasize discursive continuities between the global eras. In particular, Foucauldian discourse analyses that designate British colonial discourse to be the pedagogical origin of liberal modern Indian consciousness, and see contemporary identities as evolving from that origin,[116] ignore how worldly frames of reference interact with imagination and assumption As such, they also fail to closely read the fresh challenges facing activist thinkers under our world conditions.

Works by the feminist intellectuals Aparna Sen, Manjusri Chaki-Sircar, and Ranjabati Sircar suggest how activists continue to reprise ethical autonomies in neoliberal India. Aparna Sen's, as much as the Sircars', imaginations of agency partake in a transcultural and temporal ethical project. The cumulative complexity in Sen's works also shows the key challenge. The challenge is to remain self-aware that precisely the enabling teleologies of our political economy can reroute humane alternatives and recolonize autonomy. Sen's recent works, however, presciently point the way to meeting this challenge of appealing teleologies. The way is for each of us to cultivate a principled double eye of reference: to look upon what are commonly seen as the pleasing, the good, and the safe life-destinations and to evaluate how human solidarity is daily disintegrating both *within* these seemingly comfortable habitats and in all those other abodes that have been *cast elsewhere* in relation to here.

CONCLUSION

Women, Decolonization, and Autonomy

As the range of examples in this book should have illustrated, my position is that a study of the autonomous person as an agent of decolonization cannot but pinpoint on women's and gender issues. This applies as much to the financial and social realms of culture as to aesthetical descriptions and their communicative modes. Some social contexts tend to devalue women and conventional feminine attributes whereas others may be more inclined to glorify them. But in either case, women end up bearing a disproportionate burden of coercion and exploitation. They are routinely deprived of autonomous decisions both in material practice and in image-making. While this burden undoubtedly increases or decreases in relation to other social advantages (of class, caste, race or ethnicity, and geographic location), the correlation between a woman's social status and the options she has with regard to acting upon her own needs is far from consistent. The marginalization of a talented and wealthy performer such as Binodini, or the assignment of reproductive roles to bourgeois women travelling to the US on spousal visas present telling cases in point from the respective eras I study. Quite simply, sexual domination, in my view, stands as the last bastion of empire. Equal social agency cannot be conceived without addressing this issue.

The reasons why this modality of domination is primary, broadly speaking, are two. As my relational reading of the two eras of Indian modernity demonstrates, even though sexual divisions of labour and reward shift and adjust to changing global (local) economies, they characteristically do not alter. Second, the biopolitics of postcolonial Indian culture strengthens these divisions by adapting pre-colonial local biases as well as imperialist prejudices and interests. Vempati Chinna Satyam's choreography of Tagore's dance drama *Chandalika*, as revived in contemporary Atlanta, by disciple Sasikala Penumarthi, illustrates how the pre-colonial male-Brahmin bias regarding bodily purity and pollution evolves through nationalism into Hindu-oriented multiculturalism—it adapts to elite Victorian misogyny just as it inflects to transnational economies of progress and liberation.

In view of this, I maintain that indigenous activist-intellectuals who are committed to challenging injustices and exploitations at all levels and who brook no compromise in this regard, cannot but invest in the Enlightenment's gendered ethic of the autonomous person. None other than this speculative idea of autonomous worth can enable the fight for sexual justice within heterosexual and patriarchal frameworks. For none but this humanist notion grants to every person, irrespective of social status and biological function, the potential to choose and to develop a good life free of authoritative structures. Against this norm, we are able to evaluate all the ways that, under various orders of empire, both women and feminized underprivileged men (devalued because of the womanly work they do or the attributes they are ascribed, for example) are deprived of choices or coerced by seeming choices. At the same time, postcolonial activists no way can take autonomy as an already defined absolute. It should be taken as an only provisional norm, open to revision and extension: to struggle against global imperialism means thinking on an everyday level about which kinds of person—driven by what mentalities or outlooks—bring about sexual coercion worldwide. Those kinds who want to possess sexual objects or demarcate sexual divisions (dividing lands and peoples as well as everyday lives and labours) and also those who self-coerce to fit into these categories come under scrutiny. As I have argued and demonstrated throughout this book, such indigenous feminist thinkers as Tagore, Binodini, Aparna Sen, and Manjusri Chaki-Sircar embark on multilayered and transcultural conceptions of woman-centered autonomy. They critique dominant masculine and possessive mentalities at the same time that they want to reclaim the minimal criterion of free and mutual judgement for all gendered persons who are being coerced and dis/possessed. As I have also emphasized, cultural activists are not perfect but rather conflicted transhistorical thinkers. While self-critical, their evaluations remain partially invested in sexual privilege or in defensive anxieties about lack.

The conception of the woman as an individual is of course at the centre of debates between liberal and poststructuralist feminist thinkers, as well as of scholarly dialogues regarding cultural differences between the global North and the South. Then, how do my notions of transcultural individuation and imperfect objectivity speak to these conversations? In my view, they open a middle ground in conversations that have tended to remain somewhat polarized along the lines of sameness and difference.

At the liberal end, my approach resonates in one part with Martha Nussbaum's Kantian postulate of a 'facilitative' universalism 'committed to cross-cultural norms of justice';[1] this treats every person as an end[2] rather than an instrument of supervening structures at the same time that it wants to be sensitive to 'local particularity'.[3] Especially useful, from my viewpoint, is Nussbaum's notion that the strength of our normative universalism lies in our ability to distinguish between the moral norm and its capitalist reduction, wherein the person is seen[4] as a universal 'rational agent ... seeking to maximize [her/his] utility' irrespective of tradition or context. In another part, however, my study fundamentally disagrees with what I consider to be Nussbaum's monocultural approach to universalism and personhood.

Quite consistently, Nussbaum misrecognizes difference, reducing various Indian women's and men's conceptions of autonomy and choice to a Euro-American standard. One claim of Nussbaum's, for example, is that women everywhere—whether in village India or in urban America—command the awareness that their bodies, inclinations, and labours are separate from family and community members',[5] in other words, that they are proprietors of themselves in every respect. This synecdochal assumption that the modern person is an essentially separate and self-oriented proprietor (in a minimal sense) underlies the well-known list Martha Nussbaum has drawn up of the 'functional capabilities'[6] necessary for human flourishing, limiting the cultural relevance of this undoubtedly thoughtful list. It is not simply that some items on this list would appear to many to be odd assertions, alien to their habitual context. As foregoing chapters have illustrated, it is that any such enumeration of a person's core capabilities would appear considerably more reasonable to women and men in non-Western contexts—and presumably also cause more grievance, when at issue—if it were framed in terms irreducible to the proprietor-versus-other paradigm. When Nussbaum asserts, for example, that at core a person must be granted the capacity to relate harmoniously to 'other species', she forecloses relevance to Indian contexts wherein the separation of the rational self from nature is incomplete, that is, in tension with quotidian social and religious habits which disallow any such atomization (as amply acknowledged by Tagore in *Raktakarabi* or Aparna Sen in *Yuganto*).

Critiquing Nussbaum's monocultural framing of modern personhood along similar lines, Nivedita Menon emphasizes that the core idea of Western democracy that the individual is a separable unit is debatable in Indian culture. She draws on Sudipta Kaviraj to point out that since democracy itself took root in Indian and African societies prior to the idea of the individual, 'liberal individualism never became the uncontested core of anti-imperialist struggles for democracy'.[7] Considering the situations of impoverished women of the global South, Swasti Mitter, on her part, challenges Nussbaum's essentialism. In a 'kaleidoscopically fragmented society' such as the Indian, says Mitter, a woman's identity as a woman is often secondary to her identity as 'a citizen of a less powerful nation' or a member of a minority group therein: many Muslim women in Mumbai, for example, are ready to 'trade off their choice' to be sexually satisfied or to marry for love in order to protect their family or community.[8]

Prior discussions should illustrate that I concur with the crux of the objection these Indian feminist thinkers raise, that Nussbaum's philosophical lens ignores the material histories of how modern cultural norms are formed, come to dominate, and are adapted or rejected in non-Western postcolonial cultures. Whereas postcolonial and Marxist feminist critiques such as these assume that in Indian and other non-Western contexts personal identity is integrated to collective identity (familial, local-community-based, national-community-based), my readings add a new historical specificity. The claim I have sought to demonstrate throughout this book is that, in certain strands of modern Indian thought, the autonomous agent stands out as an ethical norm which refuses to distantiate collectivity. Since the dichotomy between the self and the world constituting possessive individualism in Euro-American contexts comes to be contested on the cultural grounds of the Indian subcontinent, the autonomous person emerges instead as an inside-outsider of the community. She strives to recreate personal and collective relationships in more egalitarian and mutual ways (between heterosexual and same-sex persons; within and across families and communities). Whereas certain aspects of the European vocabulary of the feminist individual have travelled, then, their emphasis and goal have altered and adjusted to difference.

As against Nussbaum's ahistorical monoculturalism, liberal feminist thinker Seyla Benhabib's conceptions of the individual self and interactive universalism come closer to my own. Departing from a liberal multiculturalism such as Nussbaum's, which views cultural traditions as unified and teleological,[9] Benhabib stresses that 'cultures are internally riven and contested' such that 'individuality [is] the unique and fragile achievement of selves in weaving together conflicting narratives and allegiances into a unique life history'.[10] On this view of 'deliberative democracy', which rests on Jurgen Habermas's idea of communicative ethics, feminist autonomy constitutes developing a unique life-path 'vis-à-vis ascribed identities'.[11] What also converges with my viewpoint is Benhabib's complex notion of interaction in globalized public cultures— the notion that deliberative associations occur in multiple official and unofficial public spheres which include the 'civil, cultural, religious, and artistic'.[12] As discussed earlier, Rabindranath Tagore's deliberations on feminist autonomy—hand-in-hand with his contentious involvement in Indian nationalist and feminist movements—are exemplary of this form of association. In these respects, I am in agreement with feminist historian Tanika Sarkar's position on Seyla Benhabib's model of inter-active universalism.[13] This model is most helpful for delineating those critical strands of Indian thought which drew on the Enlightenment in their efforts not to compromise with gender hierarchy on any basis. I must, however, raise a pragmatic question: how practical is it to claim, as Benhabib does, that one can 'exit'[14] an ascribed cultural identity and enter another autonomous one?

I grant that the right to exit is here formulated as a legal principle rather than conceptualized on the level of social practice. Still, my issue is that there is no room in this model of individuality to account for how a person's investments in ascribed obligations, allegiances, powers, and lack could stand in the way of her choice to exit cultural associations. In this respect, Benhabib's liberal idealism converges with Nussbaum's in that both are setting norms for feminist autonomy, as Judith Butler puts it, 'outside of a history which is always to a certain extent opaque to us at the moment of action'.[15] As I have extensively demonstrated through my readings of Aparna Sen's cinema, a feminist thinker always struggles for transhistorical clarity and against historically ascribed interests, assumptions, and biases. Autonomous critiques and corrections of self-coercive interests are at best only partial. Moreover, these limitations to feminist ethical communication if anything have been even more accentuated in our contemporary historical context of transnational networks. As my various readings of our networked status should confirm, we simply cannot invoke a model of communicative ethics in the vein of Habermas without also taking account of today's media of communication and the various ways these *mediate* dominant corporate and state interests. In this light, let me also reiterate a point I brought up in the Preface of this book: artistic texts as well as the quotidian practices in which textuality is grounded can well provide more robust critical arenas for exploring humanist norms than legal/ philosophical formulations. It is not quite enough for activist scholars to only acknowledge, as Benhabib does, that democratic interactions occur in multiple public spheres. It would be worth our while to take the interdisciplinary step of considering how differing activist public voices—of the lawmaker and the filmmaker, for example—could critique and complement each other's visions of normative agency.

Earlier in this book, I have extensively discussed that at the Poststructuralist end of this conversation, as against the Liberal, historical effects are seen as pervading the self and controlling normative language. Along these lines, we obtain from Inderpal Grewal a picture of feminist autonomy within global cultures that strikingly differs from both Benhabib's and Nussbaum's. According to Grewal, liberal feminists today must be especially wary that the 'concept of choice is essential to participation in democracy as well as to consumer culture'[16] and, as such, that social movements and their principled subjects alike[17] unwittingly collaborate with market-driven binary attitudes. Contra Nussbaum, Grewal implies that the moral individual cannot be extricated from the utility-driven capitalist individual in our transnational world. That feminist choices—notably the choice of exiting identities ascribed by patriarchal families—are highly marketable commodities in today's neoliberal Indian visual culture should be clear from my discussion in Chapter 3 of popular feminist narratives on Indian satellite television. Yet I have also demonstrated through my analyses of the visual/cognitive struggles of Manjusri Chaki-Sircar and Aparna Sen that feminist ethical approaches to choice can disagree with the marketable range of women's choices in India today, even though these disagreements are limited by proprietory interests. A materialist approach, rather than a thoroughly

Foucauldian one such as Grewal's, can illuminate these complexities of cultural difference and transcultural agency.

Saba Mahmood's study of Islamic feminine agency, on the other hand, makes historical difference and cultural 'coimbrication'[18] central to a poststructuralist analysis of ethics. Mahmood eschews the somewhat binary poststructuralist practice of studying the consolidation or the subversion of norms, which stems from a paradigm of sameness-against-difference; instead, she argues that ethical norms can also be performed, inhabited, and experienced.[19] Her point is that if we take difference seriously, we will notice that in creating life-worlds incommensurable with Enlightenment reason, women in Islamic movements treat 'socially authorized forms' of performance—of 'restraining ... sensibilities, affect, desire, and sentiments', for example[20]—as the 'potentialities ... through which the self is realized'.[21] We certainly encounter a similar investment in alternative religious norms in Rabindranath Tagore's portrayal of the self-yielding woman and the madman in a land of accumulation (*Raktakarabi*) or Manjusri Chaki-Sircar's of woman-centred Tantric rituals (*Tomari Matir Kanya*). Where the activist-indigenous thinkers depicted in this book depart from a framework such as Mahmood's is that they invoke indigenous religious norms in the domain of secular gender ethics. Their way is not a radical departure from the Enlightenment's concepts of freedom and autonomy. Rather, it is a way running through these concepts and toward their historical goal. The endeavour of these gender activists, who refuse to compromise with hierarchy as a matter of principle, is to avoid an exclusive emphasis on historical difference (such as Mahmood's); the concern, as I have shown through my readings of Tagore's works, is that this exclusive emphasis could construct an insular space for idealizing 'non-Western societies as a "resource" to meet the inadequacies of Western philosophies and lifestyles'.[22] As Rajeswari Sunder Rajan notes, anti-Western idealism has spawned in the Indian context a radical and patriarchy-friendly feminism that pits the supposedly essential Hindu feminine qualities of self-surrender and strength against the self-centredness of the Western feminist. We saw earlier that exactly along the lines suggested by Sunder Rajan the Hindu goddess is coming to be a serviceable instrument of racialized feminism both in India and in Hindu-dominant diasporas.

From the grounds of anti-imperial feminist politics what, finally, do we gain from a study such as this book? For one, we are strongly reminded that developing an activist consciousness in a world where, as Materialist feminist thinker Chandra Talpade Mohanty notes, 'relations of rule' are far from transparent is always a struggle fraught with 'contestation about reality itself'.[23] My readings have argued that, nonetheless, feminists who struggle to decolonize our neoliberal world would find especially helpful the Enlightenment's emancipatory hope in the autonomous person. If creatively conceived, this humanist norm could alert us to what, in our thought and practice, is irreducible to possessive mentalities. If we try to mutually enable this potentiality for autonomy—while we recognize imperfection and complicity—we uncover the ethical and transcultural aspects of our activist selves.

NOTES

Preface

1. *Webster's New Universal Unabridged Dictionary*, New York: Simon and Schuster (1979), p. 1117.

2. Sutapa Bhattacharya (ed.), *Bangali Meyer Bhabonamulak Gadya: Unish Shatak*, Kolkata: Sahitya Akademi (1999), p. 3.

3. Binodini Dasi, *Amar Katha O Anyanyo Rachona*, Kolkata: Subarnarekha (1987 [1913]), p. 38.

4. 'Red Oleanders: Author's Interpretation', Appendix to *Raktakarabi*, Calcutta: Viswabharati Press (1985 [1924]), p. 123; see also, 'Narir Manusatya', *Rabindra Racanabali*, Calcutta: Viswabharati Press (1961 [1928]), vol. 13, p. 28.

5. See, Trevor Montague Wade, 'Choreography as Feminist Strategy: Three Approaches to Hindu Feminism in the Dance of Chandralekha, Manjusri Chaki-Sircar and Daksha Seth', University of Chicago: Ph.D. diss. (2001); personal conversation with Chaki-Sircar, p. 225.

6. See interviews: http://www.rediff.com/entertai/2002/jul/27aparna.htm; and http://www.time.com//asia/magazine.

7. Anne McClintock, *Imperial Leather: Race, Gender, and Sexuality in the Colonial Contest*, New York and London: Routledge (1995), p. 45. Throughout this book, I am indebted to McClintock's path-breaking analysis of the modalities of race, gender, and sexuality in empire. See particularly her chapter, 'The Lay of the Land: Genealogies of Imperialism', pp. 21–74.

8. Ibid., p. 44.

9. Edward Said, *Culture and Imperialism*, New York: Vintage Books (1993), p. 9.

10. J.N. Mohanty, *Classical Indian Philosophy*, Lanham: Rowman and Littlefield, p. 70. See also, Edward C. Dimock, et al., *The Literatures of India: An Introduction*, Chicago: University of Chicago Press (1974), p. 226.

11. Bimal Krishna Motilal, 'Philosophy, Culture, and Religion: Mind, Language, and the World', in Jonardon Ganeri (ed.), *The Collected Essays of Bimal Krishna Matilal*, Oxford: Oxford University Press, 2002, pp. 311–12.

12. Raymond Williams, *Keywords: A Vocabulary of Culture and Society*, New York: Oxford University Press (1983 [1966]), p. 164.

13. This ethical aspect of liberal individualisms has been analysed by Charles Taylor. See his *Sources of the Self: The Making of the Modern Identity*, Cambridge: Harvard University Press (1989), pp. 3–107. See also, Stephen Lukes, *Individualism*; Oxford: Basil Blackwell (1984 [1973]), especially pp. 45–105.

14. Lawrence Buell, 'In Pursuit of Ethics', *PMLA Special Issue: Ethics and Literary Study*, (January 1999), p. 14. The emphasis on the *ordinary* person as an agent in the world, as against the hero or the aristocrat, is one hallmark of Enlightenment thought according to Charles Taylor, pp. 211–33.

15. Focusing on John Locke's liberalism, C.B. Macpherson finds this attitude to be at the heart of Enlightenment politics. See his *The Political Theory of Possessive Individualism: From Hobbes to Locke*, Oxford: Oxford University Press (1962), p. 3.

16. Purnima Bose, *Organizing Empire: Individualism, Collective Agency, and India*, Durham: Duke University Press (2005), p. 3.

17. 'A Vocabulary of Feminist Praxis: On War and Radical Critique', in Robin L. Riley, Chandra Talpade Mohanty, and Minnie Bruce Pratt (eds), *Feminism and War: Confronting US Imperialism*, London: Zed Books (2008), p. 23.

18. Edward Said (1993), p. 9.

19. Wai Chee Dimock, quoted in Lawrence Buell, p. 11.

20. *After Amnesia: Tradition and Change in Indian Literary Criticism*, Hyderabad: Orient Longman (1992), pp. 38–9.

21. Michel Foucault, *Ethics, Subjectivity, and Truth*, trans. by R. Hurley, et al. and edited by Paul Rabinow, New York: New York University Press (1984), pp. 224–5.

22. See, Catherine Belsey's succinct discussion of the post-structuralist critique of the sovereign subject: *Critical Practice*, London: Metheun (1980), p. 67.

23. *A Critique of Postcolonial Reason: Toward a History of the Vanishing Present*, Cambridge: Harvard University Press (1999), p. 315.

24. *Edgework: Critical Essays on Knowledge and Politics*, Princeton: Princeton University Press (2005), p. 4.

Introduction

1. For another extended version of this discussion, see my 'Decolonizing Universality: Postcolonial Theory and the Quandary of Ethical Agency', *diacritics*, vol. 32:2 (Summer 2002), pp. 42–59.

2. Quoted from Alex Aronson and Debapriya Paul, 'Tagore and the West: Modernism and Bengal', in Krishna Sen and Tapati Gupta (eds), *Tagore and Modernity*, Kolkata: Dasgupta and Company (2006), p. 104.

3. 'Red Oleanders: Author's Interpretation', Appendix to *Raktakarabi*, Calcutta: Viswabharati Press (1985 [1924]), pp. 120–3.

4. William Howe (ed.), *The Complete Works of William Hazlitt*, vol. 4, London: J.M. Dent (1930), pp. 347 and 200.

5. David B. Clark (ed.), *Shelley's Prose*, London: Fourth Estate (1988), pp. 39, 285, and 292.

6. *Nationalist Thought and the Colonial World: A Derivative Discourse?*, Minneapolis: University of Minnesota Press (1986), p. 11.

7. Ibid.

8. 'The Disciplines in Colonial Bengal', in Partha Chatterjee (ed.), *Texts of Power: Emerging Disciplines in Colonial Bengal*, Minneapolis: University of Minnesota Press (1995), pp. 23 and 26.

9. *The Politics of the Governed: Popular Politics in Most of the World*, New York: Columbia University Press (2004), p. 34.

10. Ibid., pp. 40 and 50–1.

11. 'A Preface to Transgression', in Donald Bouchard (ed.), *Language, Counter-Memory, Practice*, Ithaca: Cornell University Press (1977), p. 44.

12. 'Michel Foucault versus Noam Chomsky: Justice versus Power', in Fons Elders (ed.), *Reflexive Water: The Basic Concerns of Mankind*, London: Souvenir (1974), p. 180.

13. *The Location of Culture*, London and New York: Routledge (1994), p. 256.

14. Ibid., p. 247.

15. *Provincializing Europe: Postcolonial Thought and Historical Difference*, Princeton: Princeton University Press (2000), p. 251. See also, Chakrabarty's *Habitations of Modernity: Essays in the Wake of Subaltern Studies*, Delhi: Permanent Black (2002), p. 46.

16. *Provincializing Europe* (2000), pp. 74 and 83.

17. Ibid., p. 242.

18. Ibid., pp. 153 and 168.

19. Michel Foucault, *The Order of Things: An Archeology of the Human Sciences*, New York: Vintage Books (1994 [1970]), p. 83.

20. 'What is Enlightenment?', in Paul Rabinow (ed.), *The Foucault Reader*, New York: Pantheon Books (1984), pp. 38 and 42.

21. Ibid., p. 46.

22. *The Intimate Enemy: Loss and Recovery of Self under Colonialism*, Delhi: Oxford University Press (1983), pp. 73 and 113.

23. Ashis Nandy, *The Illegitimacy of Nationalism: Rabindranath Tagore and the Politics of the Self*, Delhi: Oxford University Press (1994), p. 41.

24. *The Savage Freud and Other Essays on Possible and Retrievable Selves*, Princeton: Princeton University Press (1995), p. 39.

25. Edward C. Dimock, 'Doctrine and Practice among Vaisnavas of Bengal', *Krishna: Myths, Rites, and Attitudes*, Chicago: University of Chicago Press (1966), pp. 47 and 57.

26. Ranajit Guha, *History at the Limit of World-History*, Delhi: Oxford University Press (2003), p. 92.

27. See 'Kaler Matra O Rabindra Natak' (The Measure of Time and Tagore Drama), *Sankha Ghosher Gadyasangraha*, vol. 5, Kolkata: Dey's Publishing (2002), p. 20.

28. See, 'Kabir Abhipryay', *Sankha Ghosher Gadyasangraha*, vol. 5, Kolkata: Dey's Publishing (2002), p. 26.

29. 'Kaler Matra', p. 23.

30. *Modernism and Tagore*, Amitava Ray (trans.), Delhi: Sahitya Akademi (1995), p. 84. This observation resonates with Promothonath Bishi's in *Rabindrakabyaprobaha* (twelfth reprint), Kolkata: Mitra and Ghosh (1985), pp. 201–10. For a succinct and insightful assessment of Tagore's drama in a vein similar to Sankha Ghosh, see also, Asitkumar Bandopadhyay, *Adhunik Bangla Sahityer Sankhipta Itibritta* (thirteenth edition), Kolkata: Modern Book Agency (1988), pp. 120–6.

31. Ayyub, *Modernism*, pp. 138–9.

32. Ibid., p. 83.

33. *History at the Limit of World-History*, Delhi: Oxford University Press (2003), p. 76.

34. Ibid., p. 86.

35. Ibid., p. 81.

36. Ibid.

37. Ibid., p. 79.

38. Ibid., p. 81.

39. 'The Poetry of Interiority: the Creation of a Language of Subjectivity in Tagore's Poetry', in Bharati Ray and David Taylor (eds), *Politics and Identity in South Asia*, Kolkata: K.P. Bagchi (2001), p. 70. For an insightful reading of Tagore's critical humanism, see also, Krishna Sen, 'The Fortress and the Raj', in Krishna Sen nd Tapati Gupta (eds), *Tagore and Modernity*, Kolkata: Dasgupta and Co. (2006), pp. 82–9.

40. Ghosh, *Gadyasangraha*, vol. 5, p. 380.

41. Ayyub, *Modernism*, pp. 182–6.

42. Tanika Sarkar, 'Mrinal Anya Itihaser Swakshar', *Desh* (August 2000), p. 35.

43. *Humanism and Democratic Criticism*, New York: Columbia University Press (2004), p. 43. For a prescient reading of postcolonial textual politics along these lines, with emphasis on South Asia, see, Aamir Mufti, *Enlightenment in the Colony*, Princeton: Princeton University Press (2006).

44. *Marxism and the Philosophy of Language*, trans. by Ladislav Matejka and I.R. Titunik, New York: Seminar (1973), p. 118.

45. Ibid., p.120.

46. Ibid., pp. 23 and 118.

47. See, Sisir Kumar Das, 'Introduction', *The English Writings of Rabindranath Tagore*, Delhi: Sahitya Akademi (1994), pp. 30–1.

48. See, Debapriya Paul, 'Tagore and the West', pp. 107–8.

49. Stuart Hall, 'The Local and the Global: Globalization and Ethnicity', in Anthony D. King (ed.), *Culture, Globalization, and the World-System: Contemporary*

Conditions for the Representation of Identity, Minnesota: University of Minnesota Press (1997), p. 20.

50. Bijoy Kumar Dutta (ed.), *Rabindranath O Nobel Purashkar: Samakalin Tathya*, Kolkata: Paschim Banga Akademi (1998), pp. 80–90.

51. *Marxism and the Philosophy of Language*, trans. by Ladislav Matejka and I.R. Titunik. Cambridge: Harvard University Press (1986), p. 23.

52. *A Letter Concerning Toleration* (1689). www.constitution.org/jl/tolerati. htm.

53. *The Ethics of Identity*, Princeton: Princeton University Press (2005), pp. 269–70.

54. (1996 [1792]), p. 18.

55. Volosinov, *Marxism* (1976), p. 159.

56. *Towards a Philosophy of the Act*, trans. by Vadim Lipunov and edited by Vadim Liapunov and Michael Holoquist, Austin: University of Texas Press (1993), p. 3.

57. Ibid., p. 47.

58. Ibid., p. 98.

59. Volosinov (1976), p. 122.

60. 'Translator's Preface and Afterword to Mahasweta Devi, '*Imaginary Maps*', *The Spivak Reader: Selected Works of Gayatri Chakravorty Spivak*, Donna Landry and Gerald MacLean (eds), New York: Routledge (1996), p. 277.

61. Ibid., p. 282.

62. Ibid., p. 280.

63. *Literary Theory and the Claims of History: Postmodernism, Objectivity, Multicultural Politics*, Ithaca: Cornell University Press (1997), p. 137.

64. Ibid., p. 139.

65. Ibid.

66. Ibid., p. 212.

67. Ibid., p. 210

68. Ibid., p. 214

69. V.N. Volosinov, 'Discourse in Life and Discourse in Art', *Freudianism: A Marxist Critique*, I.R. Titunik (trans.), edited in collaboration with Neal H. Bruss, New York: Academic Press (1976), p. 108.

70. Ibid., p. 147.

71. Mohanty, *Literary Theory*, p. 140.

72. Ibid., p. 144.

73. Ibid., pp. 214–16.

74. Ghosh, *Gadyasangraha*, vol. 5, p. 78.

75. Rabindranath Tagore, 'Rabindranather Rashtranaitik Math', *Rabindra Racanabali*, vol. 12, Calcutta: Saraswati Press (1961 [1928]), p. 270.

76. Raymond Williams, *Marxism and Literature*, Oxford: Oxford University Press (1977), p. 121.

77. Ibid., pp. 122–3.

78. Ibid., p. 12.

79. Marshall McLuhan, 'The Medium is the Message', in Marris Thorham and Sue Thornham (eds), *Media Studies: A Reader*, Paul Edinburgh: Edinburgh University Press (1999), p. 39.

80. Raymond Williams, 'Programming as Sequence and Flow', *Media Studies: A Reader*, p. 232–3.

81. Adam Smith, *An Inquiry into the Nature and Causes of the Wealth of Nations, 1776*, Adam Smith Institute: Online Edition, 1995–2005, Chapter 2, see http://www.adamsmith.org

82. John Stuart Mill's notion of moral privacy—of pursuing the good in a way not interfered by social custom—is influential on Aparna Sen's works and the indigenous Bengali liberal tradition as a whole. See, Mill, *Utilitarianism*, p. 126.

83. See interview, http://www.rediff.com/entertai/2002/jul/27aparna.htm

84. Quoted Shoma Chatterji, *Parama and Other Outsiders: The Cinema of Aparna Sen*, Calcutta: Parumita Publications (2002), p. 215.

85. Adam Smith's Economic Individualism centres upon self-love, whereas Harriet Taylor Mill's Utilitarian feminist position, for one, affirms competitive individualism. See Harriet Taylor Mill, 'Enfranchisement of Women', in Alice S. Rossi (ed.), *John Stuart Mill and Harriet Taylor Mill: Essays on Sex Equality*, Chicago: University of Chicago Press (1970), p. 105.

86. See, Paul Virilio's analysis of commercial media's role in the First Gulf War in *Desert Screen: War at the Speed of Light*, Michael Degener (trans.), London: Continuum Press (2002), p. 108.

87. Jean Comaroff and John L. Comaroff, 'Millenial Capitalism and the Culture of Neoliberalism', in Marc Edelman and Angelique Haugerud (eds), *The Anthropology of Development and Globalization: From Classical Political Economy to Contemporary Neoliberalism*, Oxford: Blackwell (2005), pp. 182–3.

88. As rightly noted by Shoma Chatterji (2002), p. 206.

89. Ibid., p. 161.

Chapter 1

1. *Bangla Sahityer Itihas*, vol. 3, 1943; Kolkata: Ananda Publishers (2003), pp. 435–48.

2. See Debipada Bhattacharya, *Bangla Charit Sahitya*, Calcutta: Dey (1982); Sudipta Kaviraj, 'The Poetry of Interiority: the Creation of Language of Modern Subjectivity in Tagore's Poetry', *Politics and Identity in South Asia*, Bharati Ray and David Taylor (eds) Kolkata: K.P. Bagchi (2001), pp. 48–76; Tanika Sarkar, *Words to Win: The Making of Amar Jiban—A Modern Autobiography*, New Delhi: Kali for Women (1999), pp. 6–8.

3. Kaviraj, 'The Poetry of Interiority: The Creation of Language of Modern Subjectivity in Tagore's Poetry', in Bharati Ray and David Taylor (eds), *Politics and Identity in South Asia*, Kolkata: K.P. Bagchi (2001), p. 52.

4. Charles Taylor, *Sources of the Self: The Making of the Modern Identity*, Cambridge: Harvard University Press (1989), p. 47.

5. Ibid., p. 289.

6. Ibid., p. 48.

7. Ibid., pp. 144, 185–7.

8. Crowford B. Macpherson, *The Political Theory of Possessive Individualism: Hobbes to Locke*, Oxford: Oxford University Press (1962), pp. 2–3.

9. Ibid., p. 2.

10. Purnima Bose, *Organizing Empire: Individualism, Collective Agency, and India*, Durham: Duke University Press (2003), p. 5.

11. Ranajit Guha, *History at the Limit of World-History*, New Delhi: Oxford University Press (2003), p. 92.

12. Ann McClintock, *Imperial Leather: Race, Gender and Sexuality in the Colonial Contest*, New York: Routledge (1995), pp. 36–56. See my discussion of 'empire' in this light in the Preface.

13. Rey Chow makes these insightful remarks about the reductive trend of the visual medium of knowledge. *Writing Diaspora: Tactics of Intervention in Contemporary Cultural Studies*, Bloomington: Indiana University Press (1993), p. 166.

14. Slavoj Zizek argues that the visual medium involves a 'mortification of the living body'. See *The Plague of Fantasies*, London: Verso, 1997, p. 108.

15. Ramond Williams, *The Long Revolution*, New York: Columbia University Press (1961), p. 48.

16. See among others the works of Sudipta Kaviraj and Tanika Sarkar (note 2 above). See also Ranajit Guha, *History at the Limit of World-History*, New Delhi: Oxford University Press (2002), pp. 75–94; Malavika Karlekar, *Voices from Within: Early Personal Narratives of Bengali Women*, Delhi: Oxford University Press (1991); Rimli Bhattacharya (ed. and trans.), *Binodini Dasi: My Story and My Life as an Actress*, New Delhi: Kali for Women, 1998. Note my discussion of the critical approaches of Kaviraj, Sarkar, and Guha in the Introduction.

17. *A Letter Concerning Toleration*, 1689. www.constitution.org/jl/tolerati.htm.

18. According to Charles Taylor, 'The language of subjective rights ... expresses ... immunities and benefits as a kind of property of the subject, which can be invoked by the subject in his or her own cause', p. 395.

19. Quoted by Sukumar Sen, *Bangla Sahityer Itihas*, vol. 3, Kolkata: Ananda Publishers (2003 [1943]), p. 443.

20. Reprinted in *Atmakatha*, vol. 2, Nareschandra Jana, Manu Jana, and Kamalkumar Sanyal (eds), Calcutta: Ananya Publications (1981), pp. 4–70.

21. First published in 1953 in serial form in the periodical *Masik Basumati*. Reproduced in *Atmakatha*, vol. 2, pp. 3–40. For an extended discussion of this autobiography, see Malavika Karlekar, *Voices from Within*, pp. 122–43.

22. Reproduced in *Bangali Meyer Bhabonamulak Gadya: Unish Shatak*, Sutapa Bhattacharya (collected and edited), New Delhi: Sahitya Akademi (1999), p. 96. The letter was written two years after the ban on *sati* immolation by Lord Bentinck in 1829. Prior to that, the idea of women's equality had been strongly promoted by Rammohan Roy. Noteworthy is his polemical tracts published in 1818 and 1819 titled *Probatak O Nibartaker Sambad* (Conference between a Proponent and an Opponent). *Rammohan Racanabali*, Calcutta: Haraf, 1973, pp. 202–3. Significant portions of the Second Conference are intertextual with Mary Wollstonecraft's

Vindication of the Rights of Women. Whether or not he had read this, he was conversant with her arguments.

23. Nareshchandra Jana, Manu Jana, and Kamalkumar Sanyal (eds), *Atmakatha,* vol. 2, Calcutta: Ananya Publications (1981 [1913]), p. 8.

24. Sukumar Sen, *Bangla Sahityer Itihas,* vol. 3, Kolkata: Ananda Publishers (2003 [1943]), p. 444.

25. Nareshchandra Jana, Manu Jana, and Kamalkumar Sanyal (eds), *Atmakatha,* vol. 2, Calcutta: Ananya Publications, (1981 [1913]), p. 8.

26. For excellent discussions of biases against women's sexuality in the Hindu codes that prohibited education and how these were re-structured by male nationalist reformers, see Uma Chakravarti, *Rewriting History: The Life and Times of Pandita Ramabhai,* Delhi: Kali for Women (1998), pp. 200–5; see also Tanika Sarkar, *Words to Win,* pp. 67–91.

27. See, for example, William Adam, 'Female Instruction', in Ananthnath Basu (ed.), *Second Report on the State of Education in Bengal, 1836.* Calcutta: Calcutta University (1941), pp. 187–8; and James Mill, *The History of British India,* annotated H.H. Wilson, London: James Madden (1840), p. 314.

28. For a succinct study of how the Aryanization of the upper caste Hindu affected the status of women in nineteenth century India, see Uma Chakravarti, 'Whatever Happened to the Vedic *Dasi?* Orientalism, Nationalism, and a Script for the Past', *Recasting Women: Essays in Colonial History,* Delhi: Kali for Women (1989), pp. 27–87.

29. See, Sarah Lamb, *White Saris and Sweet Mangoes: Aging, Gender, and Body in North* India, Berkeley: University of California Press (2000), pp. 30–7, 182–7. Lamb draws on the following studies: McKim Marriott and Ronald Inden, 'Toward an ethnosociology of South Asian caste systems', in Kenneth David (ed.), *The new wind: Changing Identities in South Asia.* The Hague: Mouton Publishers (1977), pp. 227–38; and E. Valentine Daniel, *Fluid signs: Being a person the Tamil way.* Berkeley: University of California Press.

30. The influential nineteenth century work on the ideal homemaker was John Ruskin's *Sesames and Lilies.* New Haven: Yale University Press (2002 [(1865)]), edited by Deborah Epstein Nord. See especially Lecture II, pp. 68–196. For perceptive discussions of the racial and class dimensions of the Judeo-Christian binary of chaste-and-whore, see, Sander L. Gilman, 'Black Bodies and White Bodies: Towards an Iconography of Female Sexuality in Late Nineteenth Century Art, Medicine, and Literature', *'Race', Writing, and Difference,* Henry Louis Gates, Jr. (ed.), Chicago: University of Chicago Press (1985), pp. 223–61; Patricia Hill Collins, *Black Feminist Thought: Knowledge, Consciousness, and the Politics of Empowerment.* New York: Routledge (1991), pp. 166–79; and Ann McClintock, *Imperial Leather,* New York: Routledge (1995), pp. 160–73.

31. For a concise review of the influence of colonial educators, including missionaries, on modern Indian perceptions of sexuality see Ruth Vanita and Saleem Kidwai (eds), *Same-Sex Love in India: Readings from Literature and History,* New York: St. Martin's Press (2000), pp. 194–205.

32. Benedict Anderson, *Imagined Communities: Reflections on the Origin and Spread of Nationalism*, London: Verso (1991 [1983]).

33. Debashis Majumdar and Shekhar Samaddar (eds), *Satabdir Natyachinta: Girishchandra Theke Utpal Dutta*, Kolkata: A. Mukherjee and Co. (2000), pp. 86–94.

34. Sir Surendranath Banerjea, *A Nation in the Making being the Reminiscences of Fifty Years of Public Life*, Bombay: Oxford University Press (1963 [1925]).

35. Ibid., pp. 263 and 366.

36. Ibid., p. 361.

37. Ibid., pp. 364–5.

38. Ibid., p. 10.

39. Ibid.

40. Ibid., p. 9.

41. McClintock, *Imperial Leather* (1995), p. 40.

42. Ann Stoler, 'Tense and Tender Ties: The Politics of Comparison in North American History and (Post-Colonial Studies', *Haunted by Empire: Geographies of Intimacy in North American History*, Durham: Duke University Press (2006), pp. 23–67.

43. For a careful study of how British and native gender ideologies were implicated in new notions of manhood among Bengalis in the nineteenth century, see especially Mrinalini Sinha, *Colonial Masculinity: The 'Manly Englishman' and the 'Effeminate Bengali' in the Nineteenth Century*, Manchester: University of Manchester Press (1995), pp. 33–63 and 138–172; see also, Ashis Nandy, *The Intimate Enemy: Loss and Recovery of Self Under Colonialism*, Delhi: Oxford University Press (1983), pp. 1–29.

44. David Lloyd, 'Genet's Genealogy: European Minorities and the Ends of the Canon', *Cultural Critique* (Spring 1987), 6, p. 85.

45. Ibid.

46. See, Sumit Sarkar's insightful overview, 'Calcutta and the "Bengal Renaissance"', *Calcutta: The Living City, The Past* Vol. 1, Delhi: Oxford University Press (1991), pp. 95–105.

47. Partha Chatterjee, *The Nation and Its Fragments: Colonial and Postcolonial Histories*. Princeton: Princeton University Press (1993), p. 237.

48. Purnima Bose, *Organizing Empire* (2003), p. 5.

49. Raymond Williams, *Marxism and Literature*, Oxford: Oxford University Press (1977), pp. 122–3.

50. Partha Chatterjee (1993), p. 237.

51. Ramond Williams, *The Long Revolution*, New York: Columbia University Press (1961), p. 48.

52. For example, Kumari Jayawardena notes that Rammohan Roy's arguments for women's rights echo some of Mary Wollstonecraft's in her *Vindication of the Rights of Women*; moreover he is known to have met and been influenced by the feminist thinker, Harriet Martineau. See *Feminism and Nationalism in the Third World*, London: Zed Books (1986), pp. 80–2. Sukumar Sen lists a series of

biographies of great Europeans written by Jogendranath Bidyabhushan between 1877 and 1890 that includes Giuseppe Mazzini, Giuseppe Garibaldi, and John Stuart Mill, *History of Bengali Literature*, pp. 440–1. In nineteenth and early twentieth century periodicals we find such commentaries as Swarnakumari Debi's on George Eliot, *Bharati O Balak* (July 1890), and on Percy Shelley and atheism, *Bharati O Balak* (May 1888); Jyotirindranath Tagore's on Shakespeare, Milton, and John Stuart Mill, *Bharati O Balak* (1889); and Rabindranath Tagore's on Ernest Renan's thesis of nationalism.

53. See my full discussion of this approach in the Introduction. The quotes are from Mikhail Bakhtin, *Towards the Philosophy of an Act*, (trans. by Vadim Liapunov), Vadim Liapunov and Michael Holoquist (eds), Austin: University of Texas Press (1993), p. 3.

54. Lisa Lowe and David Lloyd, 'Introduction', *The Politics of Culture in the Shadow of Capital*, Durham: Duke University Press (1997), p. 14.

55. Ranajit Guha, *History at the Limit of the World-History* (2003), pp. 72 and 73.

56. Indira Debi Chaudhurani (ed.), *Puratani*, Kolkata: Indian Associated Publishing (1957), pp. 5–42.

57. Himani Bannerji, 'Attired in Virtue: The Discourse of Shame (*lajja*) and Clothing the *Bhadramahila* in Colonial Bengal', in Bharati Ray (ed.), *From the Seams of History: Essays on Indian Women*, Delhi: Oxford University Press (1995), p. 74.

58. Partha Chatterjee, *The Nation and Its Fragments* (1993), p. 149.

59. Chandra Talpade Mohanty, *Feminism Without Borders: Decolonizing Theory, Practicing Solidarity*, Durham: Duke University Press (2003), p. 78.

60. The letter has been reproduced in Sutapa Bhattacharya, *Bangali Meyer Bhabonamulak Gadya: Unish Satak* (collected and edited) (2003), p. 3.

61. In her introductory comments, Sutapa Bhattacharya notes the virulent opposition to materials published in this periodical. She also quotes the Brahmo reformist leader Shibnath Shastri's applause of the progressive boldness of the periodical, p. 2.

62. Sutapa Bhattacharya, *Bengali Meyer Bhabonamulak Gadya* (2003), p. 6.

63. Himani Bannerji, *From the Seams of History: Essays on Indian Women*, p. 76.

64. Anindita Mukhpadhyay, *Behind the Mask: The Cultural Definition of the Legal Subject in Colonial Bengal (1775–1911)*, Delhi, New York: Oxford University Press (2006), pp. 158–62.

65. See Anindita Mukhpadhyay, pp. 160–1; Joyonto Goswami, *Patha Sahitya: Pathapustika*, Kolkata: Kamal Publishers (1982), pp. 24–30; Jyotindra Jain, *Kalighat Painting: Images from a Changing World*, Ahmedabad: Mapin Publishing (1999), 127–38.

66. Judith R. Walkowitz, *Prostitution and Victorian Society: Women, Class, and the State*, Cambridge: Cambridge University Press (1980), pp. 69–79.

67. Carole Pateman, *The Sexual Contract*, Stanford: Stanford University Press (1988), p. 196.

68. Sutapa Bhattacharya, *Bengali Meyer Bhabonamulak Gadya* (2003), p. 3.

69. Ibid.

70. E.P. Thompson, *The Making of the English Working Class*, New York: Pantheon Books (1964), 9, p. 807.

71. Carole Pateman makes the argument that prostitution proves the ubiquity of 'patriarchal right' and 'fraternal relations' in seemingly contractual domains, pp. 189 and 192.

72. Raymond Williams, *Keywords: A Vocabulary of Culture and Society*, New York: Oxford University Press (1983 [1966]), p. 164. See my discussion of this concept in the Preface.

73. Rajeswari Sunder Rajan (ed.), 'The Burden of English', *Lie of the Land: English Literary Studies in India*, Delhi: Oxford University Press (1992), p. 290.

74. Gayatri Chakravorty Spivak, *A Critique of Postcolonial Reason: Toward A History of the Vanishing Present*, Cambridge: Harvard University Press (1999), p. 310.

75. V.N. Volosinov, *Freudianism: A Marxist Critique* (translated I.R. Titunik, edited in collaboration with Neal H. Bruss), New York: Academic Press (1976), p. 105.

76. Bondini Dasi, *Amar Katha O Annanyo Rachona*, edited by Soumitra Chattopadhyay and Shankar Bhattacharya, Kolkata: Subarnarekha (1987), p. 33.

77. Marvin Carlson notes that, in his *A Short Treatise on Acting* (1744), David Garrick argues that human nature must never be simply imitated, rather 'digested' by the actor and translated by his judgment. See, *Theories of the Theatre: A Historical and Critical Survey from the Greeks to the Present*, Ithaca: Cornell University Press (1984), p. 139.

78. Bondini Dasi, *Amar Katha O Anyanya Rachona*, (1987), p. 137.

79. Ibid., p. 7.

80. Ibid., p. 138.

81. Ibid., p. 144. See also, Partha Chatterjee, *The Nation* (1993), pp. 151–4; and Sudipto Chatterjee, *The Colonial Staged*, pp. 210–11.

82. Bandini Dasi, *Amar Katha O Anyanyo Rachona*, (1987 [1913]), p. 1.

83. Ibid.

84. Ibid., p. 71.

85. Ibid., p. 3.

86. Ibid., p. 67.

87. 'Abhinetri Samālochona', *Girish Racanabali*, vol. 3, Calcutta: Sahitya Samsad (1972), pp. 823–7.

88. *Kalighat Painting: Images from a Changing World*, Ahmedabad: Mapin Publishing (1999), pp. 97–138.

89. Ashish Rajadhyaksha, 'The Phalke Era: Conflict of Traditional Form and Modern Technology', in Tejaswini Niranjana, P. Sudhir, Vivek Dhareshwar (eds), *Interrogating Modernity: Culture and Colonialism in India*, Calcutta: Seagull Press (1993), pp. 54–5.

90. Jain, *Kalighat Painting* (1999), p. 97.

91. Zizek, *The Plague of Fantasies* (1997), p. 108.

92. Jain, *Kalighat Painting* (1999), p. 97.

93. Ashish Rajadhyaksha, *Interrogating Modernity: Culture and Colonialism in India*, p. 57.

94. Rimli Bhattacharya (ed. and trans.), *Binodini Dasi: My Story and My Life as an Actress*, New Delhi: Kali for Woman (1998), p. 200.

95. *'Abhinetri Samālochona', Girish Racanabali*, vol. 3, p. 825.

96. Sumit Sarkar makes this insightful point regarding the incest taboo underneath Ramakrishna's mother worship. See his ' "Kaliyuga", "Chakri", and "Bhakti": Ramakrishna and His Times', *Economic and Political Weekly*, vols 27–9 (July 1992), pp. 1543–65 and 1551.

97. *'Abhinetri Samālochona', Girish Racanabali*, vol. 3, p. 825.

98. Bondini Dasi, *Amar Katha O Anyanya Rachona*, (1987), pp. 137–8.

99. *'Abhinetri Samālochona', Girish Racanabali*, vol. 3, p. 825.

100. Ibid., vol. 3, p. 826.

101. Ibid., vol. 4, 641–54.

102. Himani Bannerji, *From the Seams of History: Essays on Indian Women*, p. 76.

103. Ashish Rajadhyaksha, *Interrogating Modernity: Culture and Colonialism in India*, p. 35.

104. Bondini Dasi, *Amar Katha O Anyanya Rachona*, (1987), p. 35.

105. Gail Marshall, *Actresses on the Victorian Stage: Feminine Performances and the Galatea Myth*, Cambridge: Cambridge University Press (1998), p. 38.

106. Ibid.

107. Gail Marshall, *Actresses on the Victorian Stage*, p. 101.

108. Bondini Dasi, *Amar Katha O Anyanya Rachona* (1987), p. 48.

109. Ibid.

110. Bondini Dasi, *Amar Katha O Anyanya Rachona* (1987), p. 49.

111. Naliniranjan Chattopadhyay, *SriRamakrishna O Banga Rangamancha*, Calcutta: Deb Sahitya Kutir (1992), p. 9.

112. Bondini Dasi, *Amar Katha O Anyanya Rachona* (1987), p. 48.

113. Ibid., pp. 69–70.

114. Ibid., 50.

115. Ibid., p. 141.

116. See Parama Roy's insightful discussion of the "gynophobia" in the gender-crossing performances of Ramakrishna: *Indian Traffic: Identities in Question in Colonial and Postcolonial India*, Berkeley: University of California Press (1998), pp. 96–7.

117. Sumit Sarkar, 'A Religion of Urban Domesticity: Sri Ramakrishna and the Calcutta Middle Class', *Subaltern Studies VII: Writings on South Asian History and Society*, Delhi: Oxford University Press (1992), pp. 60–1.

118. Sarkar, 'Kaliyug', *Economic and Political Weekly* (1992), p. 1548.

119. Bondini Dasi, *Amar Katha O Anyanya Rachona* (1987), p. 18.

120. Ibid., 20–1.

121. Sarkar, 'Kaliyug', *EPW* (1992), p. 1547.

122. Bondini Dasi, *Amar Katha O Anyanya Rachona* (1987), pp. 4 and 66.

123. Ibid., pp. 70–1.

124. Ibid., p. 4.

125. Gayatri Chakravorty Spivak, 'The Burden of English', *Lie of the Land* (1999), p. 290.

126. Mikhail Bakhtin, *Towards a Philosophy of the Act* (1993), p. 3.

127. Rimli Bhattacharya (ed. And trans.), *Binodini Dasi: My Story and My Life as an Actress* (1998), pp. 18–19.

128. Ibid., pp. 36–7.

129. Bondini Dasi, *Amar Katha O Anyanya Rachona* (1987), p. 24.

130. Rimli Bhattacharya (ed. and trans.), *Binodini Dasi: My Story and My Life as an Actress* (1998), p. 195.

131. Bondini Dasi, *Amar Katha O Anyanya Rachona* (1987), p. 37.

132. Ibid., p. 40.

133. Ibid., p. 38.

134. Ibid.

135. Ibid.

136. As Jean Jacques Rousseau put it in *The Social Contract,* a self resting on contract gains 'civil liberty and the proprietorship of all he possesses'; on his part Immanuel Kant emphasizes social contract as an '*idea* of reason' was enabling a 'coalition of the wills of all private individuals in a nation to form a common ...'. See, Michael Lessnoff (ed.), *Social Contract Theory,* New York: New York University Press (1990), pp. 114 and 132.

137. Bondini Dasi, *Amar Katha O Anyanya Rachona* (1987), p. 47.

138. Ibid.

139. Sarkar, 'Kaliyug', *EPW* (1992), p. 1547.

140. Bondini Dasi, *Amar Katha O Anyanya Rachona* (1987), p. 47.

141. Amales Tripathi, *Trade and Finance in the Bengal Presidency, 1793–1833;* qtd., Tanika Sarkar, *Words to Win,* p. 23.

142. Bondini Dasi, *Amar Katha O Anyanya Rachona* (1987), p. 39.

143. Ritu Birla, *Stages of Capital: Law, Culture, and Market Governance in Late Colonial India,* Durham: Duke University Press (2009), pp. 35–6.

144. Ibid., p. 15.

145. Ibid., p. 237.

146. Ibid., pp. 28–9.

147. Ibid., p. 29.

Chapter 2

1. Dipesh Chakraborty, *Provincializing Europe: Postcolonial Thought and Historical Difference*, Princeton: Princeton Uni· sity Press (2000), pp. 216–17.

2. Ibid., pp. 225 and 228.

3. Ibid., p. 228.

4. Ibid., p. 218.

5. Ibid., pp. 3–23.

6. Uma Dasgupta, 'Rabindranath Tagore and Modernity', in Krishna Sen and Tapati Gupta (eds), *Tagore and Modernity*, Kolkata: Dasgupta and Co. (2006), p. 7.

7. Raymond Williams, *The Long Revolution*, New York: Columbia University Press (1961), p. 48. See my discussion: Chapter One.

8. *Rabindra Racanabali*, vol. 13, Calcutta: Saraswati Press (1961), pp. 21–9.

9. Reprinted as Sutapa Bhattacharya (ed.), 'Ramabai', in *Bangali Meyer Bhabonamulak Gadya*, Delhi: Sahitya Akademi (1999), pp. 20–1.

10. Reprinted as 'Ramabaier Baktrita Upalakshe Patra', *Rabindra Racanabali*, vol. 13, Calcutta: Saraswati Press (1961), pp. 101–5.

11. Ibid., p. 104.

12. Reprinted as 'Strilok O Purush', in *Bangali Meyer Bhabonamulak Gadya*, Delhi: Sahitya Akademi (1999), pp. 21–34.

13. 'Probartak O Nibartaker Dwitiya Sambad', *Rammohan Racanabali*, Calcutta: Harraf (1973), pp. 202–3.

14. 'Probas Patra', *Bharati* (1885), pp. 76–80.

15. Bharati Ray and David Taylor (eds), 'The Poetry of Interiority: the Creation of a Language of Modern Subjectivity in Tagore's Poetry', *Politics and Identity in South Asia*, Kolkata: K.P. Bagchi (2001), pp. 50–1.

16. Ibid., p. 49.

17. Ibid., p. 70.

18. Tagore, 'Narir Manusatya', p. 24.

19. Ibid., p. 28.

20. Ibid., p. 25.

21. Ibid., p. 24.

22. Ibid., p. 27.

23. Ibid., p. 22.

24. Ibid.

25. Ibid., p. 25.

26. Ibid., p. 21.

27. Ibid.

28. Ibid., p. 22.

29. Ibid., pp. 23–4.

30. Ibid., p. 26.

31. Ibid.

32. Ibid., p. 27.

33. Ashis Nandy, *The Illegitimacy of Nationalism*, Delhi: Oxford University Press (1994), p. 41.

34. Ibid., p. 42.

35. K.A. Appiah, *The Ethics of Identity*, Princeton: Princeton University Press (2005), p. 264.

36. 'Of Individuality as one of the Elements of Well-being', in Geraint Williams (ed.), *Utilitarianism, On Liberty, Considerations on Representative Government*, J.M. Dent: Everyman (1993), p. 125.

37. Ibid., p. 124.

38. Ibid., p. 126.

39. Ibid., p. 126.

40. Tagore, 'Narir Manusatya', p. 27.

41. Ibid.
42. Marshall Berman, *All That is Solid Melts in the Air: The Experience of Modernity*, New York: Penguin (1988 [1982]), p. 21.
43. 'Two Theories of Modernity', *Public Culture*, 11(1), pp. 153–74 and 153.
44. Tagore, 'Narir Manusatya', p. 27.
45. Ibid., p. 28.
46. Tagore, *Galpaguccha*, Kolktata: Visva-Bharati Press (1998), pp. 567–75. See also, Tanika Sarkar's insightful reading of this short story: 'Mrinal Anya Itihaser Sakshar (August 2000), pp. 35–44.
47. *Modernism and Tagore* (trans. by Amitava Ray), New Delhi: Sahitya Akademi (1995), p. 182.
48. Dasgupta, *Rabindranath Tagore and Modernity* (2006), p. 7.
49. Ghosh, *Gadyasangraha*, vol. 5, Klkata: Dey's Publishing (2002), p. 88.
50. Ibid., pp. 80–1
51. Ibid., pp. 88–9
52. Tagore, 'Narir Manusatya', p. 24.
53. Ibid.
54. Appiah, *The Ethics of Identity* (2005), p. 264.
55. Tagore, 'Narir Manusatya', p. 28.
56. See especially, Kumari Jayawardena, *Feminism and Nationalism in the Third World*, London: Zed Books (1986), pp. 73–108; Geraldine Forbes, *Women in Modern India*, Cambridge: Cambridge University Press (1996), pp. 92–156; and Ketu H. Katrak, 'Indian Nationalism, Gandhian "Satyagraha", and Representations of Female Sexuality', in Andrew Parker, Mary Russo, Doris Summer, and Patricia Yeager (eds), *Nationalisms and Sexualities*, New York: Routledge (1992), pp. 395–406. For a theoretical overview of women in anti-colonial nationalism, see also the 'Introduction' to *Nationalisms and Sexualities* by the editors.
57. Tagore, 'Narir Manusatya', p. 28.
58. 'Ethics and Politics in Tagore, Coetzee, and Certain Scenes of Teaching', *Diacritics* (Fall 2002), 32, pp. 17–31 and 30.
59. Jyotirindranath Tagore, 'Sekaler Ingraj Stree', *Bharati O Balak* (1888), p. 166.
60. Ibid., pp. 170–1.
61. Gauri Viswanathan, *Masks of Conquest: Literary Study and British Rule in India*, New York: Columbia University Press (1989). *Siting Translation: History, Post-structuralism, and the Colonial Context*, Berkeley: University of California Press (1992).
62. Tejaswani Niranjana, *Speeches and Writings of Swami Vivekananda*, Madras: G.A. Natesan (1927), p. 563.
63. Ibid.
64. Ibid., p. 568.
65. Ibid., p. 569.
66. Ibid., p. 566.
67. Ibid., p. 568.
68. Ibid.
69. Ibid., p. 567.

70. *The East and the West*, Calcutta: Advaita Ashrama (1963), p. 34–5.

71. Ibid., p. 34.

72. Indira Chowdhury, *The Frail Hero and Virile History: Gender and the Politics of Culture in Colonial Bengal*, Delhi: Oxford University Press (1998), p. 125. See also, Tapan Raychaudhuri, *Europe reconsidered: Perceptions of the West in Nineteenth Century Bengal*, Delhi and New York: Oxford University Press (1988).

73. Jyotirindranath Tagore, 'Sekaler' (1888), p. 170.

74. Vivekananda, *Speeches and Writings*, p. 566.

75. Tagore, *Sanchaita*, Calcutta: Visva-Bharati Press (1932), pp. 668–72.

76. *Saratsahityasamagra*, vol. 2, Calcutta: Ananda Publishers (1987), pp. 1929–51.

77. *Sadharan Meye*, p. 669.

78. Ibid., p. 672.

79. See my 'Decolonizing Universality: Postcolonial Theory and the Quandary of Ethical Agency', *diacritics* (2002), 32:2, pp. 42–59. This essay contains an earlier reading of *Sadharan Meye*. See also, Tagore's 'Shakuntala in 'Prachin Sahitya' *Rabindra Racanabali*, vol. 13, Calcutta: Saraswati Press (1961), pp. 661–70.

80. *Sadharan Meye*, p. 672.

81. Ranajit Guha, *History at the Limit of World-History*, New Delhi: Oxford University Press (2003), p. 82.

82. Ibid., p. 81.

83. Ibid., p. 90.

84. 'Vishwasahitya', *Rabindra Racanabali*, vol. 13, Calcutta: Saraswati Press (1961 [1906]), p. 762.

85. Ibid.

86. 'Bangla Jatiya Sahitya', *Rabindra Racanabali*, vol. 13, Calcutta: Saraswati Press (1961 [1894]), p. 793.

87. Sukanta Chaudhuri and Sisir Kumar Das (ed. and annotated), 'Literary Creation' *Rabindranath Tagore: Selected Writings on Literature and Language* (trans. by Swapan Chakravorty), New Delhi: Oxford University Press (2001 [1908]), p. 152.

88. J.N. Mohanty, *Classical Indian Philosophy*, Lanham: Rowman and Littlefield (2000), p. 135–6.

89. Ibid., p. 136.

90. Edward C. Dimock detects a certain 'deification of esthetics' in the *bhakti* tradition launched by Rupa Goswami. See, *The Literatures of India: An Introduction*, Chicago: University of Chicago Press (1974), p. 227.

91. 'Shahitya O Saundarya', *Rabindra Racanabali*, vol. 13, Calcutta: Saraswati Press (1961 [1907]), p. 780.

92. Ibid., p. 775.

93. 'Vihwasahitya', *Rabindra Racanabali*, p. 762.

94. Ghosh, *Gadyasangraha*, vol. 5, p. 58.

95. 'Discourse in Life and Discourse in Art', *Freudianism: A Marxist Critique*, trans. by I.R. Titunik edited in collaboration with Neal Bruss, New York: Academic Press (1976), p. 110.

96. *Rabindra Racanabali*, vol. 25, Calcutta: Visva-Bharati Press (1976), p. 434.

97. Ibid.

98. Partha Mitter, *Art and Nationalism in Colonial India 1850–1922*, Cambridge: Cambridge University Press (1994), p. 9.

99. Ghosh, *Gadyasangraha*, p. 34.

100. 'Rangamancho', reprinted in Debashish Majumdar and Sekhar Samaddar (eds), *Satabdir Natyachinta*, Kolkata: A. Mukherjee (2000 [1909]), pp. 24–6; Tagore commented on Sisir Bhaduri much later, in 1935 (quoted in Ghosh, p. 34).

101. *Rabindra Racanabali*, vol. 25, p. 434.

102. *Nritya*, Calcutta: Visva-Bharati Press (1993 [1949]), p. 13.

103. J.L. Styan, *Modern Drama in Theory and Practice 2: Symbolism, Surrealism, and the Absurd*, New York: Cambridge University Press (1981), p. 6.

104. Charles Taylor, *Sources of the Self: The Making of Modern Identity*, Cambridge: Harvard University Press (1989), pp. 443–4.

105. Styan, *Modern Drama*, pp. 5 and 7.

106. Sisir Kumar Das, *A History of Indian Literature, Vol. 8: 1800–1910 Western Impact, Indian Response*, New Delhi: Sahitya Akademi (1991), p. 189.

107. Kapila Vatsyayan, *Traditions of Indian Folk Dance*, New Delhi: Indian Book Company (1976), p. 9.

108. Ashoketaru Bandopadhyay, *Ashoketaru*, Rituparna Roy and Bhaswati Chakrabarty (eds), Kolkata: Praptisthan (1997), pp. 7 and 23.

109. Tagore, 'Rangamancho', *Rabindra Rachanabali*, p. 25.

110. Ghosh, *Gadyasangraha*, p. 44.

111. Ibid., pp. 44–5.

112. Tagore, *Chitrangada*, Calcutta: Visva-Bharati Press (1991), pp. 9–61.

113. *Rabindra Racanabali*, vol. 25, Calcutta: Visva-Bharati Press (1976), pp. 125–58.

114. 'Kabye Niti', *Dwijendra Racanabali*, vol. 1, Rabindranath Roy (ed.), Calcutta: Sahitya Samsad (1964), p. 213.

115. See 'Nurjahan', and 'Mebarpatan' in *Dwijendra Racanabali*, vol. 1, Rabindranath Roy (ed.), Calcutta: Sahitya Samsad (1964), pp. 151–281 and 296–350.

116. Probhatkumar Mukhpadhyay, *Rabindrajibani*, vol. 2, Kolkata: Visva-Bharati Press (1998 [1936]), pp. 378–9.

117. For details of the agreements and disagreements between Gandhi and Rabindranath Tagore, see, *The Mahatma and the Poet: Letters and Debates between Gandhi and Tagore 1915–1941*, compiled and edited, Sabyasachi Bhattacharya, New Delhi: National Book Trust (1997). Bhattacharya presents a succinct overview of the debates in his Introduction.

118. Quoted, Sarkar, 'Mrinal Anya Itihaser Sakshar', p. 35.

119. Tanika Sarkar presciently delineates the nationalist argument that education turns a woman into a pseudo-man. See especially her 'Mrinal Anya Itihaser Sakshar', p. 40. See also, Uma Chakravarti, *Rewriting History: The Life and Times of Pandita Ramabai*, New Delhi: Kali for Women (1998), pp. 200–24. See my discussion in Chapter One of women's education in colonial India.

120. *Nritya*, pp. 24–5.

121. Kapila Vastsyayan, p. 108.

122. *Nritya*, p. 25.

123. Ibid., p. 24.

124. 'Introduction', *Choreographing History*, Susan Leigh Foster (ed.), Bloomington: Indiana University Press (1995), pp. 7–11.

125. Ibid., p. 7.

126. See, Edward C. Dimock, 'Doctrine and Practice Among the Vaishnavas of Bengal', in Milton Singer (ed.), *Krishna: Myths, Rites, and Attitudes*, Chicago: University of Chicago Press (1966), pp. 48–9. See also, Sushil Kumar De, *Early History of the Vaishnava Faith and Movement in Bengal*, Calcutta: Firma K.L. Mukhopadhyay (1961 [1942]). For notions of self-surrendering versus self-loving desire (*parakiya* and *swakiya prem*), see, Ronald B. Inden and Ralph W. Nicholas, *Kinship in Bengali Culture*, Chicago: University of Chicago Press (1977), p. 24.

127. *Rabindra Racanabali*, vol. 25, Calcutta: Visva-Bharati Press (1976), p. 135.

128. Ibid., p. 136.

129. Ibid.

130. Susan Foster, *Choreography History* (1995), p. 10.

131. *Rabibdra Racanabali*, vol. 25 (1976), p. 138.

132. Ibid., p. 141.

133. Ibid., p. 143.

134. Ibid., p. 148.

135. Ibid., p. 153.

136. 'The Nationalist Resolution of the Women's Question', in Kumkum Sangari and Sudesh Vaid (eds), *Recasting Women: Essays in Colonial History*, Delhi: Kali for Women (1989), p. 238.

137. *Rabindra Racanabali*, vol. 25 (1976), p. 151.

138. Manning Marble (ed.), *Feminist Theory: From Margin to Center*, Boston: South End Press (1984), pp. 68–9.

139. Spivak, 'Ethics and Politics in Tagore', p. 30.

140. *Rabindra Racanabali*, vol. 25, Calcutta: Visva-Bharati Press (1976), p. 164.

141. Ibid., p. 166.

142. Tagore, *Chandalika*, Kolkata: Visva-Bharati Press (2004 [1933]), pp. 16–17.

143. *Rabindra Racanabali*, vol. 25 (1976), p. 170.

144. ibid., p. 172.

145. Ibid.

146. For caste- and gender-centered notions of bodily purity and pollution, see, Sarah Lamb, *White Saris and Sweet Mangoes: Aging, Gender, and Body in North India*, Berkeley: University of California Press (2000), pp. 191–4.

147. *Rabindra Racanabali*, vol. 25 (1976), p. 174.

148. Partha Chatterjee explains the various ways in which these tropes were deployed by Ramakrishna and his followers. See, *The Nation and Its Fragments*, Princeton: Princeton University Press (1993), pp. 62–4.

149. For an overview, see, Gerhard Oberhammer (ed.), *Studies in Hinduism II, Miscellnea to the Phenomenon of Tantras,* Wien: Verlag der Osterreichischen Akademie der Wissenschaften (1998).

150. *Rabindra Racanabali,* vol. 25, p. 164.

151. Ibid., p. 178.

152. Ibid.

153. Ibid., p. 180.

154. 'The mirror stage as formative of the function of the I as revealed in psychoanalytic experience', *Ecrits: A Selection,* London: Norton (1977), pp. 1–7.

155. *Rabindra Racanabali,* vol. 25 (1976), p. 179.

156. Ibid., p. 181.

157. 'Translator's Preface and Afterword to Mahasweta Devi, *Imaginary Maps*', in Donna Landry and Gerald Maclean (eds), *The Spivak Reader: Selected Works of Gayatri Chakravorty Spivak,* New York: Routledge (1996), p. 277.

158. Ibid., p. 280.

159. *Rabindra Racanabali,* vol. 25 (1976), p. 180.

160. V.N. Volosinov, *Marxism and the Philosophy of Language* (trans. by Ladislav Matejka and I.R. Titunik), New York: Seminar (1973), p. 23. See my discussion in the Introduction.

161. *Rabindra Racanabali,* vol. 25 (1976), p. 174.

162. *Rabindra Racanabali,* vol. 25 (1976), p. 242.

163. Tagore, *Raktakarabi,* Kolkata: Visva-Bharati Press (2003 [1924]), p. 22.

164. Ibid., pp. 71 and 77.

165. Walter Benjamin, *The Origin of German Drama* (trans. by John Osborne), London: Verso (1977), p. 180.

166. Tagore, *Raktakarabi,* p. 117.

167. Ibid., p. 13.

168. *Rabindra Racanabali,* vol. 25, Calcutta: Visva-Bharati Press (1976), pp. 187–205.

Chapter 3

1. Mary E. John, 'Globalisation, Sexuality and the Visual Field: Issues and Non-issues for Cultural Critique', in Mary E. John and Janaki Nair (eds), *A Question of Silence: the sexual economies of modern India,* London: Zed Books (2000), p. 368.

2. Malini Bhattacharya notes that the 'term "empowerment" entered feminist discourse in India in the course of the 1990s', especially in the wake of the Country Paper presented by the Indian government at the Beijing conference in 1995. A government-sponsored empowerment/self-help policy followed with the declaration of Stree Shakti Varsh (Women's Empowerment Year). See 'Introduction', *Talking of Power: Early Writings of Bengali Women from the Mid-Nineteenth Century to the beginning of the Twentieth Century,* Kolkata: Stree (2003), p. 1.

3. In regards to women's issues and legal change in recent decades, see Flavia Agnes, *State, Gender, and the Rhetoric of Law Reform,* Bombay: Research Centre for Women's Studies, SNDT University (1995), especially pp. 188–211; Ratna

Kapur (ed.), *Feminist Terrains in Legal Domains: Interdisciplinary Essays on Women and Law in India*, Delhi: Kali for Women (1996), especially the essays by Brenda Cossman and Ratna Kapur, Rajeswari Sunder Rajan, and Patricia Uberoi. For a historical account of gender-centred social movements, see Radha Kumar, *The History of Doing: an illustrated account of movements for women's rights and feminism in India, 1800–1990*, London; New York: Verso. For accounts of state-sponsored movements for justice through media images, see Purnima Mankekar, *Screening Culture, Viewing Politics: An Ethnography of Television, Womanhood, and Nation in Postcolonial India*, Durham: Duke University Press (1999), pp. 106–7; Rupal Oza, *The Making of Neoliberal India: Nationalism, Gender, and the Paradoxes of Globalization*, New York: Routledge (2006), pp. 46–9.

4. Slavoj Zizek, *The Plague of Fantasies*, London: Verso (1997), p. 108.

5. M.M. Bakhtin, *Towards the Philosophy of an Act*, edited by M. Holquist and V. Liapunov, Austin: University of Texas Press (1993), p. 3. This is the concept I have been working with in the previous chapters.

6. This point has been made persuasively by Stuart Hall and Arjun Appadurai. See, 'The Local and the Global: Globalization and Ethnicity', in Anthony King (ed.), *Culture, Globalization, and the World-System*, Minneapolis: University of Minnesota Press (1997), pp. 19–39; and 'The Grounds of the Nation-state: Identity, Violence, and Territory', in Kjell Goldmann, Ulf Hannerz, and Charles Westin (eds), *Nationalism and Internationalism in the Post-Cold War Era*, London: Routledge (2000), pp. 129–42.

7. Rey Chow, *Cultural Capital: Tactics of Intervention in Contemporary Cultural Studies*, Bloomington: Indiana University Press (1955), p. 169.

8. John Guillory, *Cultural Capital: The Problem of Literary Canon Formation*, Chicago: The University of Chicago Press (1992), p. 282.

9. Ibid., p. 282.

10. V.N. Volosinov, *Marxism and the Philosophy of Language*, trans. by Ladislav Matejka and I.R. Titunik, Cambridge: Harvard University Press (1973), p. 23.

11. Guillory, *Cultural Capital* (1992), p. ix.

12. Antonio Gramsci, *Selections from Prison Notebooks* edited and trans. by Quintin Hoare and Geoffrey Nowell Smith, New York: International Publishers (1971), p. 10.

13. Stuart Hall, 'The Local and the Global' (1997), p. 16.

14. Ibid., p. 29.

15. Maitrayee Choudhuri, 'Introduction', in Maitrayee Choudhuri (ed.), *Feminism in India*, Delhi: Kali for Women (2004), p. xli.

16. Rajeswari Sunder Rajan, *Real and Imagined Women: Gender and Postcolonialism*, New York and London: Routledge (1994), p. 131.

17. John, *A Question of Silence* (2000), pp. 378 and 382.

18. 'Diasporas Old and New: Women in the Transnational World', in Amitava Kumar (ed.), *Class Issues: Pedagogy, Cultural Studies, and the Public Sphere*, New York: New York University Press (1997), pp. 87–116.

19. Ibid., p. 90.

20. Ibid.

21. See, my co-written introduction in *Trans-Status Subjects: Gender in the Globalization of South and Southeast Asia,* co-edited Sonita Sarker and Esha Niyogi De, Durham: Duke University Press (2002), p. 3.

22. Ahmed et al., 'Introduction', *Uprootings/Regroundings,* Oxford: Berg (2003), p. 9. See also, Krishnendu Ray, *The Migrant's Table: Meals and Memories in Bengali-American Households,* Philadelphia: Temple University Press, pp. 5 and 12; and Rey Chow, *Writing Diaspora,* pp. 15–16.

23. A. Appadurai, *Modernity At Large: Cultural Dimensions of Globalization,* Minneapolis: University of Minnesota Press (1996), pp. 198–9.

24. *Internet,* Kolkata: Dasgupta and Company (n.d.)

25. Rabindranath Tagore, 'Red Oleanders: Author's Interpretation', Appendix to *Raktakarabi,* Calcutta: Visva-Bharati Press (n.d. [1924]), p. 121. See my discussion of this passage in the Introduction.

26. Walter Benjamin, *The Origin of German Drama,* London: Verso (1977), p. 180.

27. Michel Foucault, 'Space, Knowledge, Power', in Paul Rabinow (ed.), *The Foucault Reader,* New York: Pantheon Books (1984), p. 255.

28. T.T. Sreekumar, 'ICT's for the Rural Poor: Civil Society and Cyber-Libertarian Developmentalism in India', *Political Economy and Information Capitalism in India: Digital Divide, Development and Equity,* New York: Palgrave (2006), pp. 61–2.

29. Rey Chow, *Writing Diaspora,* p. 170.

30. See the discussion of the 'performance of ethnicity' by Ketu Katrak, 'Body Boundarylands Locating South Asian Ethnicity in Performance and in Daily Life', *Amerasia Journal,* 27:1 (2001), p. 2.

31. See, Dipesh Chakrabarty, *Provincializing Europe: Postcolonial Thought and Historical Difference,* Princeton: Princeton University Press (2000), p. 204.

32. Krishnendu Ray, *The Migrant's Table: Meals and Memories in Bengali-American Households,* Philadelphia: Temple University Press (2004), pp. 5 and 12.

33. Ibid., p. 12.

34. Satya Mohanty, *Literary Theory and the Claims of History: Postmodernism, Objectivity, Multicultural Politics,* Ithaca: Cornell University Press (1997), p. 216.

35. Ibid.

36. Ibid., p. 205.

37. Ibid., p. 211.

38. V.N. Volosinov, 'Discourse in Life and Discourse in Art', *Freudianism: A Marxist Critique,* trans. by I.R. Titunik, and edited in collaboration with Neal H. Bruss, New York: Academic Press (1997), p. 105.

39. Anannya Bhattacharjee, 'The Public/ Private Mirage: Mapping Homes and Undomesticating Violence Work in the South Asian Immigrant Community', in M. Jacqui Alexander and Chandra Talpade Mohanty (eds), *Feminist Genealogies, Colonial Legacies, Democratic Futures,* Routledge: New York (1996), pp. 308–29.

40. For a discussion of Indian Americans as a 'model minority' see, Anannya Bhattacharjee, 'The Habit if Ex-Nomination: Nation, Woman, and the Indian Immigrant Bourgeoisie', *Public Culture* 5(1) (1992), pp. 19–44.

41. Jenny Sharpe, 'Is the United States Postcolonial? Transnationalism, Immigration, and Race', *Diaspora* 4:2 (1995), p. 193.

42. Jean Comaroff and John L. Comaroff, 'Millennial Capitalism and the Culture of Neoliberalism', in Marc Edelman and Angelique Haugerud (eds), *The Anthropology of Development and Globalization*, Oxford: Blackwell (2005), p. 182.

43. Bhattacharjee, 'Public/Private Mirage', pp. 313–14.

44. Jonathan Friedman, 'Globalization, Dis-Integration, Re-organization: The Transformations of Violence', *The Anthropology of Development and Globalization* (2005), p. 162.

45. Jenny Sharpe, 'Is the United States Postcolonial?', *Diaspora* 4:2 (1995), p. 189.

46. Ibid., p. 193.

47. Karen Brodkin, 'Global Capitalism: What's race got to do with it?' *American Ethnologist* 27(2) (2000), pp. 237–56.

48. Saskia Sassen, 'Globalization After September 11', *The Anthropology of Development and Globalization* (2005), pp. 173–6.

49. Ketu Katrak, 'Changing Traditions: South Asian Americans and Cultural/ Communal Politics', *The Massachusetts Review* 75-88 (2002) (Spring), p. 77.

50. Michael Omni, 'Racialization in the Post-Civil-Rights Era', in Avery F. Gordon and Christopher Newfield (eds), *Mapping Multiculturalism*, Minneapolis: University of Minnesota Press (1996), p. 179.

51. For an insightful feminist anthropology of Bengali Indian patriarchal trends among post-1965 immigrants, see, Keya Ganguly, *States of Exception: Everyday Life and Postcolonial Identity*, Minneapolis: University of Minnesota Press (2001), pp. 95–116.

52. Sucheta Mazumdar, 'The Politics of Religion and National Origin: Rediscovering Hindu Indian Identity in the United States', in Vasant Kaiwar and Sucheta Mazumdar (eds), *Antimonies of Modernity: Essays on Race, Orient, Nation*, Durham: Duke University Press (2003), p. 241.

53. Mohammed A. Bamyeh, *The Ends of Globalization*, Minneapolis: University of Minnesota Press (2000), p. 155.

54. Vinay Lal, 'The Politics of History on the Internet: Cyber-Diasporic Hinduism and the North American Hindu Diaspora', *Diaspora* 8:2, pp. 137–71 and 157.

55. Tanika Sarkar, *Hindu Wife, Hindu Nation: Community, Religion, and Cultural Nationalism*, New Delhi: Permanent Black, p. 281.

56. Tapan Basu et al. (eds), *Khaki Shorts and Saffron Flags: Tracts for the Times*, Bombay: Orient Longman (1993), p. 8.

57. See, for example, http://www.zmag.org. This controversy was extensively covered in the news magazine, *India West*.

58. 25 August 2006, A6.

59. Vinay Lal, 'The Politics of History on the Internet', *Diaspora*, p. 141.

60. Jean Comaroff and John L. Comaroff, 'Millennial Capitalism and the Culture of Neoliberalism', p. 182.

61. For a succinct discussion of Sanskrit *rasa* aesthetics, see, J.L. Mohanty, *Classical Indian Philosophy*, Lanham: Rowman and Littlefield (2000), pp. 133–7. For

the elaboration of *rasa* theory in classical Indian dance Jon B. Higgins, *The Music of Bharat Natyam,* in Shubha Chaudhuri (ed.), *AIIS-ARCE Series on Ethnomusicology,* New Delhi: AIIS and Oxford (1993), pp. 10–17; and Bimal Mukherjee and Sunil Kothari (eds), *Rasa: the Indian Performing Arts in the Last Twenty-Five Years,* Calcutta: Anamika Kala Sangam (1995).

62. Ketu Katrak, 'Body Boundarylands', *The Massachusetts Review* (2002), p. 11.

63. Arvind Rajagopal, *Politics After Television: Hindu Nationalism and the Reshaping of the Public in India,* Cambridge: Cambridge University Press (2001), pp. 49–50.

64. http://gandhifoundationusa.com/ChandalikaArticle.html

65. http://www.hindunet.org

66. Mohammed A. Baymeh, *The Ends of Globalization* (2000), p. 155.

67. See, the essays by Tanika Sarkar and Amrita Basu in *Women and the Hindu Right,* in Tanika Sarkar and Urvashi Butalia (eds), Delhi: Kali for Women (1995), pp. 158–215.

68. Ibid., 'Heroic Women', *Women and the Hindu Right,* p. 208.

69. Basu, *Women and the Hindu Right,* p. 167.

70. This history carries the biases of the anti-Nautch movements and subsequent nationalist revisions of temple dance. See, Avanthi Meduri, *Nation, woman, representation: The Sutured History of the Devadasi and Her Dance,* New York University, Ph.D. dissertation (1996). See also, Frederique Apffel Marglin, *Wives of the God King: The Rituals of the Devadasis of Puri,* Delhi: Oxford University Press (1985).

71. 'Choreographing History', in Susan Leigh Foster (ed.), *Choreographing History,* Bloomington: Indiana University Press (1995), p. 7.

72. Uma Chakravarti, 'Inventing Saffron History: A Celibate Hero Rescues an Emasculated Nation', *A Question of Silence: The Sexual Economies of Modern India,* London: Zed Books (2000), p. 258.

73. Ibid., p. 256.

74. See, Sarah Lamb, *White Saris and Sweet Mangoes: Aging, Gender, and Body in North India,* Berkeley: University of California Press (2000), p. 183; and the two essays by Frederique Apffel Marglin in *Purity and Auspiciousness in Indian Society,* Leiden: E.J. Brill (1985), pp. 1–10 and 65–83.

75. Leela Venkataraman, 'Chadralekha and Her Bodyline Approach', *Sruti* 102 (1993), p. 31.

76. Mazumdar, 'The Politics of Religion and National Origin', *Antimonies of Modernity* (2003), p. 241.

77. Mary E. John, 'Globalisation, Sexuality and the Visual Field: issues and non-issues for cultural critique', *A Question of Silence* p. 385.

78. Roland Barthes, *Mythologies,* translated by Annette Lavers, London: Paladin Books, pp. 138 and 141. See also, Anannya Bhattacharjee, 'The Habit of Ex-Nomination: Nation, Woman, and the Indian Immigrant Bourgeoisie', *Public Culture* 5(1) (1992) (Fall), pp. 19–44.

79. Marshal McLuhan, *Understanding Media: The Extensions of Man,* London: Routledge and Kegan Paul (1964).

80. Gramsci, *Selections from Prison Notebooks* (1971), p. 10.

81. See, Sumit Sarkar, 'Calcutta and the "Bengal Renaissance"', *Calcutta: The Living City*, vol. II (1990), pp. 100–1; and Partha Chatterjee, *The Nation and Its Fragments*, Princeton: Princeton University Press (1993). See my discussion in Chapters One and Three.

82. Comaroff and Comaroff, *The Anthropology of Development and Globalization* (2005), p. 183.

83. Ibid.

84. For a recent summary of figures of West Bengal's economic growth, see 'From Red to Riches', *India Today*, 25 September 2006. http://www.indiatoday.com/20060925/state-westbangal.shtml. For an overview of the changing trends of economy in West Bengal and Kolkata, see the essays by Omkar Goswami and Bhabatosh Datta in *Calcutta: The Living City*, vol. II, edited by Sukanta Chaudhuri, London and Delhi: Oxford University Press (990), pp. 88–108.

85. Uma Chakravarti, *Rewriting History: The Life and Times of Pandita Ramabhai*, Delhi: Kali for Women (2000), pp. 200–45; see also, Tanika Sarkar, 'Hindu Conjugality and Nationalism in Nineteenth Century Bengal', in Jasodhara Bagchi (ed.), *Indian Women: Myth and Reality*, Calcutta: Sangam Books (1995), pp. 98–115.

86. Nandi Bhatia, *Acts of Authority/ Acts of Resistance: Theater and Politics in Colonial and Postcolonial India*, Ann Arbor: Michigan University Press (2004), p. 88.

87. See, Kumar Roy, 'Five Decades of Calcutta Theatre', Samik Banerji, 'The Early Years of Calcutta Cinema', and Moinak Biswas, 'Modern Calcutta Cinema', *Calcutta: The Living City*, vol. II (1990), pp. 283–315.

88. Nandi Bhatia, *Acts of Authority/ Acts of Resistance* (2004), p. 97.

89. Samik Banerji, 'The Early Years of Calcutta Cinema', *Calcutta: The Living City*, vol. II (1990), p. 296; Moinak Biswas, 'Modern Calcutta Cinema', *Calcutta: The Living City*, vol. II (1990), pp. 308–9.

90. Sumita S. Chakravarty, 'Introduction', in Sumita S. Chakravarty (ed.), *The Enemy Within: The Films of Mrinal Sen*, Wiltshire: Flick Books (2000), pp. 1–10; and Satyajit Ray, *Our Films, Their Films*, Bombay: Orient Longman (1976).

91. Arun Kumar, 'Globalization and the Indian Economy-1', in Achin Vanaik (ed.), *Globalization and South Asia: Multidimensional Perspectives*, New Delhi: Manohar (2004), p. 23.

92. Govindan Parayil, 'Introduction: Information Capitalism', *Political Economy and Information Capitalism in India: Digital Divide, Development and Equity*, New York: Palgrave (2006), p. 2.

93. See, Fredric Jameson, 'Reification and Utopia', *Social Text*, vol. 1 (1979) (Winter), p. 135.

94. http://www.etv.co.in

95. See, Thomas Elsaesser's well-known formulation of the family melodrama in 'Tales of Sound and Fury: Observations on the Family Melodrama', in Bill Nichols (ed.), *Movies and Methods*, vol. 1, University of California Press (1985); reprinted, Calcutta: Seagull Press (1993), pp. 168 and 172.

96. Bishnupriya Ghosh, 'Melodrama and the Bourgeois Family: Notes on Mrinal Sen's Critical Cinema', *The Enemy Within*, p. 67.

97. Elsaesser, 'Tales of Sound and Fury', *Movies and Methods*, vol. 1 (1993), p. 169.

98. As Ghosh, p. 71, observes drawing on other feminist film critics, and we will see below, feminist cinema mobilizes these generic conflicts of melodrama.

99. Christian Metz works out important distinctions between conversational communicative give-and-take and filmic signification that works by analogy and compounds different codes: 'On the Notion of Cinematographic Language', *Movies and Methods*, vol. 2, pp. 583–7.

100. Purnima Mankekar, *Screening Culture, Viewing Politics: An Ethnography of Television, Womanhood, and Nation in Postcolonial India*, Durham: Duke University Press (1999).

101. John Stuart Mill, 'Of Individuality as One of the Elements of Well-Being', *Utilitarianism*, London: Everyman (1993), pp. 126–7 and 131; and 'Early Essays on Marriage and Divorce (1832)', in Alice S. Rossi (ed.), *Essays on Sex Equality*, Chicago: University of Chicago Press (1970), p. 73.

102. Uma Chakravarti, 'Introduction', *The Enemy Within*, p. 7.

103. Kathleen L. Komar, 'Feminist Curves in Contemporary Literary Spaces', in Margaret Higonnet and Joan Templeton (eds), *Reconfigured Spheres: Feminist Explorations of Literary Space*, Amherst: University of Mass. Press (1994), p. 90.

104. Mary Ann Doane, 'The Voice in the Cinema: Articulations of Body and Space', *Movies and Methods*, vol. 2, p. 574.

105. Portrayals of women's strength that break social myths of desirable women (beautiful, educated, etc.) is an important trend on commercial Indian television. See, for example, Waheeda Sultana, 'Women in Indian Soap Operas', *Women and Media: Challenging Feminist Discourse*, Delhi: The Woman Press (2005), pp. 114–18.

106. Arun Kumar, *Globalization and South Asia* (2004), p. 278.

107. This is a common trend in commercial visual publics. See Robin Andersen, 'Introduction', in Robin Andersen and Lance Strate (eds), *Critical Studies in Media Commercialism*, New York: Oxford University Press (2000), p. 8.

108. Delicia Harvey and Lance Strate, 'Image Culture and the Supermodel', *Critical Studies in Media Commercialism*, p. 204.

109. Ibid., p. 78.

110. Ibid.

111. Stephen Neale, *Cinema and Technology: Image, Sound and Colour*, London: Macmillan/ British Film Institute Publishing (1985), p. 155.

112. Foster, *Choreographing History* (1995), p. 7.

113. *The Laws of Manu [Manusmriti]*, trans. by Wendy Doniger and Brian K. Smith, Hammondsworth: Penguin (1991), vol. 2, p. 66.

114. 'Is the Hindu Goddess a Feminist?' in Maitrayee Chaudhuri (ed.), *Feminism in India*, New Delhi: Kali for Women (2004), p. 330.

Chapter 4

1. Satya Mohanty, *Literary Theory and the Claims of History: Postmodernism, Objectivity, Multicultural Politics*, Ithaca: Cornell University Press (1997), pp. 205 and 211. See my discussion of this approach in the Introduction.

2. In pre-modern communities of the Indian subcontinent 'small-scale' changes in caste status were possible, especially if people migrated to other regions of the subcontinent. This was so despite that caste- and religion-based identities were central in social hierarchies, and in determining a person's status in agrarian economic arrangements. See, Sudipta Kaviraj, 'Introduction', in Sudipta Kaviraj (ed.), *Politics in India*, Delhi: Oxford University Press (1997), pp. 5–7.

3. *Communications*, Hammondsworth: Penguin Special (1962), p. 10.

4. Raymond Williams, 'The Technology and the Society', in John Thornton Caldwell (ed.), *Electronic Media and Technoculture*, New Jersey: Rutgers University Press (2000), pp. 36–9.

5. Antonio Gramsci, *Selections from Prison Notebooks*, edited and trans. by Quintin Hoare and Geoffrey Nowell Smith. New York: International Publishers (1971), p. 10.

6. Ibid.

7. I am grateful to Gayatri Chakravorty Spivak for clarifying for me Gramsci's notion of the organic intellectual.

8. M. Jacqui Alexander and Chandra Talpade Mohanty, 'Introduction', in M. Jacqui Alexander and Chandra Talpade Mohanty (eds), *Feminist Genealogies Colonial Legacies, Democratic Features*, New York: Routledge (1997), p. xxviii.

9. 'The Tutor-Code of Classical Cinema', *Movies and Methods*, vol. 1, Calcutta: Seagull (1993), p. 447.

10. V.N. Volosinov, *Marxism and the Philosophy of Language*, trans. by Ladislav Matejka and I.R. Titunik. New York: Seminar (1973), p. 23.

11. Dayan, 'The Tutor-Code', p. 443.

12. Ibid., pp. 448-9.

13. See Chapter 3, especially note 48.

14. I derive this definition of choreography from Susan Leigh Foster's idea of the body in motion as 'written upon' but also as writing and meaning: *Choreographing History*, Bloomington: Indiana University Press (1995), p. 15, and Janet O'Shea, *At Home in the World: Bharat Natyam on the Global Stage*, Middleton, Connecticut: Wesleyan University Press (2007), p. 180.

15. www.dancersguild.org

16. Kapila Vatsyayan, *Traditions of Indian Folk Dance*, New Delhi: Indian Book Company (1976), pp. 9 and 13–14. See also my discussion of the Tagore dance drama form in Chapter 2.

17. See, Trevor Montague Wade, *Choreography as Feminist Strategy: Three Approaches to Hindu Feminism in the Dance of Chandralekha, Manjusri Chaki-Sircar, and Daksha Seth*, University of Chicago: Ph.D. diss. (2001), personal conversation with Chaki-Sircar, p. 225. Since both Manjusri and Ranjabati have passed away, I have relied on Wade's excellent ethnographic work.

18. Manjusri Chaki-Sircar, 'Tagore and Modernization of Dance', in Bimal Mukherjee and Sunil Kothari (eds), *Rasa: The Indian Performing Arts in the Last Twenty-Five Years*, Calcutta: Anamika Press (1995), p. 247.

19. For a succinct overview of the dance traditions in metropolitan Kolkata, see Sunil Kothari, 'Classical Dance in Calcutta', *Calcutta: The Living City*, vol. II, Delhi: Oxford University Press (1990), pp. 280–2.

20. McKim Marriott and Ronald Inden, Towards an Ethnosociology of South Asian Caste Systems', in Kenneth David (ed.), *The New Wind: Changing Identities in South Asia*, The Hague: Mouton Publishers (1977), pp. 232–3.

21. Vatsayan, *Traditions of Indian Folk Dance*, p. 9.

22. Video for television, produced by G.D. Ghoshal, New Delhi: Central Production Centre (1991).

23. Foster, *Choreographing History*, p. 10

24. *This Sex Which Is Not One*, trans. by Catherine Porter. Ithaca: Cornell University Press (1977), p. 28.

25. Mary Gregor (ed.), *Groundwork of the Metaphysics of Morals*, Cambridge: Cambridge University Press (1998), p. 42.

26. Wade, *Choreography as Feminist Strategy*, p. 239.

27. J.L. Mohanty, *Classical Indian Philosophy*, Lanham: Rowman and Littlefield (2000), p. 67.

28. Wade, *Choreography as Feminist Strategy*, p. 238.

29. 'Staber Mater', in Susan Rubin Suleiman (ed.), *The Female Body in Western Culture: contemporary perspectives*, Cambridge: Harvard University Press (1985), p. 99.

30. See the essays by David R. Kinsley and Patricia Dodd in Rachel Fell McDermott and Jeffrey J. Kripal (eds), *Encountering Kali: In the Margins, At the Center, In the West*, Berkeley: University of California Press (2003), pp. 23–59; and Ajit Mookerjee, *Kali the Feminine Force*, Rochester: Destiny Books (1988), pp. 25–84.

31. *Dancers' Guild Brochure*, Kolkata: Salt Lake (2006).

32. Laura Mulvey defines scopophilia as looking at an erotic object as a source of pleasure. See, 'Visual Pleasure and Narrative Cinema', *Movies and Methods*, vol. 2, p. 307.

33. See, Shantideb Ghosh, *Gurudev Rabindranath O Adhunik Bharatiya Nritya*, Calcutta: Ananda Publishers (1983), pp. 3–4.

34. 'Discourse in Life and Discourse in Art', *Freudianism: The Marxist Critique*, trans. by I.R. Titunik, edited by I.R. Titunik and Noel H. Bruss, New York: Academic Press (1976), pp. 109–10.

35. Wade, *Choreography as Feminist Strategy*, pp. 187–92.

36. Marta E. Savigliano, 'Fragments for a story of tango bodies (On Choreocritics and the Memory of Power)', in Susan Leigh Foster (ed.), *Corporealities: Dancing Knowledge, Culture and Power*, New York: Routledge (1996), p. 224.

37. Marta E. Savigliano, *Angora Matta: Fatal Acts of North-South Translation*, Middletown, Connecticut: Wesleyan University Press (2003), p. xvi.

38. See the chapters on Hindutva by Thomas Blom Hansen in T.B. Hansen and C. Jaffrelot (eds), *Omnibus: Hindu Nationalism and Indian Politics*, New Delhi: Oxford University Press (2004).

39. Purnima Mankekar, *Screening Culture, Viewing Politics: An Ethnography of Television, Womanhood, and Nation in Postcolonial India*, Durham: Duke University Press (1999), pp. 105–7.

40. Jonaki Sarkar, *Artistic Director, Dancers Guild*, personal conversation, 15 July 2006.

41. Arvind Rajagopal, *Politics After Television: Hindu Nationalism and the Reshaping of the Public in India*, Cambridge: Cambridge University Press (2001), pp. 47–51.

42. Quoted by Shoma Chatterji, *Parama and other Outsiders: The Cinema of Aparna Sen*, Calcutta: Parumita Publications (2002), p. 21.

43. Alan Ryan (ed.), *On Liberty and the Subjection of Women*, London: Penguin (2006 [1859]), pp. 26–7.

44. Linda Steiner, 'Feminist Media Ethics', in Lee Wilkins and Clifford G. Christians (eds), *The Handbook of Mass Media Ethics*, New York: Routledge (2009), p. 377.

45. 'The Life in a Day of Aparna Sen!' http://www3.estart.corn./india/women/aparnasen.html

46. See, Ipshita Chanda, 'Birthing Terrible Beauties:Feminisms and "Women's Magazines"', in Maitrayee Chaudhuri (ed.), *Feminism in India*, New Delhi: Kali for Women (2004), pp. 228–45.

47. Ashish Rajadhyaksha and Paul Willemen, *Encyclopaedia of Indian Cinema*, Oxford and New Delhi: Oxford University Press (1994), p. 195.

48. See, Darius Cooper, *The Cinema of Satyajit Ray: Between Tradition and Modernity*, Cambridge: Cambridge University Press (2000), especially the chapter titled 'From Gazes to Threat: the Odyssean Yatra (Journey) of the Ray Woman'.

49. Bishnupriya Ghosh, 'Melodrama and the bourgeois family: notes on Mrinal Sen's critical cinema', in Sumita Chakravarty (ed.), *The Enemy Within: The Films of Mrinal Sen*, Wiltshire: Flick Books (2000), pp. 66–7.

50. Geeta Kapur, 'Articulating the Self into History: Ritwik Ghatak's Jukti takko ar gappo', in Jim Pines and Paul Willemen (eds), *Questions of Third Cinema*, London: British Film Institute (1989), pp. 179 and 182.

51. Ashish Rajadhyaksha, 'Debating the Third Cinema', in Jim Pines and Paul Willemen *Questions of Third Cinema*, London: British Film Institute (1989), p. 174.

52. Ashish Rajadhyaksha, *Ritwik Ghatak: A Return to the Epic*, Bombay: Screen Unit (1982), pp. 53 and 60.

53. See, Moinak Biswas, 'Modern Calcutta Cinema', *Calcutta: the Living City*, vol. II (1990), pp. 308–9.

54. Gayatri Spivak, 'Ethics and Politics in Tagore, Coetzee, and Certain Scenes of Teaching', *Diacritics* 32: 3/4 (2002) (Fall), pp. 17–31: 6. Spivak draws on Mieke Bal's notion of 'focalization' as 'the relation between the vision and that which is "seen" to formulate in what way a reader becomes active and "transactional." The

metaphor of counter focalization is especially helpful for thinking about visual texts', in my view.

55. Ibid., p. 6.

56. Pam Cook, 'Melodrama and the Woman's Picture', *Imitations of Life: A Reader on Film and Television*, Detroit: Wayne State University Press (1991), p. 251.

57. Thomas Elaesser, 'Tales of Sound and Fury: Some Observations on the Family Melodrama, Movies and Methods', vol. 1. Edited by Bill Nichols, University of California Press (1985); reprinted, Calcutta: Seagull Press (1993), p. 169.

58. Cook, 'Melodrama', p. 251.

59. Chuck Kleinhans, 'Notes on Melodrama and the Family under Capitalism', *Imitations of Life: A Reader on Film and Television*, Detroit: Wayne State University Press (1991), p. 201.

60. The film coincides with the new urban development plan of Calcutta, and the massive real-estate developments that preceded this in the early 1980's. See, Bhabatosh Datta, 'The Economy of Calcutta: Today and Tomorrow', in Sukanta Chaudhuri (ed.), *Calcutta: The Living City*, vol. II, Delhi: Oxford University Press (1990), pp. 104–8.

61. http://www.feminaindia.com/articleshow/38053182.cms

62. An inquiry into the Nature and Causes of the Wealth of Nations, 1776 (Adam Smith Institute: Online Edition, 1995–2005) Chapter II http://www.adamsmith.org

63. Michel Foucault, *The Foucault Reader*, edited by Paul Rabinow, New York: Pantheon Books (1984), p. 144.

64. Tonsuring and desexualizing of a widow signifies continuing control by the patriline of a feminine sexuality that had been opened and heated through marital sex. See, Sarah Lamb, *White Saris and Sweet Mangoes: Aging, Gender, and Body in North India*, Berkeley: University of California Press (2000), p. 220.

65. Chatterji, *Parama and Other Outsiders*, p. 86.

66. Thomas Elsaesser, 'Tales of Sound and Fury Observations on the Family Melodrama, Movies and Methods', vol. 1. Edited by Bill Nichols, University of California Press (1985); reprinted, Calcutta: Seagull Press (1993), pp. 168 and 172.

67. Betty Friedan, *The Feminine Mystique*, New York: Norton and Co. (1997 [1963]), p. 18.

68. Poonam Arora, 'Third World Subjects for First World Consumption', in Diane Carson, Linda Dittmar, and Janice R. Welsch (eds), *Multiple Voices in Feminist Film Criticism*, Minneapolis: University of Minnesota Press (1994), p. 303.

69. E. Ann Kaplan, *Looking for the Other: Feminism, Film, and the Imperial Gaze*, New York: Routledge (1997), pp. 61–2.

70. 'Can the Subaltern Speak?' in C. Nelson and L. Grossberg (eds), *Marxism and the Interpretation of Culture*, Bassingstoke: Macmillan (1988), pp. 273–4.

71. See, Immanuel Kant's discussion of 'dignity', in Christine M. Korsgaard (ed.), *Groundwork of the Metaphysics of Morals*, 'Introduction' edited by Mary Gregor, Cambridge: Cambridge University Press (1997), p. 42.

72. Mohanty, *Literary Theory*, p. 212.

73. Ibid., pp. 210, 212.

74. Ibid., 212.

75. Mary Ann Doanne, 'The Voice in the Cinema: The Articulation of Body and Space', in Bill Nichols (ed.), *Movies and Methods*, vol. 2, Calcutta: Seagull Press (1993 [1985]), p. 574.

76. *Provincializing Europe*, Princeton: Princeton University Press (2000), p. 214.

77. ibid., p. 226.

78. Ibid.

79. Ibid., p. 225.

80. Ibid., p. 147.

81. Ibid.

82. Chatterji, *Parama and Other Outsiders*, p. 245

83. Quoted Chatterji, *Parama and Other Outsiders*, p. 219.

84. The most well-known early exponent of this notion is St. Augustine. See, *The Confessions of St. Augustine*, trans. by E.B. Pusey, London: Everyman Library (1926).

85. For example, see, Hannah Arendt, *The Human Condition*, Garden City: Anchor Books (1959), pp. 35–42.

86. Mill, *On Liberty*, p. 81.

87. Bimal Krishna Matilal, 'Philosophy, Culture, and Religion: Mind, Language, and the World', in Jonardon Ganeri (ed.), *The Collected Essays of Bimal Krishna Matilal*, Oxford: Oxford University Press (2002), p. 312.

88. http://www.mybindi.com/arts-netertainment/WHATSON/interview-aparnasen.cfm

89. Arjun Appadurai, *Modernity at Large: Cultural Dimensions of Globalization*, Minneapolis: University of Minnesota Press (1996), pp. 132–3. The general concept of biopolitics is drawn from Michel Foucault: 'The Rights of Life and Power over Death', in Paul Rabinow (ed.), *The Foucault Reader*, New York: Pantheon Books (1984), pp. 258–72.

90. *The Ethics of Identity*, Princeton: Princeton University Press (2005), p. 64.

91. http://www.mybindi.com/arts-netertainment/WHATSON/interview-aparnasen.cfm

92. For a discussion of the rasas, see, Dimock, et al., *The Literatures of India: An Introduction*, Chicago: University of Chicago Press (1974), p. 226. See also Chapter 2 for an elaborate discussion.

93. David Hume, *Enquiries Concerning Human Understanding and Concerning the Principles of Morals*, 'Introduction' by I.A. Sigby-Bigge, Oxford: Clarendon Press (1990); Adam Smith, *The Theory of Moral Sentiments*, edited by D.D. Raphael and A.L. Macfie, Indianapolis Liberty Fund (1984).

94. Spivak, 'Ethics and Politics', p. 30.

95. Jean Comaroff and John Comaroff suggest the characteristic of the 'autonomic impulse' of neoliberal capitalism is that it decontextualizes and distantiates people from the 'workings of power'. 'Millienial Capitalism and the Culture of Neoliberalism', *The Anthropology of Development and Globalization: From Classical Political Economy to Contemporary Neoliberalism*, Oxford: Blackwell (2005), pp. 182–3. See my discussion in the Introduction.

96. Bal, qtd. Spivak, p. 20.

97. 'Groundwork', p. 47.

98. http://www.time.com/asia/magazine

99. Walter Benjamin, *The Origin of German Tragic Drama*, trans. by John Osborne, London: Verso (1977), p. 180.

100. Ibid.

101. 'Discourse in Life and Discourse in Art', in I.R. Titunik and Neal H. Bruss (eds), *Freudianism: The Marxist Critique*, trans. by I.R. Titunik, New York: Academic Press (1976), pp. 98–9.

102. Sukumar Sen, *Bangla Sahityer Itihas*, vol. 4, Kolkata: Ananda Publishers (1995 [1946]), p. 122.

103. The lecture notes were taken down by Pradyotkumar Sen and published serially in the periodical Shantiniketan in 1922–3 (Balaka, 1998, p. 115). They appear with the poems in subsequent editions of Balaka.

104. Balaka, Calcutta: Visva-Bharati Press (1998 [1916]), p. 115.

105. Balaka (1998), p. 122.

106. Ibid., pp. 88 and 91.

107. Ibid., p. 91.

108. Ibid., p. 88.

109. Ibid., p. 90.

110. See, Balaka (1998), pp. 170–1. This teleological and invariably self-referential spirituality coincides with dominant readings of the Upanishadic past in the Brahmo Samaj, wherein Tagore and his family took leading roles. See also, Chapter Two.

111. Balaka (1998), pp. 92–3. Co-translated with Pushpanjali Niyogi and Suranjan De.

112. Ibid., p. 171.

113. Ibid., p. 89.

114. Ayyub, p. 182.

115. Savigliano, 'Fragments', p. 224.

116. A noteworthy recent example is Inderpal Grewal's *Transnational America: Feminisms, Diasporas, Neoliberalisms*, Durham: Duke University Press (2005), especially pp. 38–41.

Conclusion

1. *Women and Human Development: The Capabilities Approach*, Cambridge: Cambridge University Press (2000), pp. 7 and 59.

2. Ibid., p. 5.

3. Ibid., p.7.

4. Ibid., p. 32.

5. Ibid., p. 57.

6. Ibid., pp. 78–80.

7. 'Universalism without foundations?', *Economy and Society*, vol. 31(1) (February 2002), pp. 152–69.

8. 'Universalism's Struggle', *Radical Philosophy: A Journal of Socialist and Feminist Philosophy* 108 (July/August 2001), pp. 40–2.

9. This view accounts for Nussbaum's surprising assertion that modernists such as Tagore, Rammohun Roy, or Rokeya Hossain are the spokespeople of authentic (insular) Indian Hindu and Muslim traditions, *Women and Human Development*, pp. 44–8.

10. *The Claims of Culture: Equality and Diversity in the Global Era*, Princeton: Princeton University Press (2002), p. 16.

11. Ibid., p. 86.

12. Ibid., p. 21.

13. See, *Hindu Wife, Hindu Nation*, Delhi: Orient Longman (2000).

14. Ibid., p. 19.

15. 'For a Careful Reading', in Linda Nicholson (ed.), *Feminist Contentions: A Philosophical Exchange*, New York: Routledge (1995), p. 129.

16. *Transnational America*, Durham: Duke University Press (2005), p. 28.

17. Ibid., p. 17.

18. *Politics of Piety: The Islamic Revival and the Feminist Subject*, Princeton: Princeton University Press (2005), p. 25.

19. Ibid., p. 22.

20. Ibid., p. 188.

21. Ibid., p. 31.

22.'Is the Hindu Goddess a Feminist?', in Maitrayee Chaudhuri (ed.), *Feminism in India*, New Delhi: Kali for Women (2004)

23. *Feminism without Borders: Decolonizing Theory, Practicing Solidarity*, Durham: Duke University Press (2003), p. 78.

INDEX